Virtual Education: Cases in Learning & Teaching Technologies

edited by

Fawzi Albalooshi
University of Bahrain, Bahrain

IRM Press
Publisher of innovative scholarly and professional
information technology titles in the cyberage

Hershey • London • Melbourne • Singapore • Beijing

KH

Acquisitions Editor:	Mehdi Khosrow-Pour
Senior Managing Editor:	Jan Travers
Managing Editor:	Amanda Appicello
Copy Editor:	Maria Boyer
Typesetter:	Amanda Appicello
Cover Design:	Weston Pritts
Printed at:	Integrated Book Technology

Published in the United States of America by
    IRM Press (an imprint of Idea Group Inc.)
    701 E. Chocolate Avenue, Suite 200
    Hershey PA 17033-1240
    Tel: 717-533-8845
    Fax: 717-533-8661
    E-mail: cust@idea-group.com
    Web site: http://www.irm-press.com

and in the United Kingdom by
    IRM Press (an imprint of Idea Group Inc.)
    3 Henrietta Street
    Covent Garden
    London WC2E 8LU
    Tel: 44 20 7240 0856
    Fax: 44 20 7379 3313
    Web site: http://www.eurospan.co.uk

Library of Congress Cataloging-in-Publication Data

Virtual education : cases in learning & teaching technologies / [edited by] Fawzi Albalooshi.
        p. cm.
Includes bibliographical references and index.
    ISBN 1-931777-39-X (softcover) -- ISBN 1-931777-55-1 (ebook)
    1. Education, Higher--Computer network resources. 2. Education, Higher--Effect of technological innovations on. 3. Educational technology. 4. Distance education. I. Albalooshi, Fawzi.
    LB1044.87.V57 2003
    378.1'734--dc21

                                                    2002156225

British Cataloguing in Publication Data
A Cataloguing in Publication record for this book is available from the British Library.

11/22/04

New Releases from IRM Press

- **Multimedia and Interactive Digital TV: Managing the Opportunities Created by Digital Convergence**/Margherita Pagani
  ISBN: 1-931777-38-1; eISBN: 1-931777-54-3 / US$59.95 / © 2003
- **Virtual Education: Cases in Learning & Teaching Technologies**/ Fawzi Albalooshi (Ed.), ISBN: 1-931777-39-X; eISBN: 1-931777-55-1 / US$59.95 / © 2003
- **Managing IT in Government, Business & Communities**/Gerry Gingrich (Ed.)
  ISBN: 1-931777-40-3; eISBN: 1-931777-56-X / US$59.95 / © 2003
- **Information Management: Support Systems & Multimedia Technology**/ George Ditsa (Ed.), ISBN: 1-931777-41-1; eISBN: 1-931777-57-8 / US$59.95 / © 2003
- **Managing Globally with Information Technology**/Sherif Kamel (Ed.)
  ISBN: 42-X; eISBN: 1-931777-58-6 / US$59.95 / © 2003
- **Current Security Management & Ethical Issues of Information Technology**/Rasool Azari (Ed.), ISBN: 1-931777-43-8; eISBN: 1-931777-59-4 / US$59.95 / © 2003
- **UML and the Unified Process**/Liliana Favre (Ed.)
  ISBN: 1-931777-44-6; eISBN: 1-931777-60-8 / US$59.95 / © 2003
- **Business Strategies for Information Technology Management**/Kalle Kangas (Ed.)
  ISBN: 1-931777-45-4; eISBN: 1-931777-61-6 / US$59.95 / © 2003
- **Managing E-Commerce and Mobile Computing Technologies**/Julie Mariga (Ed.)
  ISBN: 1-931777-46-2; eISBN: 1-931777-62-4 / US$59.95 / © 2003
- **Effective Databases for Text & Document Management**/Shirley A. Becker (Ed.)
  ISBN: 1-931777-47-0; eISBN: 1-931777-63-2 / US$59.95 / © 2003
- **Technologies & Methodologies for Evaluating Information Technology in Business**/ Charles K. Davis (Ed.), ISBN: 1-931777-48-9; eISBN: 1-931777-64-0 / US$59.95 / © 2003
- **ERP & Data Warehousing in Organizations: Issues and Challenges**/Gerald Grant (Ed.), ISBN: 1-931777-49-7; eISBN: 1-931777-65-9 / US$59.95 / © 2003
- **Practicing Software Engineering in the 21ˢᵗ Century**/Joan Peckham (Ed.)
  ISBN: 1-931777-50-0; eISBN: 1-931777-66-7 / US$59.95 / © 2003
- **Knowledge Management: Current Issues and Challenges**/Elayne Coakes (Ed.)
  ISBN: 1-931777-51-9; eISBN: 1-931777-67-5 / US$59.95 / © 2003
- **Computing Information Technology: The Human Side**/Steven Gordon (Ed.)
  ISBN: 1-931777-52-7; eISBN: 1-931777-68-3 / US$59.95 / © 2003
- **Current Issues in IT Education**/Tanya McGill (Ed.)
  ISBN: 1-931777-53-5; eISBN: 1-931777-69-1 / US$59.95 / © 2003

Excellent additions to your institution's library!
Recommend these titles to your Librarian!

To receive a copy of the IRM Press catalog, please contact
(toll free) 1/800-345-4332, fax 1/717-533-8661,
or visit the IRM Press Online Bookstore at: [http://www.irm-press.com]!

Note: All IRM Press books are also available as ebooks on netlibrary.com as well as other ebook sources. Contact Ms. Carrie Skovrinskie at [cskovrinskie@idea-group.com] to receive a complete list of sources where you can obtain ebook information or IRM Press titles.

Virtual Education: Cases in Learning & Teaching Technologies

Table of Contents

Part II: E-Collaboration

Part III: Web-Based Learning & Teaching

Part IV: Effective E-Learning

Part V: IT Teaching Cases

Preface

Early computer researchers sought ways to use the new invention for learning and teaching purposes. Instructional computing at that time took place on mainframes in the form of typing and reading text, but serious efforts were made to further utilize the computer power to serve education. Examples include the Programmed Logic for Automated Teaching Operations (PLATO) (Alpert & Bitzer, 1970) project, which managed to integrate text and graphics, and the Time-shared, Interactive, Computer-Controlled Information Television (TICCIT) (Merril, Schneider, & Fletcher 1980) project, which introduced the concept of learner-controlled instruction. A major advantage in such environments is the availability of information in the centralized system that was sharable by all users. The invention of microcomputers in the late '70s made it possible for businesses, schools, and homes to enjoy computing. The new small size computers were not restricted to text, but allowed colored graphics, animation, and voice. Input became possible through the mouse, touch screens, scanners, and microphones, in addition, to the keyboard. Various forms of output became possible (in addition to the black-and-white monitor) such as colored monitors, LCDs, colored printers, and speakers. Although at first the new computers were stand-alone and information could not be shared, networking solved this problem. In the late '70s and early '80s Apple computers were the first widely available microcomputers that had most of the early courseware, only to be superseded by IBM-compatible computers that gained wide popularity and continued to grow its market share up to present day. Network technologies allowed PCs to communicate and share information and processing power. At first, Local Area Networks (LANs) were developed followed by the Wide Area Networks (WANs), and then the Internet made of LANs and WANs started to grow rapidly. Today, millions of people use the Internet to pursue various businesses, pleasure, and learning activities. However, a major setback in computer-based instruction is the unavailability of tools that make use of the new multimedia technologies to develop the software. Developers tend to glue together various technologies to build the system and struggle to overcome the incompatibilities of software and hardware.

With regard to learning, there is an ongoing debate on the effectiveness of computers to facilitate learning. Research findings vary: some researchers report considerable improvements in learning levels through the use of the computer as a learning medium, while others found little or no improvements. Many researchers believe that the benefits are attributed to the way computer-based instruction is designed. Alessi and Trollip (2001) emphasize that in order to facilitate learning in an efficient way, the process must include: information presentation, learning guidance, practice, and assessment. Information should be presented using verbal, pictorial, and/or textual representation. Skills to be learned must be modeled, especially the ones that involve following a certain procedure to carry out a task.

Another important approach is the use of examples to illustrate the applications of a concept, rule, skill, or procedure. Learner guidance can be implemented through interaction between the learner and the medium. The learner may answer questions about factual information, apply rules, principles in problem-solving activities, or practice procedural skills. The teaching medium observes the learner going through the lesson and corrects errors, as well as giving suggestions and hints. Practice sessions can be offered to improve the learners' speed, fluency, and retention. During these sessions the medium may observe and make short corrective statements. Ending a learning session with tests may prompt the start of a new session. Finally, tests give feedback to the level of learning and quality of teaching. Intelligent programs must assess the learner's knowledge and must decide on the weak areas that need to be enforced. It should offer the learner the chance to continue using parts of the program to improve on those specific areas. Additionally, alternative modes of presentation, examples, and drills could also be useful and may be more suitable to the learner.

Common types of interactive multimedia, as reported by Alessi and Tropllip (2001), include tutorials, hypermedia, drills, simulations, and games. Programs that present information and guide the learner are classified as tutorials. Hypermedia programs are more open-ended and allow the learners to choose their own paths through the material. Drills are specifically designed for practice to gain speed, fluency, and retention. Simulations are more complex and can be used for direct instruction. In addition to information presentation, they guide the learner and offer practice sessions. Games are used as discovery environments and may be combined with simulations and drills. They may be used to integrate learning across a number of areas as is often done in adventure gaming. They can be combined with drills and simulations.

Another important question we are often faced with is when to use computers to improve learning. Many believe it is more effective when other media have shortcomings. Example situations in which computer-based instruction can be useful is when the use of other means of learning are either expensive or dangerous, such as in the case of simulators to train pilots, when safety is in concern as in chemistry laboratories, or the need for 3-D and other computer effects that are not supported by other media. Other reasons could be intended learners' special needs such as visual or auditory disabilities.

In recent years the powers of computers have increased exponentially and the technology related to developing multimedia systems is continually advancing. These advancements, coupled with that of network technologies, made it possible to build virtual learning environments that can simulate real-life situations and provide a safe, controlled place to learn. Such environments simulate the real world, providing the students with the context for the learning process to take place. They can represent a virtual laboratory in which experiments can be conducted; virtual worlds in any time and place; or virtual office, plant, or store for a company. These allow the student to control the learning process, develop an ability to solve high-level problems, make learning a personal experience, model the complexities and uncertainties of working in the real world, and can also accommodate a wide range of student learning styles.

Another newcomer to the world of education is the virtual university that became possible with the advances of the Internet and the World Wide Web. These offer the learner anywhere in the world a variety of courses and study programs that s/he can access and interact with in the comfort of her/his home. All real university services and functions are simulated on the Internet so that no physical interaction will be needed to complete a program. Such a setup allows learning to reach any person, anywhere, at any time; facilitates group learning; and makes a wide body of learning material timely available.

In recent years multimedia computing has expanded from being a research area to become a field of study taught in universities. It became important for students to learn the development and application of this technology in the field of education and many others, and at the same time researchers continue to offer solutions and improvements. This book presents a collection of the latest research findings in the field of virtual education that is carried out by researchers around the globe. They have been carefully selected from five tracks in the IRMA (Khosrow-Pour, 2002) conference titled, "Issues & Trends of Information Technology Management in Contemporary Organizations." The book is made up of 18 chapters and organized into the following five parts: The Virtual University, E-Collaboration, Web-Based Learning and Teaching, Effective E-Learning, and IT Teaching Cases.

Four papers related to virtual universities are grouped under the first part. In Chapter One Barjis presents an overview of virtual university studies pertaining to issues, concepts, and trends, and provides recommendations for future designers. The second chapter by Lassila and Howell examines information systems (IS) education criteria and sets guidelines as a framework for the development of online IS programs. The third, by Valenti, Panti, and Leo, addresses the issue of quality assurance of Web-based degrees through the MODASPECTRA (MOtor Disability Assessment SPECialists TRAining) Web-based degree. In the fourth Durrett, Burnell, and Priest present a Smart Agent-based Resource for virtual Advising (SARA).

Papers related to collaboration via the Web are grouped under the E-Collaboration part. Chapter Five, by Fernandes, Holzer, Forte, and Zaerpour, identifies key factors that motivate to share and reuse pedagogical documents. Chapter Six, by L. Gouveia and J. Gouveia, proposes a model for developing a World Wide Web-based system that allows interaction between users and contents. In Chapter Seven Klein explores normative influence as a barrier to creative idea generation that is present in small groups and suggests IT-based solutions to remove barriers. Chapter Eight by Forzi and Laing presents a new approach for a customer-oriented e-business modeling with specific attention on inter-organizational cooperative networks and re-intermediation, as well as on information management within distributed manufacturing networks.

Part Three gathers a number of papers that address the general use of the Web in teaching and learning. Chapter Nine Stein examines whether gender and age factors affect students' ICT literacy and Web usage. Chapter 10, by Freedman, Tello, and Lewis, identifies potential communication barriers between instructor and students in an online educational environment, and suggests ways to reduce or eliminate them. Chapter 11, by Espejo, Mana, and Bato, looks into the use of the Internet in the Philippines in education. The paper investigates the reasons behind the difference in the levels of education provided by public and private schools.

The Effective E-Learning part gathers papers that suggest ways to improve computer-based learning. In Chapter 12 Frick, Sautter, and Øverbekk suggest the use of modeling techniques to gain understanding of causes and relationships in learning environments. Chapter 13 by Alkhalifa and Albalooshi introduces a three-dimensional framework aimed at evaluating educational software. Born and Jessup in Chapter 14 discuss the concept of performance assessment in a virtual classroom environment, including the proposition that using traditional assessment processes alone is not sufficient. Chapter 15 by Webster explores the use of cognitive styles and meta-cognitive skills in the design and development of E-Learning environments.

Part Five gathers three selected cases of teaching in IT. Chapter 16, by Asoh, Belardo, and Crnkovic, presents a case study of the Multi-Purpose Access for Customer Relations and Operational Support (MACROS) project, designed to help implement a new vision of business of state agencies within New York State. In Chapter 17 Murtuza discusses the benefits of literary works in systems analysis courses, and management information system curriculum in general. Chapter 18, by Martin, illustrates the problems that can develop quickly when an organization does not have defined goals, effective management, and supporting information systems.

REFERENCES

Alessi, M.S. & Trollip, R.S. (2001). *Multimedia for Learning, Methods and Development, 3rd Edition.* Allyn & Bacon.

Alpert, D. & Bitzer, D.L. (1970). Advances in computer-based education. *Science,* 167, 1582-1590.

Khosrow-Pour, M. (Ed.). (2002). Issues & trends of information technology management in contemporary organizations. *Proceeding of the 13ᵗʰ International IRMA Conference,* May 19-22. Hershey, PA: Idea Group Publishing.

Merril, M.D., Schneider, E.W., & Fletcher, K.A. (1980). *TICCIT.* Englewood Cliffs, NJ: Education Technology.

Fawzi Albalooshi
University of Bahrain, Bahrain

Acknowledgments

The editor would like to acknowledge the help of all involved in the collection and review process of the book, without whose support the project could not have been satisfactorily completed. I wish to thank all of the authors for their insights and excellent contributions to this book.

A further special note of thanks goes to all the staff at Idea Group Inc., whose contributions throughout the whole process, from inception of the initial idea to final publication, have been invaluable. Special thanks go to Amanda Appicello, the Managing Editor, for her prompt support throughout the process. Final words of thanks go to Abdulla Alderzi and Eshaa Alkhalifa for proof reading the preface and providing useful comments.

Part I

The
Virtual
University

Chapter I

An Overview of Virtual University Studies: Issues, Concepts, Trends

Joseph Barjis
The University of Reading, UK

ABSTRACT

This chapter provides an overview of virtual university studies pertaining to issues, concepts and trends. Although numerous papers, reports and booklets are published with respect to that, there is still lack of an overview of virtual universities. In this chapter, the author tries to draw basic directions of the virtual university studies and developments. These basic directions grasp virtual universities' issues, concepts and trends in general, model, definition and basic characteristics of virtual universities in particular. The author goes on giving some educational and financial features of future higher education. It is discussed that virtual universities and distance learning are currently lacking in some areas that need to be paid attention to in the future. The chapter concludes with some recommendations for the future designers of virtual universities and distance learning programs.

INTRODUCTION

Numerous papers, books, seminars workshops and conferences are dedicated to the introduction and study of virtual universities (VUs). However, there is still lacking a profound concept and overall view of VUs, and their related issues and aspects. This chapter is a starting work to present an overview of important aspects of VUs, where most related issues and aspects are categorized, classified, defined and briefly studied.

Virtual University: What is the Meaning of "Virtual"?

Recently many universities have started projects, written papers, and organized meetings and workshops dealing with the development of "virtual university." Analyzing what is really done or meant with this, you may find the following activities:

- Teaching materials—programs, syllabi, courses, assignments, etc.—are posted to the intranet/Internet in a way that allows students to access them from anywhere at anytime.
- All the course and teaching materials could be accessible by all branches of the university and other partner universities in order to deliver them simultaneously to different students at different locations.
- Study programs could be as selectable and flexible, as they on one hand meet the demands of quality education; on the other hand, they meet exactly the needs and goals of the students.
- All university services and functions (such as administration, library, social life, meetings with staff and lecturers, cafes and so on) are simulated on the Internet so that no physical interaction will be needed any more to complete a study program.
- A central institution offers combinations of study programs or courses from different universities to create one's own curriculum (**broker institution**).

The above mentioned are just some representative features of a VU. They don't claim to be complete coverage of such features. In reality, VUs and related features progress and change so dynamically that it is hard to make any ultimate list of features.

The Information Age and the ICT developments provided an opportunity for new levels of multi-institutional, multistate and multinational collaboration to provide postsecondary education and training through existing and emerging global networks. Collaborating institutions can deliver modules, courses and degrees to individuals and groups of learners who interact with faculty and with organized learning materials, in both real-time and delayed-time (asynchronous) modes. This enriched educational environment envisioned by many academic leaders is captured in the phrase "the virtual university" (Twigg & Oblinger, 1996).

What is the Mission of VU?

The mission of a VU is explained by the **challenge of our time to the higher education system**, which is formulated as follows: *Evolving from an Industrial*

Age University to an Information Age University—from bricks-based university to electronic components-based university—from walls surrounded university to wires surrounded university—from human professors to digital professors—from hard books to electronic books....

Why VU?

In our ever-continuing changing life and ongoing technology application to all spheres of the life of the society, sustainable self-development is a key to competitiveness in the information age.

With application of new and modern information communication technology, more and more possibilities become accessible to each member of the society. Worldwide use of the Internet makes it possible for educators and learners to reach each other without barrier of space and time. In its turn, it opens the door to continuing education, sharing experience and knowledge, learning as often as the modern technology demands for new and new skills.

In-depth discussion and arguments about the mentioned issues will be given later on in the related sections of this chapter.

This chapter is designed as three sections, each dedicated to one of three key directions of the virtual university study. The first section focuses on the virtual university **ISSUES** (problems, obstacles, lacks). The second section covers the virtual university **CONCEPTS** (basic definitions, concepts and ideas behind a virtual university). In addition, the section introduces some models of VU. The third section is dedicated to current **TRENDS** of virtual universities from educational and technical perspectives. It concludes with brief information about some existing VU. The conclusion summarizes results of this chapter and indicates future research related to the topic.

ISSUES

As the title itself suggests, this section addresses some social, legal and technical problems, obstacles and lacks in virtual learning. In order to disclose these issues, let's start this section from a healthy skepticism. Doing this, the author cites the following question from Gladieux and Swail (1999):

> Will management pundit Peter Drucker's prediction that the residential university will cease to exist within 30 years come true? Will "virtual instruction" replace face-to-face lectures, office hours and review sessions? How will the expanding, interactive computer networks of today change the global market for higher education? And more importantly, will the new technologies expand opportunities for those who have been

traditionally underrepresented in higher education or deepen the divide between the educational haves and have-nots?

Answers to these questions depend on how the idea of "virtual university" is implemented, how "virtual instruction" takes place and what will be the range of an average virtual university. Most virtual universities are limited to the boundary of their own state or country. Many virtual universities, at the present stage, serve only a limited population, which makes it unfair to state that they have reached the basic goal, *"learning anytime and from anyplace."*

An important issue is recognition of diplomas and degrees achieved through "virtual universities." There is a great distrust about the quality of education via "virtual universities." Concerning this issue, very little progress is made to grant recognition of degrees awarded through virtual universities. Definitely, first of all, there should be developed, defined and established clear and sound criteria for degrees to be recognized. Probably, there is also a need for classification of fields, where students are allowed to get degrees, and fields where it is not possible to completely study via virtual universities—i.e., fields of study like medicine, biology, chemistry, etc., where virtual education is very hard, if not impossible.

Another issue is social justice. With total emphasis on ICT and Internet access, again education remains a privilege of children with better family income, support and technological awareness, especially in countries where the Internet is still treated as a privilege rather than a daily means of communications.

Very little is known about the number of students and employers who make use of online course offerings. However, individuals who are poor, minority and whose parents are less educated have less access to the Internet either at home or at school; thus, disparity between those who can benefit from virtual education and training and those who cannot is created. In addition to having limited experience with technology, traditionally underrepresented students may benefit more from the traditional delivery systems than the virtual campus (Gladieux & Swail, 1999).

As of yet, no one is regulating the quality and relative utility of each of these providers, and as such, whether or not virtual education and training truly "levels the playing field" is yet to be determined.

Another serious issue is social, cultural and psychological aspects—how to prevent that distance learning will not cause further isolation of a human being from the society. Just recall your college years spent at a traditional university environment and remember how much you have benefited from attending courses along with other fellow students; how much you have learned about various cultures, people and countries studying along with other fellow students from different countries; how you mastered teamwork through joint assignments and projects.

Though it should be also understandable that virtual universities are demands of the time, it is dictated by tremendous demand for facilities and possibilities for adults to participate in ever-lasting education without disrupting from industry. The best thing in this respect is to take advantage of both traditional and virtual universities. So, the above statement by Peter Drucker could be interpreted as: traditional universities have to undergo serious changes to meet the requirements of our time. It means to mix the traditional education system with a virtual one. Here, probably, it is necessary to distinguish between continuing/distance education for adults, and college education for young students. At this stage, virtual universities are directed more towards an adult population rather than young college students.

Despite healthy skepticism stated at the beginning of this section, there are very promising results created by virtual universities and distance learning in this short period.

Some experiments which directly compare Web-based learning with traditional institutions have been conducted within academic settings in recent years. These experiments consistently indicate that students can learn via the Web just as effectively, or in some cases more effectively, than those in traditional classroom (Hall, 1999).

Distance learning has gotten a bad rap. The perception of the public is that online courses are easier (e-learning).

Ed Klonoski, Executive Director of the Connecticut Distance Learning Consortium, concurs with Gunn: "The public does not understand distance education. What does distance learning mean? The Net is like a giant elephant. Everyone touches one part of it. Some use e-mail. Some use other delivery forms." As in the parable of the blind men and the elephant, people promulgate opinions concerning e-learning and whether or not it ought to be trusted based on the isolated part of the beast that they have touched.

So, summarizing all above, virtual universities' specialists need to worry about the standards for virtual education, appropriate interactive technologies, public awareness, etc. It must be stressed that despite the all existing obstacles and problems, the future dictates in favor of distance and virtual education.

CONCEPTS

If, just a few years ago, VU was discussed as an idea, now it is a reality. Today there exist hundreds of VUs in almost all continents, every state of the USA and many European countries.

The VU system is designed for working adults who cannot afford the time away from jobs and families, people who want to study in the USA from their home country Africa or in Europe for their home country in Asia. Finally, this system is designed for those who want to make education their lifelong learning business. Furthermore, this system is designed to transform your life experience and practical skills into academic credits and achieve your goal faster, easier and better. In a word, the VU idea is to bring the university to students instead of calling on students to universities, to adapt the university to students instead of adapting students to the university—this is not anymore an instructor-centric process, but student-centric. To use the power of modern information technologies to dramatically increase access to global educational resources throughout the world—this must be top priority in the mission of virtual universities.

Online learning gives you the flexibility to meet your education goals at your convenience—anyplace, anytime! All you need is access to a computer and the Internet, and you're ready to take advantage of the many online programs and courses offered by the best colleges and universities and other providers.

VU Models

An important role in the success and growth of VUs is information technology. It is technology that makes it possible for distance learning universities to be successful, just in time and up-to-date. Some of these technological components, that comprise a technical environment for virtual universities, are graphically represented in Figure 1. These components are the most important technological aspects of a virtual university system that together provide a Distance Learning Support System (DLSS).

Figure 1: A Model and Components of a Virtual University

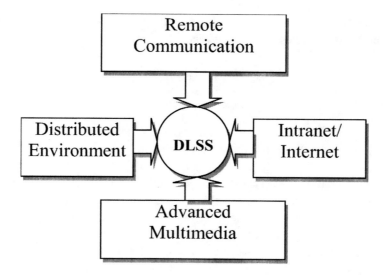

Model: The African Virtual University (http://www.avu.org)

The African Virtual University's (AVU's) delivery model combines a creative integration of satellite and Internet technologies that allows it to provide quality educational content from all over the world at an affordable cost, while taking into account the technological and infrastructure limitations that currently prevail in Africa. AVU places a high premium on interactivity and local learner support so as to ensure pedagogical effectiveness.

World-class professors from universities around the globe deliver classes from a studio classroom. The course is transmitted to AVU's central uplink facilities in Clarksburg, Maryland, and then beamed by satellite to its learning centers all across Africa, which are each equipped with an inexpensive satellite dish required to receive the signal.

The typical AVU classroom has between 25-30 students, sitting at their desks watching the broadcast on large-screen projectors, television monitors or computers. During the class, students have the opportunity for real-time interaction with the instructor using phone lines or e-mail. This framework allows a student in Rwanda, for example, to pose a question to a professor in Togo or Paris that can be heard and commented upon by students in Benin and Senegal. At each participating AVU learning center, on-site moderators guide the students through the materials and act as liaison with course instructors.

Each AVU learning center is equipped with at least 50 computers and Internet access.

Model: New Jersey Virtual University (http://www.njvu.org)

Distance learning opportunities available through New Jersey Virtual University (NJVU) are designed to meet the varied educational needs of a broad range of students using a mix of methods and technologies. You should consider what delivery methods are best suited to your individual educational needs and learning style.

For example, if you need the flexibility to work at odd hours and enjoy using your computer to interact with others electronically, then asynchronous online courses may work well for you. If you are interested in regular feedback and discussion, you should seek out offerings that will afford the greatest opportunity to interact with faculty and other students, such as courses delivered over the Internet or via interactive television.

Types of VU

- Granting a degree
- Mediating for a degree/serving as a Web-based clearinghouse for courses and degrees offered by member institutions

Basic Concepts

Listed below are primary considerations for any institution desiring to become information age (Childs, n.d.):

Customized education, where each individual receives basics, then tailors the educational experience to meet their own needs and learning style.

Just-in-time education, where knowledge is sought at a time and location relevant to the learner's need.

Facilitated learning options, where the teacher structures the learning environment/resources/activities.

Learning organizations, where new, timely information constantly forces the reevaluation and restructuring of processes, fundamental beliefs and databases.

Collaborative efforts, where individuals interact in such forums as town meetings or virtual conferences.

Connectivity, where individuals have open access to a variety of information and databases (LANs, WANs, internets, extract) as well as experts and other students.

The following are the most important opportunities that a VU provides:

Variety of programs/extensive curricula/great choice

You don't need to wait until next semester for the desired course. You are not forced to get the required amount of credits within the curricula of one university. You are free to choose the cheapest courses, from the favorite colleges and professors.

Usually, virtual universities consist of numerous member institutions, in which case they serve as clearinghouse for courses and programs. When you enroll in one of these programs, you can select courses offered by any of the participating universities. For example, just for the sake of comparison, here we look at some facts of virtual universities.

- The California Virtual Campus (http://www.cvc.edu) has 131 schools, 3,692 courses and 170 programs.
- The Canadian Virtual University (http://www.cvu-uvc.ca/english.html), comprising 13 universities, offers 2,000 courses to choose from, and the list is growing.
- The New Jersey Virtual University (http://www.njvu.org) provides an easy-to-use index to over 1,300 credit and noncredit distance learning courses offered by 42 of the state's public and independent higher education institutions.
- Virtual University (http://www.vu.org) claims to be the world's largest online learning community, serving half a million students and alumni in 128 countries.

VU Web Manager Richard Dean says, "Nearly 60% of our students at Virtual University are in the 40-59 age bracket, and this is by far our largest audience."

None of the traditional universities can afford such a great opportunity, variety of program and extensive curricula including the world largest universities.

You may complete your degree from anywhere in the world.

Here's what to expect as a student at a VU:

Program Convenience—Earn your master's or doctoral degree from the convenience of your home or workplace. The WIDU degree programs make it easy for you to further educational goals and professional objectives.

Rigorous, Flexible Curricula—Guide your own course of study with the help of the faculty mentors. Relate research to your personal interest and design projects that satisfy curriculum requirements and your professional objectives.

Personalized Support—Expect regular and frequent one-on-one interaction with faculty mentors, who provide mentorship and collegial guidance.

Strong Faculty Mentors—Carefully recruited scholars, highly skilled academicians and working professionals, our faculty members bring strong credentials and practical experience to the development of each student.

Global learning community

A good distance learning program should adhere to the same academic standards as the institution's traditional courses and programs. The institution should provide students with complete information regarding: the course and degree requirements, the nature of faculty/student interaction, assumptions about technological competence and skills, technical equipment requirements, and any difference between on-campus and distance learning tuition and fee charges.

Students should also expect equivalent access to academic and administrative support services, such as library and learning resources, advisement and counseling, registration, financial aid resources and other appropriate services.

Distance learning offerings that provide for discussion groups and other opportunities for participants to share ideas and learn from each other further enrich the academic experience, as does timely interaction with faculty. In most cases, distance education is learner-centered, with faculty functioning as a facilitator or moderator rather than a lecturer. It is a mistake, however, to think that distance learning will be easier than learning in conventional classes; you may find it requires more work, and it certainly requires self-discipline.

To summarize all the mentioned concepts, definitions and features related to virtual universities, the following statement can be made: each institution strictly following the following characteristics can be considered as an information age university, consequently as a virtual university.

Main Characteristics of a VU

- The university is completely based on ICT facilities with constant access to the Internet.
- The university provides selectable and flexible study programs everywhere and at any time in the range of its coverage (city, state, country or continent).
- Students, staff and faculty are IT competent…on the desktop, in the classroom and lecture hall, and in the simulation "center."
- State-of-the-art hardware and software are at hand (Chilcoat, n.d.).
- Institutional IT infrastructure (classroom, lecture hall, campus) is state-of-the-art (Chilcoat, n.d.).
- Academic programs are IT-based, "as appropriate" (Chilcoat, n.d.).
- University is a "learning organization"…shared vision…shared situational awareness…everyone contributes…is flat, seamless, tailorable and virtual (Chilcoat, n.d.).
- Students are taught and practiced in the art and science of "thinking in the information age" (Chilcoat, n.d.).

Delivery Methods/Modes, Means, Technology

The courses and programs in virtual universities are offered using various means of technology. In some cases, courses are provided online, requiring access to a computer with a modem. Others may need a VCR, access to an interactive classroom or other technology. The following are the most used terms for delivery methods/modes.

Audio Tapes—Taking a class by listening to all or part of it on your tape cassette machine.

Video Tapes—Taking a class by listening to all or part of it on your VCR player.

CD/Multimedia—A class, some or all of whose content is stored on a CD-ROM disk. This content can contain text, sound, video, graphics, animations and files to be downloaded (which means to receive a file into your computer from a remote computer and store it there).

Interactive TV—A class where you are seated in a specially equipped room where you can see, hear and converse back and forth with your professor and fellow classmates who may be located in one or more similarly equipped rooms no where near yours.

TV/Cable TV/Public TV/Satellite TV—Taking a class by watching all or part of it on your television set.

Correspondence Mail—Taking a class, some or all of whose content and discussions between you and your professor are carried out via printed communications, which are largely exchanged through surface mail.

E-Mail—Taking a class by communicating in part or entirely by using electronic mail or messages sent from one person, such as your professor, to another via computer networks.

Internet/Web—Taking a class where you will be asked to find information on numerous topics including, for example, your course curriculum, course content and course notes by visiting designated websites.

PC-Based Interactive—Taking a class, which involves your taking part in computer-based electronic discussions and dialogs among yourself, your professor and your classmates.

TRENDS

Generally, there three trends that must be mentioned as virtual universities progress. These are educational, technical and legal (social cultural) trends. The last trend is about how virtual universities are accepted by the society and people. How progresses recognition of this type of universities? Do these universities represent the actual future of the higher education system? For further discussions, we take a look at some works by other authors.

Creanor et al. (1996) introduce Clyde Virtual University as Europe's first virtual university. Although this article is focused on this particular university, some results and conclusions can be extended to any VU. For example, in this work the authors define VU trends in two aspects—educational and technical trends having a profound influence on higher education.

Educational Trends

- Increasing student numbers
- Wider diversity of student backgrounds
- Reaching out to the wider community—lifelong learning
- Tighter funding
- Movement towards a standard curriculum

Technical Trends

- Increased bandwidth
- Massive increase in the use of the Internet
- The development of 'virtual' libraries, laboratories and campuses

Some other important trends in the development of virtual universities are as follows; however, due to limited space and scope of the chapter, they are listed without detailed description. For a detailed list and description, interested readers are referred to Twigg (1997).

Lifelong learning

Due to rapid changes taking place in business and industry, in addition to the rightsizing of corporations, the average worker can anticipate having six or seven different careers in the course of a lifetime. Reskilling is becoming a requirement for employees. Companies are reengineering themselves and revamping fundamental work processes, resulting in fewer people left to do more things.

New competencies

Proficiency in using technology is now, for all practical purposes, a required competency in the workforce; it is becoming another basic skill. Ninety-five, if not 100% of all workers use some type of information technology in their jobs. The capacity for individuals to use technology both independently and collaboratively in their work is increasingly required. No one person has all the competencies needed in today's high-performance workplace; collaboration is essential. Is higher education staying abreast of these new competencies?

Telecommuting or telework

Millions of people around the world work from a home office. This number dramatically grows with each month and year. In a near future, most of working population of our society will be employed in home-based businesses. Telecommuting/ teleworking is becoming a way of life.

Changing demographics

The changing demographics of higher education are placing new demands on institutions. A million working adults are currently enrolled part time in American and European colleges and universities.

Increasing demand

Current studies show an incredible growth in older and employed students seeking skills enhancement and continuing education, and the numbers go much higher each month and year.

Knowledge explosion

The world's volume of new information is increasing at such a rapid pace that a class of this year will be exposed to more new data in a year than their grandparents encountered in a lifetime. Knowledge doubles every seven years.

Globalization

Globalization of the world's economies is leading to increased emphasis on internationalization of the curriculum.

Productivity

With declining budgets and increasing enrollments in higher education, there is a continuing push to find ways to get more scholars for the Dollar/Euro. Demands for greater productivity in higher education continue to be heard with greater frequency than anytime in the past.

New definitions of quality

Students expect to participate in a learning environment that fosters measurable improvement in their skill development, not just during college but also throughout their careers. Students are increasingly selecting curricula that enhance their chances of both initial and sustained employment.

A more competitive environment

Students are using their purchasing power to be more selective about which institutions they attend. Colleges challenge each other's strategic positions for funds and students.

Future and Financing of VU

Greater competition in the learning marketplace has the potential to benefit learners by offering more choices, more delivery options, lower costs and increased flexibility.

In the debate over the changes higher education must make to respond to the needs of 21st-century learners, two distinct viewpoints dominate. One view is that the role of the university should not be lost in an effort to compete with nontraditional providers such as training institutes. Advocates argue there is more to education than learning specific job-related skills. For instance, students may not know what they want or need, and the traditional institution provides guidance, structure and organization. More importantly, students may not appreciate enough the college atmosphere, whereby meeting other students, doing joint works, conducting team projects, they can develop themselves in the sense of sociability, team spirit, ability to work with different people and in different environments.

The following are some features of future higher education:

Most students are not seeking degrees. Instead, modularization enables them to meet their particular learning needs, often tied to job or career goals.

Curricular materials are outcome oriented. Some outcomes relate to the *goals of a liberal arts education;* others are defined more along the lines of *skills.*

The faculty role has changed. As a greater amount of codified knowledge is captured in courseware, the role of the faculty member is increasingly that of mentor or leader in the learning process.

Faculty labor is applied at times and in circumstances when it is needed—*that is, on-demand*—rather than on a fixed schedule such as the three-lectures-per-week model (Massy, 1997).

The **economics of supply and demand** in the new competitive environment keep the **costs of basic courses and programs low.**

Unique offerings garner higher incomes for their providers.

In addition to faculty salaries, **institutional resources are expended on course materials, instructional technologies and academic support.** Some or all of those may be *purchased* from other higher education institutions and from private providers. The proportion of the budget allocated to faculty salaries is declining.

The move away from site-based educational delivery has required **different kinds of capital investments** for infrastructure.

Educational **funding now follows the learner** rather than the institution.

Because employers have continued to reduce their numbers of core, benefited employees in favor of part-time workers or contracted/outsourced services, most students pay directly for the education they need.

Because more students are in the workforce than in the initial college-going population, more **students pay directly** for the education they need.

Public institutions **no longer receive a substantial amount of state funding.** Revenue sources include tuition, contracts with employers and other agencies of state government for training, sale of courses and courseware to other institutions, and low-interest state loans.

SOME INFORMATION AGE UNIVERSITIES

The following are some of virtual universities spread all over the world. Information about these universities are retrieved from their websites, therefore some facts could be valid only at the moment of retrieval—for example, number of courses, programs, collaborative institutions, etc. Although the choice of these virtual universities was mainly dictated by Internet search engines, they do represent leading virtual universities at the moment. It should be noted immediately that due to space restriction, just a few universities are introduced in this part. The purpose is to give readers an idea and brief information about some virtual universities, without interrupting the reading by visiting the sites in search of such information. However, for interested readers the website addresses are provided for further investigation.

University of Phoenix (http://www.phoenix.edu)

Founded in 1976, the University of Phoenix is now one of the United States' largest private accredited universities. It provides a relevant, real-world education to working adults at more than 107 campuses and learning centers in the U.S., Puerto Rico and Canada, and via the Internet. Currently, the university enroll 103,200 degree-seeking students.

DeVry Institutes (http://www.devry.edu/)

DeVry's historical roots lie in the technical education movement of the early 1900s. In 1931, Dr. Herman DeVry established DeForest Training School in Chicago to prepare students for technical work in electronics, motion pictures, radio and, later, television. The name was changed to DeVry Technical Institute in 1953, and it became the flagship of the current system of campuses. In 1968, the name was once again changed, to DeVry Institute of Technology.

The 21 DeVry campuses in the United States and Canada compose one of the largest private higher education systems in North America. Currently, DeVry campuses are located in Arizona, California, Florida, Georgia, Illinois, Missouri, New Jersey, New York, Ohio, Texas, Virginia, Washington, Alberta and Ontario, Canada, serving some 47,000 students.

The DeVry system has expanded in curriculum and degree offerings as well. In 1957, the DeVry Institutes achieved associate-degree-granting status in electronics engineering technology and 12 years later were authorized to grant bachelor's degrees in the same discipline. Computer Science for Business (later renamed Computer Information Systems) was introduced in 1979 as DeVry's second bachelor's degree program.

U.S. DeVry campuses are accredited by The Higher Learning Commission and are members of the North Central Association (NCA).

The California Virtual Campus (http://www.cvc.edu/)

The California Virtual Campus was created under the auspices of the Chancellor's Office for the California Community Colleges. One of its major responsibilities is the continuation of the Web-based distance-education catalog developed by the California Virtual University. CVU ceased operations in March 1999. CVC is maintained by El Camino College and Santa Monica College.

The CVC has 131 schools, 3,692 courses and 170 programs. The California Virtual Campus does not grant degrees or certificates. Through its service, learners can find out about courses and certificate or degree programs offered at a distance by California's leading institutions of higher education; and it connects learners to the appropriate campus to enroll and find out more information.

The mission of the California Virtual Campus (CVC) is to bring the best of California higher education to full- and part-time students in California, the United States and throughout the world. CVC is intended to expand access within California to post-secondary education and assist the state in meeting the needs of a significant portion of the nearly 500,000 additional students projected to enter California's higher education institutions over the next decade.

Additionally, CVC seeks to provide to California employers a means by which they can improve the productivity of their workforce through an extensive network of high-quality, distance-education programs and services. As California's large corporations launch sophisticated intranets and small businesses utilize the Internet, CVC can provide access to a wide range of courses and programs delivered over these new platforms.

New Jersey Virtual University (http://www.njvu.org/)

NJVU provides an easy-to-use index to over 1,300 credit and noncredit distance learning courses offered by 42 of the state's public and independent higher education institutions. The index also includes more than 40 complete degree and certificate programs, at the undergraduate and graduate level. NJVU coordinates distance learning for the state, but is not a degree granting institution. After finding the right course or program for you, registration takes place at the host institution.

The index allows users to search for desired courses or programs by institution, subject area, mode of instruction or other criteria. It enables users to combine criteria to locate the precise offerings that best meet their needs. The index also enables users to link directly to an institution's distance learning Web page or online catalogue for specific information regarding courses, admission, registration, cost and other facts about the institution. In addition to course and program information, NJVU provides valuable resources to faculty members interested in online teaching and technology-mediated instruction.

Distance learning through New Jersey's colleges and universities provides flexibility and an increased opportunity to meet individual and workforce needs. The courses and programs offered by New Jersey higher education institutions respond to the needs of a diverse population of learners requiring flexible timeframes and convenient ways to access education.

The African Virtual University (http://www.avu.org/)

The African Virtual University (AVU) is a "university without walls" that uses modern information and communication technologies to give the countries of sub-Saharan Africa direct access to some of the highest quality academic faculty and learning resources throughout the world. AVU is bridging the digital divide by training world-class scientists, engineers, technicians, business managers and other professionals who will promote economic and social development and help Africa leapfrog into the Knowledge Age.

Since the launch of its pilot phase in 1997, AVU has provided students and professionals in 15 African countries with more than 2,500 hours of interactive instruction in English and in French. More than 12,000 students have completed semester-long courses in engineering and in the sciences, and over 2,500 professionals have attended executive and professional management seminars on topics such as strategy and innovation, entrepreneurship, global competencies, e-commerce and Y2K.

AVU also provides students access to an online digital library with over 1,000 full-text journals, and more than 10,000 free e-mail accounts have been opened and can be accessed through the AVU website.

Kentucky Virtual University (http://www.kyvu.org)

The Kentucky Virtual University (KYVU) was created in 1997 with passage of the Kentucky Postsecondary Education Improvement Act. Opening its doors to 235 students in the inaugural Fall 1999 term, the virtual university grew quickly to over 3,200 students by Spring 2001. KYVU plays a critical role in achieving the goals for 2020 outlined in that legislation. The virtual university is dedicated to playing a major role in fulfilling the Council on Postsecondary's goal of adding 80,000 more students to the college ranks by the Year 2020.

Western Governors University (http://www.wgu.edu)

In late 1998, Western Governors University (WGU) began operation as the United States' first exclusively virtual university. WGU was formed by the governors of 17 states (plus Guam), along with a number of business partners including Microsoft, Sun Systems, IBM and AT&T. It has no plans to hire faculty, but will procure its online academic materials from businesses and institutions of higher education in the U.S. or other countries. Students anywhere in the world can enroll. WGU's mission is to "expand educational opportunities for learners everywhere" and provide access to a "dispersed population of students who might not otherwise have access to higher education and to those needing workplace training."

On June 6, 2001, the Accrediting Commission of the Distance Education and Training Council (DETC) announced that WGU has been granted accreditation. There are more than 50 institutions offering courses or degrees through WGU.

Canadian Virtual University (http://www.cvu-uvc.ca)

Canadian Virtual University (CVU) is a partnership of universities across Canada, committed to delivering university-level programs that can be completed from anywhere in the country or beyond. CVU comprises 13 Canadian universities offering over 175 programs available through the Internet or by distance education.

Clyde Virtual University (http://cvu.strath.ac.uk/)

Clyde Virtual University (CVU) was founded in 1995 with funding from the Scottish Higher Education Funding Council to develop and deliver Internet-based teaching materials to students registered at five institutions in the West of Scotland. Founded in 1995 as Europe's first virtual university, CVU combines the academic and technical strengths of Glasgow, Strathclyde, Glasgow Caledonian and Paisley universities, together with the Glasgow School of Art. It has become the central repository for learning material for these institutions.

Virtual University (http://www.vu.org)

Virtual University claims to be the world's largest online learning community, serving half a million students and alumni in 128 countries. VU Web Manager Richard Dean says, "Nearly 60% of our students at Virtual University are in the 40-59 age bracket, and this is by far our largest audience."

The World Information Distributed University (http://www.widu.ru)

WIDU takes advantage of both VU and conventional universities. VU means that WIDU has professors from other universities, collaboration with other universities, distance learning opportunity, etc. Conventional means that WIDU has campuses, departments, educational sites, etc. Another big difference, WIDU confers degrees upon outstanding personalities, political and public figures. It also awards honorary degrees to outstanding professors.

But, what is most important, WIDU is a degree-granting institution that offers degrees at all high levels—MSc, PhD and Grand PhD (this is a Postdoctoral Degree, equivalent to Doctor of Science, or German Habilitation).

CONCLUSION

From the study in this chapter, the first important conclusion that can be derived is, distance learning will not replace the traditional classroom setting, but it provides extraordinary opportunities for students, particularly those constrained by time or location.

Concerning quality programs, the programs should include a number of the same elements contained in a traditional university: technical support, individualized attention to students, mentoring and faculty-student exchanges.

Based on the view of various authors and experts, the following recommendation could be helpful for the designers of future virtual university systems, curricula and programs; makers and providers of technology; and public policymakers: make access a central concern, keep the allure of technology in perspective and learn from past ventures in distance education. Try to keep traditional universities open for those who will prefer to get their degrees in the traditional environment and enjoy studying along with other fellow students.

As future work, the author is planning to capture the mentioned issues and aspects in separate and in more detail. Each of the mentioned issues is a topic for a profound research work.

REFERENCES

Blumenstyk, G. (1995). Campuses in cyberspace. *Chronicle of Higher Education,* 42(16), A19, A21.

Chilcoat, R. (n.d.). *"Visioning" An Information Age University (In An Information Age JPMESystem).* Source: http://web.nps.navy.mil/FutureWarrior/Presentations/Chilcoat/Default.htm.

Childs, R.D. (n.d.). *An Informational Age University: A Living Organism Based on Intellectual Capital.* Source: http://www.ndu.edu/irmc/faculty/childs.htm.

Creanor, L., Sclater, N. & Whittington, D. (1996). Clyde Virtual University. *Proceedings of the Fifth International World Wide Web Conference,* May 6-10, Paris, France.

E-Learning—The Other White Meat? Industry-Wide Promotion Campaign Takes Shape. Source: http://www.geteducated.com/vugaz.htm.

Forman, D.C. (1995). The use of multimedia technology for training in business and industry. *Multimedia Monitor,* 13(7), 2227.

Gladieux, L.E. & Swail, W.S. (1999). *The Virtual University and Educational Opportunity: Issues of Equity and Access for the Next Generation.* Washington DC: The College Board, April. Source: http://www.aera.net/gov/archive/i0499-01.htm.

Hall, R.H. (1999). Instructional website design principles: A literature review and synthesis. *Virtual University Journal,* 2(1).

Massy, W. (1997). Life on the wired campus: How information technology will shape institutional futures. In Oblinger, D. & Rush, S. (Eds.), *The Learning Revolution.* Bolton, MA: Anker Publishing.

Tuller, C. (1997). Another paradigm shift. In Oblinger, D. & Rush, S. (Eds.), *The Learning Revolution.* Bolton, MA: Anker Publishing.

Twigg, C.A & Oblinger, D.G. (1996). *The Virtual University: A Report from a Joint Educom/IBM Roundtable,* Washington, DC, November 5-6. Reporter Patricia Bartscherer, Administrative Assistant, Educom.

Verville, A.L. (1995). What business needs from higher education. *Educational Record,* 76(4), 46-50.

Vigilante, R. (1994). *The Virtual College.* New York: New York University.

Wagner, E.C. (1998) A virtual university in a traditional environment. *Proceedings of the 7th European Distance Education Network,* June 24-26, University of Bologna, Italy.

Wendy Rickard Bollentin, President, The Rickard Group, Inc.

Willums, J.O. (n.d.). *Life-Long Learning in the New Economy.* Source: http://www.foundation.no/vus/newecon.htm.

Chapter II

A Framework for the Development of an Accredited Web-Based Computer Information Systems Degree

Kathy S. Lassila
Colorado State University–Pueblo, USA

Kris Howell
Colorado State University–Pueblo, USA

ABSTRACT

The Web-based delivery of online IS baccalaureate programs is a recent innovation. While IS researchers have identified a number of key factors related to the effective online delivery of individual courses, little empirical evidence exists to suggest "best practices" in the development and delivery of a complete four-year IS online degree program. This chapter examines and synthesizes IS education criteria from two sources: the Computer Sciences Accreditation Commission, which recently established criteria for accrediting programs in information systems, and the Regional Accrediting Commissions, which issued guidelines for the evaluation of electronically offered degree and certificate programs. The result is a set of guidelines that act as a framework for the development of online baccalaureate programs in computer information systems that addresses both IS and online accreditation requirements.

INTRODUCTION

The current and projected nationwide shortage of information systems (IS) professionals is driving a renewed interest in IS education, as companies strive to hire new IS graduates and retrain existing employees. One solution to the growing demand for IS education is the use of the World Wide Web as an educational delivery mode. The proliferation of commercially available Web-based training products is evidence of the potential of this educational delivery mode to address the needs of industry and the economy. In addition, Web-based educational delivery has been widely accepted as an effective learning platform by students, teachers and academic administrators (Tillett, 2000). Colleges and universities are entering the online education arena in increasing numbers. While much is known about how to effectively deliver individual courses online, what do we know about how to effectively deliver the entire IS degree online? What do we need to know to provide a quality IS educational experience via the Internet?

This chapter addresses the questions posed above by presenting a framework for the development of the online IS baccalaureate degree expressed as a set of quality guidelines. The guidelines are developed through a synthesis of drafts from two relevant authorities on IS and online education: the Computer Sciences Accreditation Board (CSAB) of the Accrediting Board for Engineering and Technology (ABET), and the Council of Regional Accrediting Commissions (C-RAC), comprising eight United States regional accrediting bodies.

The next section discusses the background and development of draft guidelines by both the CSAB and C-RAC and their current status. The synthesis of the draft guidelines from both accrediting entities creates the basis for a set of guidelines to direct the development of online baccalaureate programs in IS which are presented in the following section. The model is then discussed, along with its implications for effective Web-based IS degree delivery. Future directions for research and practice are then presented, followed by key conclusions.

BACKGROUND

Web-based education has been touted as the new teaching paradigm for over six years. In the IS field, most faculty use the Web to facilitate and enhance existing courses, while few use it as a replacement for traditional teaching approaches. Darbyshire and Burgess (2002) report that educators have found the Web useful for supporting teaching in a variety of ways. These include: assignment distribution, collection and grading (Boysen & Van Gorp, 1997); grade/performance distribution and reporting; and informing students of important notices (Landon, 1998). Some of the key advantages of Web-based teaching assistance include: support for interactivity between students and educators, ease of course information dissemination, use as a real-time communication medium, and the support for text, graphics, audio and video tools (Kaynama & Keesling, 2000).

The online delivery of complete four-year IS programs is a recent innovation. While many institutions offer a number of IS courses online, few offer an accredited IS baccalaureate degree online. As such, little empirical research exists that provides evidence for a set of "best practices" in IS online degree delivery. Much of the literature is anecdotal or based on limited case study. Given the lack of empirical research on effective Web-based delivery of IS programs, the framework presented in the next section is principally derived from the key guidelines established for electronically offered degrees accepted by the Council of Regional Accrediting Commissions (initially drafted by the Western Cooperative for Educations Telecommunications/ Western Interstate Commission for Higher Education (WICHE), 1999); and from the criteria for accrediting programs in information systems developed and adopted by the Computer Sciences Accreditation Board (CSAB) of the Accrediting Board for Engineering and Technology (ABET). Since accreditation of academic programs is highly desirable to most institutions and prospective students, the guidelines drafted by the C-RAC and the criteria drafted by the CSAB form a reasonable basis for the guidelines for the development of a Web-based IS degree. Each of these criteria are discussed below.

The Computing Sciences Accreditation Board (CSAB) produced Version 5.2 of "Draft Criteria for Accrediting Programs in Information Systems" in August 2000 (CSAB, 2000). The criteria were adapted for information systems programs from the previously established accrediting criteria for programs in computer science. The key objectives of the criteria are "to assure an adequate foundation in business, general education, mathematics, social sciences and information systems fundamentals, and to assure appropriate preparation in advanced information systems areas" (CSAB, p. 1).

Overall, an information systems program must be designed to provide a broad general education at the baccalaureate level and prepare students to function effectively in the information systems profession in order to be considered for CSAB accreditation. While the CSAB draft criteria do not specifically address distance education or online degree programs, these programs are eligible for evaluation and accreditation review.

The criteria address eight major categories: program objectives and assessments, students, faculty, curriculum, technology infrastructure, institutional support and financial resources, program facilities and institutional facilities. These categories, summarized in Table 1, were to be applied to CSAB evaluation of information systems programs beginning in 2001.

The Western Cooperative for Educational Telecommunications/Western Interstate Commission for Higher Education (WICHE), recognized for its substantial expertise in the field of distance learning, initially developed a draft of guidelines for electronically offered degree programs in 1999 with the purpose of reflecting current best practice in online program delivery (Academe, 2001; WICHE, 1999). The eight regional accrediting commissions responsible for accrediting United States colleges and universities used the WICHE draft as the basis for developing "Guidelines for the Evaluation of Electronically Offered Degree and Certificate Programs" for accrediting degree programs offered electronically. The Council of Regional Accrediting Commissions (C-RAC), the organizational body for the eight commissions, undertook the development of the draft to respond to the ongoing emergence of technologically mediated instruction offered at a distance (C-RAC, 1999).

Table 1: Comparison of CSAB IS Criteria and C-RAC Guidelines

Category	CASB IS Criteria	C-RAC Guidelines
(1) **Institutional Context, Support and Financial Resources**	• Sufficient support for faculty to enable program to attract/retain high-quality faculty capable of supporting the program's objectives • Sufficient support/financial resources to allow faculty members to attend technical meetings to maintain competence as teachers and scholars • Support and recognition of faculty scholarly activities • Sufficient office support for faculty members • Adequate time assigned for administration of the program • Sufficient program resources and atmosphere to function effectively with the rest of the institution • Sufficient resources to acquire/maintain adequate laboratory facilities • Sufficient resources to support library and information retrieval facilities that meet the needs of the program • Evidence of continuity of institutional support and financial resources	• Program is consistent with the institution's role and mission • Notification/consultation with accrediting commission if program represents a major change to educational goals, intended student population, curriculum, modes/venue of instruction • Institution budgets/policies reflect commitment to target students of electronically offered programs • Articulation/transfer policies judge courses/programs on learning outcomes, not modes of delivery • Assure consistent/coherent technical framework for students/faculty; minimize impact of technological change on students/faculty • Technical support provided to students for all hardware, software and delivery systems required in a program • Selection of technologies is based on appropriateness for the students and the curriculum • Institution observes the legal and regulatory requirements of the jurisdictions in which it operates
(2) **Institutional Facilities**	• Library adequately staffed with professional librarians and support personnel • Library technical collection includes up-to-date texts, reference works, and publications of professional and research organizations • Systems for locating/obtaining electronic information available • Classrooms adequately equipped for courses taught in them • Faculty offices adequate to enable faculty members to meet their responsibilities	

Table 1: Comparison of CSAB IS Criteria and C-RAC Guidelines (continued)

Category	CASB IS Criteria	C-RAC Guidelines
(3) **Program Objectives and Assessment**	• Educational objectives are documented and consistent with the mission of the institution • Objectives include expected outcomes for graduating students • Process exists for periodic review of program/courses • Program assessment results used to identify/implement program improvement • Results of program review/actions taken must be documented	• As part of institution's overall assessment, student performance is compared to intended learning outcomes in each course and at program completion; assessment results of student achievement are documented • Examinations are administered in circumstances that include firm student identification • Security of personal information is assured and security procedures are documented • Overall program effectiveness includes measures such as: - Match between student learning and intended outcomes - Extent to which student intent is met - Student retention rates - Student satisfaction, measured by periodic surveys - Faculty satisfaction, measured by periodic surveys - Extent to which access is provided to students not previously served - Extent to which library/learning resources are used appropriately by students - Student competence in fundamental communication, comprehension and analysis skills - Cost effectiveness of program to students, compared to campus-based alternatives • Program and results are reflected in the institution's ongoing self-evaluation process • Institutional evaluation of the program takes place in the context of the regular evaluation of all academic programs
(4) **Faculty**	• Interests, qualifications and scholarly contributions of the faculty members are sufficient to teach/plan/modify courses and curriculum • Faculty members are current and active in the discipline • Majority of faculty hold terminal degrees; some must be in IS or closely related field • Faculty members have level of competence that would normally be obtained through graduate work in IS	• Institution and participating faculty develop policies/agreements on workload, compensation, ownership of intellectual property resulting from the program, implications of program participation for faculty professional evaluation processes • Institution provides ongoing program of appropriate technical, design and production support for participating faculty members • Institution provides orientation/training on technologies/pedagogy to those responsible for program development and those working directly with students

The guidelines focused on providing assistance to institutions in planning distance education activities, and on providing a self-assessment framework for institutions already involved in such endeavors (C-RAC, 1999).

Table 1: Comparison of CSAB IS Criteria and C-RAC Guidelines (continued)

Category	CASB IS Criteria	C-RAC Guidelines
(5) Curriculum	• Curriculum combines professional requirements with general education requirements and electives to prepare students for a professional career in IS • Curriculum covers basic and advanced topics in IS as well as an emphasis on the IS environment • Curricula consistent with widely recognized models and standards • Specific requirements: - At least 30 semester-hours in IS topics - At least 15 semester-hours in an IS environment, such as business - At least 9 semester-hours in quantitative analysis beyond pre-calculus, including statistics and calculus or discrete mathematics - At least 30 semester-hours of study in general education • Oral and written communications skills, and collaborative skills must be developed and applied in the program • Sufficient coverage of global, economic, social and ethical implications of computing	• Program of study results in collegiate-level learning outcomes appropriate to the degree • Program is coherent and complete, leading to undergraduate degrees that include general education requirements • Academically qualified persons participate fully in the decisions concerning program curricula and program oversight • Institution includes all courses necessary to complete the program • If some program components are supplied by consortia partners or outsourced, the institution must establish criteria for their selection and means to monitor/evaluate their work • Program design reflects the importance of appropriate interaction between instructor and students, and among students
(6) Program Delivery	• Enough full-time faculty members with primary commitment to the program to provide continuity and stability • Full-time faculty must oversee all course work • Full-time faculty must cover most of the total classroom instruction • Full-time faculty must remain current in the discipline • Full-time faculty have sufficient time for scholarly activities and professional development • Advising duties are recognized part of faculty members' workloads	
(7) Technology Infrastructure	• Each student must have adequate/reasonable access to systems needed for each course • Documentation for hardware/software must be readily accessible to faculty and students • Faculty members must have access to adequate computing resources for class preparation and scholarly activities • Adequate support personnel to install and maintain computing resources	

The C-RAC guidelines address five separate components: institutional context and commitment, curriculum and instruction, faculty support, student support, and

Table 1: Comparison of CSAB IS Criteria and C-RAC Guidelines (continued)

Category	CASB IS Criteria	C-RAC Guidelines
	• Instructional assistance provided for computing resources	

(8) Students	• Courses offered with sufficient frequency to all students to complete program in reasonable amount of time
	• Effective interaction between teaching faculty and students is ensured by program structure
	• Advising on program completion, course selection and career opportunities made available to all students
	• Standards and procedures are established to ensure that graduates meet the program requirements
		• Institution has commitment to continuation of the program for a period sufficient to enable all admitted students to complete the degree in the publicized timeframe
		• Prior to admission of student to electronically delivered program, student is qualified via prior education or equivalent experience, and institution provides information to student on:
		  - Required access to technologies used in the program
		  - Technical competence required in the program
		  - Estimated or average program costs and associated payment and refund programs
		  - Curriculum design and timeframe in which courses are offered
		  - Library and other learning services available
		  - Full array of other support services available from the institution
		  - Arrangements for interaction with the faculty and fellow students
		  - Nature and potential challenges of learning in the program's technology-based environment
		  - Estimated time for program completion
		• Appropriate services must be available for students of electronically offered programs
		• Institution recognizes the importance of a "sense of community" to students' success

evaluation and assessment. The five components of the C-RAC guidelines are summarized in Table 1 and synthesized with the CSAB draft criteria in the next section.

ONLINE IS DEGREE FRAMEWORK

The C-RAC guidelines show that well-established standards of institutional quality are applicable to electronically mediated distance learning environments. The CSAB draft criteria provide educational standards for high-quality post-secondary education in information systems. The synthesis of CSAB draft criteria and C-RAC guidelines results in recommendations for online information systems programs across seven key categories: (1) institutional context, support, financial resources and facilities; (2) program objectives and assessments; (3) faculty; (4) curriculum; (5) program delivery; and (6) students. Each of these categories and their implications for online IS baccalaureate programs are discussed below.

Institutional Context, Support, Financial Resources and Facilities

The online IS program should be consistent with the role and mission of the institution. Specifically, offering the program to students at a distance should contribute to the institution's fulfillment of its stated mission. By ensuring consistency with institutional mission, commitment to the targeted students of the online IS program should be reflected in institution budgets and policies. In particular, sufficient institutional support for faculty should be available to enable the program to attract and retain high-quality faculty capable of supporting the program's objectives. Program faculty should receive financial support to attend technical meetings to maintain currency in the field and in teaching, as well as recognition for scholarly activities and sufficient office support. Online IS programs should receive adequate program resources to function effectively with the rest of the institution, acquire and maintain adequate laboratory facilities, and support library and information retrieval needs of the program. The institution should also show ongoing institutional support and financial resource commitments for the program.

The technological context and infrastructure provided for the online IS program by the institution is extremely important, and supersedes the institutional facility requirements of on-campus programs. Selection of technologies to support the online IS program must be based on the appropriateness of the technologies for the students and the curriculum. A consistent, coherent technical framework for students and faculty will minimize the impact of technological change on these parties. In addition, technical support must be provided to all students for all hardware, software and the delivery system required for completion of the online IS program.

Also within the institutional context, articulation and transfer policies must judge courses and programs on learning outcomes and not on modes of delivery to ensure that students receive the greatest benefit from the online IS program. And finally, the institution must observe the legal and regulatory requirements of the jurisdictions in which it operates.

Program Objectives and Assessment

Educational objectives and expected outcomes for graduating IS students must be specified and documented for online IS programs. The online IS program and its results must be reflected in the institution's ongoing self-evaluation process, and institutional evaluation of the program must take place in the context of regular evaluation of all academic programs. A clear process must exist for the periodic review of the online IS program and its related courses. In addition, the results of program reviews must be used to identify and implement program improvements, and the review and actions taken must be documented.

A variety of effectiveness measures should be incorporated in the assessment of online IS programs, including: match between student learning and intended outcomes; extent to which student intent is met; student retention rates; student satisfaction; faculty satisfaction; extent to which access to the online IS program reaches previously unserved students; extent to which library/information resources are used appropriately by students; student competence in fundamental communication, comprehension and analysis skills; and cost effectiveness of the program to students compared to campus-based alternatives.

In the online program environment, it is also important that the security of personal information is assured and that security procedures are documented. Also, when examinations are administered via electronically mediated distance formats, circumstances must include accurate student identification measures.

Faculty

Faculty face a number of issues when moving from traditional classroom-based delivery to online IS course delivery. In online IS programs, the institution and participating faculty must develop policies and agreements on workload, compensation, ownership of intellectual property resulting from the program and implications of program participation for faculty professional evaluation processes. The institution must also provide an ongoing program of technical design and production support for online IS faculty members. Training in technologies and pedagogies appropriate for online course delivery is also essential for those developing courses and working directly with students online.

Faculty members participating in the online IS program should demonstrate interests, qualifications and scholarly contributions sufficient to teach, plan and modify online IS courses and the curriculum. In addition, the majority of faculty in the program must hold terminal degrees, some of which must be in IS or a closely related field. In short, faculty members must have a level of competence that would normally be obtained through graduate work in IS. All faculty members are expected to remain current and active in the discipline.

Curriculum

The CSAB draft criteria establish curricular guidelines for programs in IS (CSAB, 2000). The focus of the recommended curriculum is on combining professional, general education and elective requirements to prepare graduates for a professional IS career. The specific curriculum requirements include:

- At least 30 semester hours of IS topics
- At least 15 semester hours in an IS environment, such as business
- At least 9 semester hours in quantitative analysis beyond pre-calculus, including statistics and calculus or discrete mathematics
- At least 30 semester hours of study in general education

In addition, the online IS program must assist students in the development of oral and written communication skills, and collaborative skills. It must also provide sufficient coverage of global, economic, social and ethical implications of computing.

The curriculum requirements specified by the CSAB draft criteria have serious implications for the online IS program. It is not sufficient for the IS major courses to be offered online. Online offerings must be extended to general education, mathematics, statistics and business or some other appropriate environment if the online IS baccalaureate degree will be available to students. Ideally the institution has made a commitment to providing online baccalaureate degrees, and the online IS program will have a variety of courses from which to choose.

Program Delivery

Program delivery refers to the involvement of full-time faculty with the online IS program. A sufficient number of full-time faculty members with primary commitment to the IS program must exist to provide continuity and stability to the program. Full-time faculty must oversee all course work, cover most of the online instruction, remain current in the discipline, and have sufficient time for scholarly activities and professional development. Advising duties must also be a recognized part of the faculty members' workloads.

Students

The online IS program must offer courses with sufficient frequency and continuity to ensure that students can complete the degree in a reasonable amount of time. Prior to admission of the student to the online IS program, the student must be determined to be qualified via prior education or equivalent experience to participate in the program. The student must also be provided information on: required access to technologies used in the program; technical competence required to participate in the program; estimated program costs and associated payment and refund programs; curriculum design and timeframe in which courses are offered; availability of library and other learning services; availability of full array of support services available at the institution; arrangements for interaction with the faculty and fellow students; nature and potential challenges of learning in the program's technology-based environment; and estimated time for program completion.

The institution must also make appropriate services available to online students, such as advising on program completion, course selection and career opportunities. The institution must also recognize the importance of a "sense of community" to students' success, and ensure effective interaction between teaching faculty and students throughout the program. Finally, standards and procedures must be established to ensure that graduates meet program requirements.

DISCUSSION

In synthesizing the IS degree criteria and the electronically offered program accreditation guidelines, several distinct differences between traditional classroom IS education and online IS programs emerged.

First, institutional facilities obviously become less important for off-campus students enrolled in the online IS program. Instead, the technological context provided by the institution is of major importance. It is this technological context that will mediate the student's connection to the program and directly affect student interaction with the course, instructor and fellow students. Technological context must be suitable, reliable, flexible and easily adaptable for students and for faculty.

Second, interactions between online IS students and faculty, and among IS students, must be more directly facilitated. Little facilitation is necessary for students in a face-to-face classroom environment. To nurture the potential benefits from faculty-student and student-student interaction, more deliberate, planned actions must be taken in the online IS program. These actions may involve scheduling chat rooms, interactive chat appointments, or facilitating small group projects and communication.

Third, student assessment as a part of overall program assessment is difficult. When examinations, assignments and other evaluative activities are part of the online course, action must be taken to ensure the student enrolled in the class is the student completing the activity. This is not as easily accomplished as it is in typical classroom interactions.

Finally, faculty in online IS programs face unique challenges. Not all faculty will be effective teaching in online IS programs. Special training in online techniques and pedagogy is necessary to ensure that all participating faculty have the skills necessary to develop and facilitate online learning experiences.

FUTURE DIRECTIONS

Online IS baccalaureate programs are in their infancy. The guidelines provided here are based on current knowledge of effective IS education and effective electronically offered degree programs. As more four-year IS degree programs go online, research opportunities will be created. Some of the key research questions of interest to institutions, faculty, students and prospective employers of graduates include:

- Do online IS program students perform at the same level as students in traditional IS classroom programs?
- Do online IS program students show higher levels of satisfaction with their educational experience than traditional IS program students?
- Are online IS graduates as well-prepared for the IS profession as graduates of traditional IS classroom programs?
- Are employers as satisfied with graduates of online IS programs as they are with graduates of traditional IS programs?
- Do online IS program graduates achieve the same success as graduates of traditional programs?
- Are online IS degree programs as effective as traditional classroom programs?

The most pressing need is to empirically determine a set of "best practices" for the online IS degree program, rather than extrapolating these best practices from prior experiences in distance learning.

CONCLUSION

Online IS baccalaureate programs are an emerging educational experience. Established institutional standards for high-quality educational delivery apply to electronically mediated learning experiences as well as to more traditional classroom models. Prior experience in distance learning also provides guidance for the development of online IS programs. By synthesizing approaches from the institutional guidelines as delineated by the CSAB draft criteria and the distance learning best practices identified by the C-RAC, this chapter develops a set of worthwhile guidelines for the development of online IS baccalaureate degree programs. As more programs are developed and implemented, additional research must be conducted to empirically determine the efficacy of online IS programs.

REFERENCES

Academe. (2001). Accrediting bodies draft distance education guidelines. (January-February), 6.

Boysen, P. & Van Gorp, M.J. (1997). ClassNet: Automated support of Web classes.

Paper presented at the *25ᵗʰ ACM SIGUCCS Conference of University and College Computing Services,* Monterey, California.

Computer Sciences Accreditation Board. (2000, August). *Draft Criteria for Accrediting Programs in Information Systems. (Version 5.2).* Available at: http://www.csab.org. Accessed October 4, 2001.

Council of Regional Accrediting Commissions. (2000, September). Statement of the Regional Accrediting Commissions on the Evaluation of Electronically Offered Degree and Certificate Programs and Guidelines for the Evaluation of Electronically Offered Degree and Certificate Programs. Available at: http://www.wiche.edu/telecom/Article1.htm. Accessed October 15, 2001.

Darbyshire, P. & Burgess, S. (2002). Using the Internet to add value to tertiary education: A comparison between the use of IT in business and education. *Proceedings of IRMA 2002,* Seattle. Hershey, PA: Idea Group Publishing, 139-142.

Kaynama, S.A. & Keesling, G. (2000). Development of a Web-based marketing course. *Journal of Marketing Education,* 22(2), 84-89.

Landon, B. (1998, October 4). *On-Line Educational Delivery Applications: A Web Tool for Comparative Analysis.* Centre for Curriculum, Transfer and Technology, Canada. Available at: http://www.ctt.bc.ca/landonline/. Accessed October 10, 1998.

Tillett, S.L. (2000). Educators begin to reach out—The Net cuts costs, simplifies management and could make distance learning a winner. *InternetWeek,* 835(October 30), 49-56.

Chapter III

Quality Assurance Issues for a Web-Based Degree in Motor Disability Assessment

Salvatore Valenti
Università di Ancona, Italy

Maurizio Panti
Università di Ancona, Italy

Tommaso Leo
Università di Ancona, Italy

ABSTRACT

The growth of credit-bearing distance learning offerings and enrollments at accredited, degree-granting colleges and universities has been astonishing in the last few years. This growth raises the demand for reliable information about quality. According to Kess et al. (2002), quality in education should not be forced into one single definition, but rather a collection of smaller elements, processes, which contribute to education quality in different dimensions. These elements, when chained together, constitute the overall quality in training, and the improvement of quality is achieved through simultaneous action on all these levels. Furthermore, accreditation and quality assessment in education should not be considered as separate systems. They are an integral part of the continuous quality improvement context on the road to total quality.
In this chapter we will discuss the approach adopted for ensuring the quality of the MODASPECTRA (MOtor Disability Assessment SPEcialists' TRAining) Web-based degree: a research and technology development project funded by the European Union. More in detail, the procedures enacted for ensuring the

quality of contents and the quality of the software tools developed, and of their documentation, will be discussed.

INTRODUCTION

The growth of credit-bearing distance learning offerings and enrollments at accredited, degree-granting colleges and universities has been astonishing in the last few years. According to Eaton (2001), "During the academic year 1997-98, approximately 1.6 million students were enrolled in credit-bearing distance learning courses (whether electronic, television-based, or print- and mail-based, and including both synchronous and asynchronous instruction) in degree-granting post-secondary colleges and universities in the United States. That year, 54,000 college-level credit-bearing distance-learning courses were offered in 1,680 institutions. Thirty-five states currently operate virtual universities or participate in a regional virtual university, typically created by existing degree-granting colleges and universities."

Klaus (2002) reports about a comprehensive funding program launched by the German government regarding the promotion of new media in education. Federal funds up to the amount of 175 million euro, corresponding to about a hundred euro for each student in the country, have been allotted for the program covering the period from 2000 to 2004. The objective is "to develop a new quality of Web-based training arrangements with digital content using the potential of multimedia technology." A similar program, the Swiss Virtual Campus Impulse Programme, involves the higher-level academic institutions in Switzerland (Universities, Federal Institutes of Technologies and Universities of Applied Sciences). For the years 2000-2003, a budget close to 50 million of CHF has been made available by the Confederation and the various institutions involved, to be used for a total of approximately 50 projects. The goal of the program is the formation of responsible bodies for the development and use of Internet-based e-study modules for higher education (Stucki, 2002).

This growth raises the demand for reliable information about quality.

Quality is defined in ISO 9000 as "the totality of features and characteristics of a product or service that bear on its ability to satisfy stated or implied needs." According to the Higher Engineering Education for Europe working group, quality in higher education can be interpreted as "specifying worthwhile learning goals and enabling students to achieve them." Specifying worthwhile learning goals involves paying attention to academic standards, to the expectations of society, to students' aspirations, to the demands of industry and other employers, to the requirements of professional institutions, to the fundamental principles of the subject, etc. Moreover, enabling students to achieve these goals involves making use of research into how students learn, adopting good course design procedures and building on successful teaching experience, all of which may require professional development for lecturers (H3E, 1999).

The previous definition of quality does not help very much in the evaluation of the quality of distance learning courses. In this chapter, we discuss a possible approach in assuring both the quality of contents and the quality of the Internet-based application for a Web-based degree in Motor Disability Assessment. In the next section a short overview of the degree will be provided, while in the following section the quality assurance procedures enacted will be described.

AN OVERVIEW OF THE MODASPECTRA PROJECT

The MODASPECTRA (MOtor Disability Assessment SPEcialists' TRAining) project was a research and technology development project pertaining to the "Telematics Application Programme - Education and Training" sector of the fourth Framework Program for R&D of the European Union. The project was a joint activity of the Department of Electronics and Automatics from the University of Ancona (Italy), the School of Physiotherapy of the University College Dublin (Ireland), the Medical Faculty of the University Montpellier - I (France), the Roessingh Research and Development (The Netherlands), and the TSR consortium (Telematica per il Sistema Riabilitativo) in Italy. It started in December 1998 and ended in March 2002. It was aimed at providing a Web-based open and distance learning course for training specialists in Motor Disability Assessment (MDA). The specialists targeted come from a background of physiatry, physical therapy and bioengineering. The aim was to offer to the European professionals involved in Motor Disability Assessment both a complete degree and a number of courses on Clinical Applications of Movement Analysis in a Life Long Learning (LLL) context as a means for upgrading their skills in the line of good practice dissemination and standardization (Valenti, 2002). Currently available courses on MDA are characterized by the following drawbacks:

- are of limited scope, often covering single arguments only;
- provide polarized education, according to the views of the schools driving the delivery of the material;
- are mainly of residential nature, thus occupying some consecutive working days and implying costs for travel, for accommodation and for attending the course itself.

Therefore, it seemed important to prepare specialists in MDA, and in particular specialists able to exploit information technology and telematics, for enhancing their own efficacy and effectiveness and for improving the rehabilitation system efficiency.

MODASPECTRA provides common and homogenization courses as shown in Table 1. The common courses extensively discuss movement analysis and clinical measurement. The courses "Instrumented measurement for clinical movement analysis" and "Clinical measurement for clinical movement analysis" belong to the area of "Fundamentals of measurement" and describe state-of-the-art methods and techniques in the field of clinical measurement, but also methodological aspects such as their validity and reliability. Because not all existing methods and techniques can be addressed in the courses, a limited but practically relevant set of measurement tools are presented to the students. The selection of the techniques discussed is guided by the requirements that appeared in the user needs analysis (MODASPECTRA, 1999). Especially the users from a clinical background expressed the view that the course content should be oriented towards practical application.

The course "Clinical applications of clinical movement analysis" presents clinically useful case studies on the use of the movement analysis and clinical measurement techniques that were introduced in the courses belonging to the area of "Fundamentals of measurement." The material presented in the above mentioned courses will enable the student to apply the measurement techniques properly for a given clinical problem using the presented protocols. Also, the student will not be able to interpret the resulting data. This requires a substantial body of background knowledge that will include knowledge about normal movement patterns, important abnormalities, compensation and adaptation mechanisms, etc. These issues are covered by the course "Fundamentals of normal and pathological movement." Finally, the separate course "Telematics for clinical movement analysis" addresses the use of telematics for the rehabilitation process.

The Homogenization Courses are meant to provide basic knowledge to professionals having different backgrounds in order to allow them to attend in a homogeneous manner the common courses (see Table 1).

Table 1: The Learning Offer of MODASPECTRA

Category	Name
Common Courses	Telematics for clinical movement analysis
	Fundamentals of normal and pathological movement
	Instrumented measurement for clinical movement analysis
	Clinical measurement for clinical movement analysis
	Clinical applications of clinical movement analysis
Homogenization Courses for Medical Doctors and Physical Therapists	Basic biomechanics
	Fundamentals of measurements and signal processing
	Basic informatics
Homogenization Courses for Bioengineers	Functional anatomical basis of motor system
	Basic physiology
	Fundamentals of pathology and procedures for interaction with patients (to be implemented)

To attain the degree, a pathway composed by eight courses is drawn: five Common Courses that should be attended by all the students and three out of six Homogenization Courses, which will be selected according to the previous academic career of the learners.

The pedagogical philosophy followed by MODASPECTRA, with respect to the use and development of its Electronic Learning Environment, stays between the "Content + Support Model" and the "Wrap-around Model" as defined in Mason (1998).

The pedagogical approach adopted is based on three main phases of accretion, tuning and restructuring. These phases correspond, overall, to the three phases of conceptualization, construction and dialogue of the Open University Model. In accretion, learning takes place by means of accumulation of new information. Real-world situations are evaluated, matched with some appropriate set of schemata, representation for the current situation is formed and the newly acquired knowledge is stored into the long-term memory of the learners. The newly created schema of knowledge is an instantiation of the previously existing one, changed only in that the values of the variables which are stored in the schema (the relationships between these variables are still the same). In restructuring, learning occurs when existing memory structures (net work of schemata) are not adequate to account for new knowledge and new structures are created. New structures are created by erecting new schemata specifically designed for the troublesome information or by modifying (tuning) old ones. In tuning, learning occurs when existing schemas are used as the base for the development of new ones by minor changes. This mode of learning is restricted to the cases where the basic relational structure of the schemas remains unchanged. Through practice or consistent use of schemata, they are tuned or finely adjusted to meet specific task demands or adapted to particular knowledge domains or contexts.

The indications provided by learning technologies standardization committees, such as CEN/ISSS/WS LT (2000), have been followed: thus, the content material has been structured in a set of learning resources (LRs), i.e., content units, composite units and courses. A content unit represents a piece of information not divisible anymore without losing its economic or didactic significance from the user's point of view (e.g., a number of HTML pages treating a specific and self-contained set of information). Content units are grouped in composite units through an index page. With the help of composite units, it is possible to provide a uniform navigation within the learning technology system on the one side, and on the other side to allow the usage of a content unit in more than one arrangement. Composite units are similar to a table of contents in a book and may be dynamic in terms of adding or removing entries at any time. This allows high re-usability and modularity within a learning technology system and gives a clear added value for its users.

About 10 composite units compose a course of the MODASPECTRA degree. Each course is meant as self-contained from the point of view of the instructional design, even if logically related to the others. A specific entry test for each course is devised to provide the learner with a personalized pathway within the degree. The entry test will explore the existing competence of the learner on the topics addressed by the composite units of the course. In the LLL perspective, each course has been designed as a self-contained LR.

Another key issue faced by the project has been the re-use of the learning material (Valenti, 2002a). If learning content is to be reused between systems, and if systems are to be interoperable, then there is considerable advantage in having indexing methods that conform to presently available open standards. Metadata is information about an object, be it physical or digital. In the MODASPECTRA realm an LR is a digital object that needs to be described and indexed by metadata. The IEEE LTSC Learning Object Metadata proposal for metadata has been adopted (IEEE-LOM, 1999) in agreement with other standardization initiatives (ARIADNE http://www.ariadne-eu.org and PROMETEUS http://www.prometeus.org).

Thus, the knowledge pool (KP) of MODASPECTRA system is constituted by two different data stores: a data repository holding the learning resources and a database storing the metadata.

The results of the project and the MODASPECTRA system are available at the URL: http://www.modaspectra.org.

QUALITY ASSURANCE PROCEDURES

According to Kess et al. (2002), quality in education should not be forced into one single definition, but rather a collection of smaller elements, processes, which contribute to education quality in different dimensions. These elements, when chained together, constitute the overall quality in training, and the improvement of quality is achieved through simultaneous action on all these levels. Furthermore, accreditation and quality assessment in education should not be considered as separate systems. They are an integral part of the continuous quality improvement context on the road to total quality. In this section our approach adopted for ensuring the quality of contents and the quality of the software tools developed and of their documentation will be discussed.

Quality of Contents

Three main classes of procedures have been defined and followed in the implementation of the educational system: authoring procedures for content creation and/or learning material construction, teaching procedures to guarantee proper monitoring and support/assistance to the learning process, and didactic/administrative procedures. Every procedure is meant to be implemented by one or more actors,

whose operation is inserted in a proper organization framework. It appears that the
most effective way of describing the whole operation is by the UML tools, as shown
in Figure 1.

Authoring procedures

The stakeholders of the authoring procedures are the editor-in-chief, the editors
and the authors.

The editors are appointed by the faculty and have the responsibility of organizing
courses. They define the instructional design of the course they are in charge of, and
define its structure in term of composite units. Furthermore, the editors appoint one

Figure 1: The MODASPECTRA Scenario of Operation

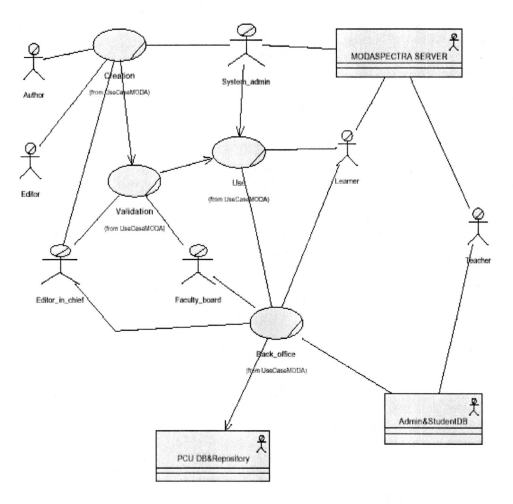

or more authors to produce the composite units. The editors verify the learning material produced by the authors and authorize its storage in the databases.

The editor-in-chief manages the validation of the learning material and takes care of the relationships with the faculty in order to decide the acceptance of a course and its activation within the degree.

The authors are in charge of producing the contents of one or more composite units of a course together with the relative assessment procedures, remedial teaching, glossary and metadata. They have to respect constraints both in the time and in the formats allowed for producing the learning material. They interact with the editor during the verification of the produced material. Authors must define the instructional design of the assigned composite and content units. The instructional design has to be coherent with the learning objectives of the course selected by the editor and has to be defined according to procedures that must be coherent with the pedagogical model adopted.

The quality of the procedure is guaranteed by the traceability of the decisions taken in this respect by the faculty and communicated to the editor-in-chief. The communication is actually performed by e-mail. The trace mechanism is based on the daily back up of the incoming messages. Possible improvement of the communication traceability, if needed, will be implemented by means of a specific telematic procedure.

The consortium has chosen an iterative approach in the development of the MODASPECTRA courses. This means that this development is a continuous cycle of specifying improvements over the present edition of the courses, making the appropriate changes to courseware and evaluating the results. In the first and the third step of this development cycle, good contacts with both the scientific and user community are crucial.

Therefore, an evaluation system has been implemented using selected question-naires and structured interviews that provide feedback from the users that allow improvement of the MODASPECTRA material. This feedback has been obtained from students, but also from the professional organizations that are interested in using the course to fulfill their education role (Valenti, 2002b).

A second goal in this iterative development is to keep track of the scientific and clinical state of the art. Worldwide, there is a considerable ongoing research and development activity both in the technical and clinical areas. Thus, it is important that the consortium is continuously aware of new relevant developments that could have implications for the learning material. To achieve this result, the consortium will frequently discuss the learning material with members of the scientific community in the application area.

The basic mechanism in assuring quality of the contents is independent peer review. Three experts are involved in the review of each course: two domain experts, variable from course to course, and one MDA expert, to be involved in all the courses' review to guarantee the needed levels of homogeneity. The frequency of consultation will be once every two years. The editors of the individual courses will process the comments and recommendations related to the contents. It is the responsibility of these editors to find the most appropriate measures for modifying the contents according to these comments. The procedure for updating the learning material implies the traceability of the various successive versions by means of the explicit indication of the version in the metadata. Moreover, internal and external procedures have been defined at a preliminary level.

Teaching procedures

The teaching procedures include discussion management, assessment and tutoring.

The teacher/tutor activates specific bulletin boards in order to foster the discussion with the students on specific topics via "Questions of the week." The discussion lists are open for contributions during limited time slots. The teacher interacts asynchronously with the students by answering their questions and/or by suggesting some correction on the discussion items. The schedule of the discussions is communicated to the students by means of the Calendar of Course Events provided by the delivery platform (WebCT). At the end of the time allotted for the discussion, the teacher summarizes its results and includes the summary in an addendum to be used at suitable times to upgrade the learning material.

Personal communication between teachers and students is performed using the internal e-mail system.

The discussion tools are used mainly during the restructuring phase of learning and provide the student with significant feedback on the learned concepts.

The assessment occurs by means of a discussion with the teacher performed either face to face or by videoconference. In this latter case, the presence of the tutor at the student site is needed in order to guarantee the transparency of the assessment. The assessment policy foresees the verification of the achievement of the learning objective at the desired level of competence.

In the perspective of the whole degree attended by the student, a final dissertation has to be produced in order to demonstrate the capability to face a specific MDA issue at the evaluation level of Bloom's taxonomy. Students should also be able to demonstrate the awareness of the multi-disciplinary character of MDA.

The tutors have the responsibility of enforcing the effectiveness of the learning path of groups of students. They are committed to monitoring such paths and assisting the students in overcoming educational and/or technical obstacles. The tutors interact with the students face to face, by e-mail and by videoconference.

Didactic/administrative procedures

The didactic/administrative procedures involve the activities of student enrollment, faculty operation and back-office operation.

Students intending to enroll either to the whole degree or to one or more courses in an LLL perspective contact the back office via the Web and provide their curriculum vitae. A section containing explanatory pages and a form, compliant with the administrative office specifications, to be filled out online by the applicant learner has been included into the MODASPECTRA server. Once submitted, the form is resent to the applicant for verification, modified if needed and finally confirmed. At this point, the learner will be inserted in a student database and will be recognized by the administrative office and by the teacher. Once the enrollment is finalized, the learner is allowed to interact with the teacher for performing the placement assessment and for receiving the assignment of composite units corresponding to his/her entry level. This initial phase is done in two steps. During the former, the teacher invites the learner to perform the placement assessment procedure; during the latter, the interactions between student and teacher occur within the delivery environment, using its own facilities.

The faculty states the award policies both from the didactic and managerial point of view. It appoints the editor-in-chief and provides him/her with the specifications for the quality of the courses and of the composite units. The faculty appoints the editors, the teachers and the tutors, too.

The faculty authorizes the activation of the courses, on the basis of the results of the validation provided by the editor-in-chief. The faculty manages the authorization of the learning material via an ad-hoc procedure. The quality of the procedure is guaranteed by the traceability of the decision taken in this respect by the faculty and communicated to the editor-in-chief. The communication is actually performed by e-mail. The trace mechanism is based on the daily backup of the incoming messages. Possible improvements of the communication traceability depend on the specific implementation enacted by the faculty that will exploit the results of the project.

Among the operations performed by the back office, it is worth mentioning a) the communication of the appointments to the editors, to the teachers and to the tutors; b) the processing of the registration requests from the learners and the evaluation of the adequacy of the curriculum for the requested courses; c) the communication of the acceptance to the course(s) and of their plan and scheduling to the learners, and the verification of the payment of the fees. Furthermore, the back office is in charge of communicating the list of the students attending a course to the teachers/tutors and of managing the storage of the results attained by the students.

Accreditation of the learning material

The learning material has to be accredited by third parties active the educational field such as, for instance, academic institutions. Such institutions define the procedures for the accreditation; consequently, no quality assurance specifications have been defined in this respect. As a first step in the accreditation of the learning material, the Dublin School of Physiotherapy has received approval from University College Dublin, Ireland, to offer one of the courses belonging to the MODASPECTRA educational package as a distance learning certificate course from the coming academic year. The course has been renamed to "Outcome Assessment in Motor Disability." Directed mainly at physiotherapists throughout Ireland and Europe, the course consists of standardized and validated measures to be used before and after treatment to evaluate the effectiveness of the intervention. It could also be relevant to the practice of other health professionals.

Quality Assurance of the Web-Based Implementation

As a general reference, QA procedures for software development are based on the relevant IEEE standards (IEEE, 1997). The quality policy of the project with respect to Web-based software implementation (computer programs, procedures, information, data, records) is to satisfy quality requirements suitable for the establishment of a running Life Long Learning system at the completion of the project. In particular, the prototype of the MODASPECTRA Course focused the attention to the key elements of the quality plan: quality of the software tools and of their documentation, security services and security networks. Each of these issues will be discussed in the following sub-sections.

Quality of software tools and their documentation

The software quality characteristics to be attained are functionality, reliability, usability, efficiency, maintainability and portability, as defined by the ISO/IEC 9126

Figure 2: The QUINT Quality Assurance Methodology

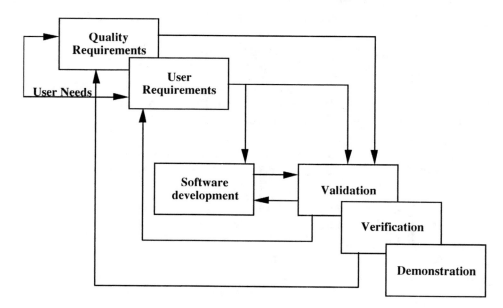

(ISO, 1998). The software implementation has been performed taking into account the satisfaction of quality requirements at each phase of the software development cycle and in particular IEEE-1061 (IEEE, 1997). The QUINT—QUality in INformation Technology model (van Zeist et al., 1996) has been adopted for the software development process (see Figure 2).

In this chapter, the software documentation is meant as the description of the design solutions and of the implementation of the Metadata dB and Communication Tools. The information is organized in:

- a section introducing the reader to the scenarios of the MODASPECTRA Teaching and Training System reported in UML code;
- a section describing the design and implementation of the knowledge pool of the system with particular reference to Metadata dB and the tools devoted to its management;
- a section describing the design and the implementation of the MODASPECTRA course delivery with particular reference to the adopted electronic learning environment (WebCT);
- an annexed volume containing the "Editor Manual" and the "Learner User Manual" sections constituting a 'help' for the users.

The format of documentation is the standard requested by the European Community for the production of the project deliverables. The quality of documentation is based on the application of ISO-9000-3 "Guidelines for the application of ISO-9001: 1994 to the Development, Supply, Installation and Maintenance of Computer Software," section 4.5. It has been assured by the supervision of the work package responsible and by the peer review process of the related deliverable (MODASPECTRA, 2001).

Security issues

The problem of security has been faced taking into account the indications provided by the Information Technology Security Evaluation Criteria (ITSEC), the European standard for the evaluation of security. According to such standard, the MODASPECTRA degree has been classified in the E2 category: "An informal detailed design and test documentation must be produced. Architecture shows the separation of the Target of Evaluation into security enforcing and other components. Penetration testing searches for errors. Configuration control and developer's security is assessed. Audit trail output is required during start up and operation" (ITSEC, 2001).

The security aspects implemented in the demonstrator are relative to availability, confidentiality and data/information integrity: a proper access control policy, based on the definition of different levels of passwords with the relative privileges for the access to the data, has been defined and implemented according to the scenarios. The following classes of users, having different (decreasing) privileges of accessibility to the stored data, have been implemented:

Content creation side	Course delivery side
Web administrator	Web administrator
Editor-in-chief	Teacher
Editors	Student
Authors	

The access control policy adopted assures also the confidentiality of the system with respect to the protection of the information relative to the learners.

A second aspect of confidentiality, not yet implemented, is security of the transactions possibly needed for the online payment of the course fee. This aspect will be considered in the final version of the demonstrator when the enrollment procedures will be completely implemented.

A proper data management policy has been defined and implemented. This involved on one hand associating a specific identifier of each version of CU and metadata to allow the traceability of the development of the content material. On the other hand, standard back-up (every week) and maintenance procedures for re-creating data lost or disrupted have been adopted.

The two main issues to be considered at the networking level are the protection of the integrity of the data stored in the MODASPECTRA repositories and the protection of data and system availability.

At present, quality assurance procedures to guarantee integrity of data stored have been implemented by means of a proper access control policy, adequate anti-virus and weekly back-up procedures.

Moreover, a back-up server is permanently available in order to substitute the main one in the case of its serious malfunction. Data and software of the back-up system are aligned to the last back up of the main system.

To protect against attacks from the outside world, a security policy has been adopted at the TCP/IP and application levels so that:

- only the HTTP and S-HTTP traffics are authorized from the Internet to the Web server;
- no traffic is authorized from the Internet to the Relational Database Management System (RDbMS) and vice versa;
- only the HTTP server can perform requests to the RDbMS;
- IP spoofing and denial-of-service attacks are not possible.

With this architecture no external person has a direct access to the system, thus preventing data interception and intrusion.

FINAL REMARKS

MODASPECTRA is probably one of the first Web-based degrees whose structure and organization are fully available to the scientific community. The various aspects of the system have been presented in a number of conferences (Leo et al., 2000; Valenti et al., 2002a, 2002b 2002c, 2002d) and in academic journals (Valenti et al., 2002). Furthermore, access to the deliverables is granted from the MODASPECTRA site at http://www.modaspectra.org, provided that a username and a password are requested to the system administrator. This is an indirect way of enforcing the quality of the design approach and of the solutions adopted. Moreover, the quality of the contents is ensured by the iterative procedure adopted as discussed earlier in this chapter. Finally, the quality of the software tools developed and of their documentation, along with the security of services and networks, has been ensured via proper procedures that refer to well-known standards coming from the field of software engineering.

A point that remains open yet is the verification of the quality assurance procedures enacted for the operation of the system. These procedures will undergo a true verification only when the prototype will be transformed in an engineered system and used in real life.

REFERENCES

CEN/ISSS/WS-LT Project 1 Draft Report, March 22, 2000.

Eaton, J.S. (2001). *Distance Learning: Academic and Political Challenges for Higher Education Accreditation.* CHEA—Council for Higher Education Accreditation, Monograph Series 1. Available at: http://www.chea.org.

ECTS. (1998). *European Credit Transfer System—Users' Guide.* Available at: http://europa.eu.int/comm/education/socrates/guide-en.doc.

H3E. (1999). *H3E-wg2 Position Paper on Quality and Quality Assurance—A Proposal for a Formalised Procedure for Achieving Good Quality Teaching of Engineering in European Universities.* Available at: http://www.hut.fi/Misc/H3E/wg2/wg2p1_F0.html.IEEE. (1997). *IEEE Standards Collection: Software Engineering, 1997 Edition.*

IEEE LOM.(1999). *IEEE Learning Technology Standards Committee (LTSC) Learning Object Metadata.* Working Draft Document 3. Available at: http://ltsc.ieee.org/doc/wg12/LOM-WD3.htm.

ISO. (1994). *Guidelines for the Application of ISO-9001:1994 to the Development, Supply, Installation and Maintenance of Computer Software.* Section 4.5.

ISO. (1998). *ISO/IEC 9126 IHS/Infodoc.* Englewood, CO: World-Wide Standards Service.

ITSEC (2001). *Information Technology Security Evaluation Criteria. Assurance Levels.* Available at: http://www.cesg.gov.uk/assurance/iacs/itsec/criteria/itsec-levels/index.htm.

Kess, P., Haapasalo, H. & Pyykonen T. (2002). Quality of university education in complex learning environments. *Proceedings of the World Conference on Networked Learning in a Global Environment: Challenges and Solutions for Virtual Education (NL2002).* Canada/The Netherlands: ICSC-NAISO Academic Press.

Klaus, H.G. (2002). New media in education: A German government program and its implementation. Special session on "National and International E-Learning Programs" of the *World Conference on Networked Learning in a Global Environment: Challenges and Solutions for Virtual Education (NL2002).* Canada/The Netherlands: ICSC-NAISO Academic Press.

Leo, T., Marini, M., Maurizi, M., Panti, M. & Valenti, S. (2000). Web-based teaching and training on motor disability assessment. In Jin, Q. (Ed.), *Emerging Technologies and New Challenges in Information Society: Proceedings of the 2000 International Conference on Information Society in the 21st Century, Special Session on Virtual Universities and Distance Education (IS2000),* The University of Aizu, Japan, 516-524.

MODASPECTRA. (1999). *User Requirements. Deliverable 2.1.* Joint Call Educational Multimedia.*

MODASPECTRA. (2001). *MODASPECTRA Educational System (Teaching and Training Tools of a Specialist's Training Course in MDA). Deliverable 4.2—Second Edition.* Joint Call Educational Multimedia.*

Stucki, P. (2002). The Swiss Virtual Campus Impulse Programme. Special session on "National and International E-Learning Programs" of the *World Conference on Networked Learning in a Global Environment: Challenges and Solutions for Virtual Education (NL2002).* Canada/The Netherlands: ICSC-NAISO Academic Press.

Valenti, S., Fioretti, S., Maurizi, M., Panti, M. & Leo, T. (2002). Teaching motor disability assessment over the Web: MODASPECTRA. *Educational Technology & Society,* 5(1), 184-192.

Valenti, S., Fioretti, S., Panti, M. & Leo T. (2002b). Preliminary results from the validation of a specialist's degree in motor disability assessment. To appear in Kinshuk, initial. (Ed.), *Proceedings of the International Conference on Computers in Education,* December 3-6, Auckland, New Zealand. IEEE CS Press.

Valenti, S., Fioretti, S., Panti, M. & Leo, T. (2002c). A Web-based ODL system in motor disability assessment. In Wagner, E. & Szucs, A. (Eds.), *Research and Policy in Open and Distance Learning: Proceedings of the 2nd Research Workshop of the European Distance Education Network (EDEN),* European Distance Education Network, 84-87.

Valenti, S., Fioretti, S., Panti, M. & Leo, T. (2002d). MODASPECTRA: A learning system for teaching motor disability assessment. *Proceedings of 4th International Conference on New Educational Environments (ICNEE02),* Lugano, Switzerland.

Valenti, S., Panti, M. & Leo, T. (2002a). Design for reuse in a Web-based degree. *Proceedings of the World Conference on Networked Learning in a Global Environment: Challenges and Solutions for Virtual Education (NL2002).* Canada/ The Netherlands: ICSC-NAISO Academic Press.

van Zeist, B., Hendriks, P., Paulussen, R. & Trienekens, J. (1996) Kwaliteit van softwareprodukten. *Praktijkervaringen met een Kwaliteitsmodel.* Kluwer Bedrijfswetenschappen.

ENDNOTE

(*) Access to the MODASPECTRA deliverables is restricted via a username and password that may be requested to the web administrator.

Chapter IV

A Virtual Advisor Utilizing Multi-Agent Software Teams and Contingency Theoretic Coordination Models

John R. Durrett
Texas Tech University, USA

Lisa J. Burnell
Texas Christian University, USA

John W. Priest
University of Texas, USA

ABSTRACT

Few tools are available for managing distributed educational support processes, from answering "quick" student questions, to degree planning and course scheduling. The dual purpose of our work is to analyze the viability of synthesizing two well-established paradigms (agent-based systems and Information Processing Theory) to create a distributed Web-based support system for a virtual university. Currently, we are developing a smart agent-based resource for advising (SARA) that will serve different departments at multiple universities. This effort allows the investigation of distributed advising systems in a virtual university, along with providing a platform for investigating utilization of brick-and-mortar research on coordination and control of human employees in a completely virtual world. In this chapter, we present SARA to argue for the benefits derived from integrating agent-based systems development and information-processing theory for creating rapidly customizable Web-based support systems.

INTRODUCTION

Problem Motivation

Our motivation for this chapter comes from two sources: first, to test the viability of distributed system design steps generated from a synthesis of research in Multi-Agent Systems (MASs) and in Organizational Theory (OT); and second, to create a prototype virtual advising system. Our focus is on the design environment and architecture, and not on the details of the individual agents or other components generated.

The growing popularity of distributed education has produced a variety of interesting research in the production and presentation of educational materials. Distributed education consists of much more than simply putting PowerPoint slides on a website and receiving student homework or term papers by e-mail (Dumont, 1996). Optimally, it consists of a dynamic environment in which students and teachers can communicate and both can learn. Teaching in such an environment is at its best when the instructor is viewed as a facilitator for interested, motivated students (Graf, 2002). This fact is especially true for the fastest growing segment of eLearning, the busy adult who has too many demands on his or her time to attend a "traditional" classroom (Symonds, 2001). A viable virtual university also consists of the infrastructure and background coordination tasks necessary to successful educational efforts (Howell & Lassila, 2002). Among these tasks is student advising.

From any perspective, university student advising is an extremely complex and time-consuming process that is made up of many sub-tasks. A recent survey conducted at Texas Tech (Durrett, 2001) showed that 60% of an advisor's time was spent helping students perform long-term degree planning and current semester scheduling (e.g., course approval). The remaining time was evenly divided among evaluating transcripts; responding to requests for information concerning degree programs, course content, how to apply, kinds of jobs available to graduates; and mentoring students. Human advisors are inundated with "quick questions" to the point that there is often little time remaining for other important duties.

Attempting to automate advising for virtual universities is a risky proposition, given the difficulty of advising in person. The traditional advising process, especially in larger departments, is fraught with miscommunications, misunderstandings and misconnections. Policies and requirements are dynamic and difficult to maintain.

Advisors are inundated with "quick questions" that often result in little time remaining for mentoring and advising students. Example questions are:

- What courses do I still have to take?
- What's the fastest I can graduate (and is such a plan advisable given my life situation and past performance)?
- Do I have to take four hours, four classes or four semesters of PE?

Even with the dedication shown by most human advisors, the process can be tedious, time-consuming and error-prone. From a student's perspective, the task of deciding what courses to take and when to take them can leave many students frustrated and confused. Designing a degree plan for a given time period and creating a schedule each semester requires an understanding of all the policies and regulations within a university, college and department. From a faculty member's perspective, the advising process includes not only an understanding of the policies and rules of the university, but also an understanding of the rules explicitly, and many times implicitly, defined within their own department. These problems are as true, if not more so, in virtual universities as they are in traditional brick-and-mortar universities.

For an advising system of a virtual university to be effective, it must at the very minimum possess the same capabilities as brick-and-mortar universities. To provide these capabilities, we are creating a smart agent-based resource for advising (SARA). Our research in the creation of SARA focuses on a synthesis of advances in software agents and OT. The creation of a usable advising system utilizing this synthesis will allow us to investigate the viability of distributed advising systems in a virtual university, along with providing a platform for investigating utilization of brick-and-mortar research on coordination and control of human employees in a completely virtual world.

BACKGROUND

In order to deliver effective, efficient services to students who are geographically and experientially diverse, university advising functions need to be accessible and adaptable. This particular task environment is complex, dynamic and thus interesting for our research because of (1) the dynamic, complex, numerous rules that vary widely across departments and universities, making standard maintenance in conventionally designed systems difficult; (2) the wide diversity of course content; and (3) a heterogeneous user base ranging from brand-new college students to experienced professionals to instructors and advisors. Given this type of task environment, most universities offering distance-learning programs still primarily utilize human beings for advising students (CHEA, 1999). To provide the flexibility necessary for our software to adapt to this task environment, we are implementing SARA using smart agents guided by business rules. To provide the inter-agent coordination necessary in such a "virtual organization," we are utilizing guidelines from OT research, specifically Information Processing Theory (IPT). While not exclusively for virtual universities, SARA is particularly valuable for such environments. We are developing SARA to work in three different departments at three different universities.

Smart Software Agents

An agent is an entity that represents a user by performing human-like tasks, such as gathering information known to be of interest to a user or responding to changes in the environment to maintain certain user goals. Multiple agents cooperate in multi-agent systems (MASs), performing tasks on the behalf of a community of users. These systems can include combinations of software, hardware and humans. Variations of the definitions given here exist, but the above are suitable for our purposes. Smart agents (Figure 1) use and learn knowledge about user goals and preferences, the domain and the environment (which may include other agents). For example, business rules may be used to represent domain knowledge within an agent. Preferences and goals allow an agent to respond to changes in the environment, e.g., to notify a student of a new course and the impact of modifying a degree plan to add or substitute the course.

The development of MASs, particularly in complex, multi-user domains, is a challenge. In part, MAS development is difficult because of software engineers' relative inexperience in developing such systems and the complexity of designing asynchronous, multi-user systems.

Most of the software available today has been designed primarily to solve problems that were suitable for a single program. Now the focus is on software that

Figure 1: Agent Typology (Adapted from Nwana & Azarmi, 1997)

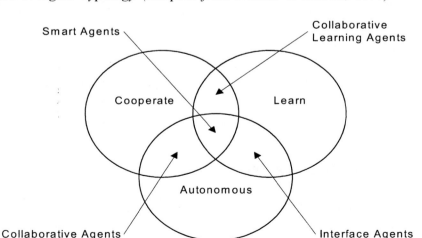

will be able to communicate and access multiple programs in order to solve a specific problem that is difficult or incapable of being solved by a single program. This concept of programming is called agent-oriented programming. Agents "interoperate," or have the ability to exchange information and services with other programs (Genesereth & Ketchpel, 1994). Implementing agents requires a language in which to construct the individual agents, an ontology for providing a shared understanding of terms and concepts, an agent communication language to exchange data and a shared model for determining the appropriate types of exchanges.

An early approach to distributed intelligent problem solving composed of multiple knowledge sources was the blackboard system. The blackboard model has been used to approach "ill-defined" problems. As Butterfield and Cooprider (1994) elaborated, "the blackboard model was developed originally as a means of sharing distributed information. It assumes that for many ill-defined problems, solutions are partitioned among a number of different experts or knowledge sources. Rather than presenting a predefined problem and soliciting possible answers, blackboard models prompt the experts for information about the problem.... [Blackboard models] provide an appropriate framework of and system for helping to resolve conflicts in the requirements analysis process" (Butterfield, Cooprider & Rathnam, 1994).

More recent approaches are based on distributed systems of rational agents using frameworks such as JADE (Bellifemine, Poggi & Rimassa, 2001), Jackal (Cost et al., 1998) and JATLite (Jeon, Petrie & Cutkosky, 2000). Individual agents are sometimes conceptualized as having beliefs, desires and intentions that can communicate with other agents to satisfy their goals. In these distributed systems, agents communicate using languages such as KQML or the FIPA ACL (Labrou, Finin & Peng, 1999).

Just as human systems created to achieve complex goals are conceived of as organizations, MASs such as those described above can be reconceptualized as "software organizations." In both types of systems, the individual components, human employees or software agents need to be controlled, guided toward a constructive goal and coordinated toward the completion of the necessary individual tasks. Individual agents have specific goals and tasks to perform, possess specialized knowledge and have access to particular data. Agents accomplish their goals by communicating with other agents to acquire data, request tasks to be performed or to notify other agents of environmental changes they have affected. This conceptualization allows us to use well-established research from OT in creating guidelines for the design of our agent-based advising system.

Contingency-Theoretic Systems Development

OT is a field of study that examines an organization's structure, constituencies, processes and operational results in an effort to understand the relationships involved in creating effective and efficient systems (Scott, 1992). A major division of OT,

Contingency Theory (CT) states that the structure of a successful organization is dependent upon the environment in which it operates (Van de Ven, 1985). IPT postulates that this environment-determines-organizational-structure dependency is the result of the coordination requirements among the basic elements and tasks that make up the organization (Cyert, 1963; Galbraith, 1973).

IPT states that the adaptations that organizations may utilize to solve the information processing requirements in an organizational structure can be generalized into two broad categories: planning and mutual adjustment. The more heterogeneous, unpredictable and dependent upon other environmental resources a task is, the greater the information processing that the organization must be able to do in order to successfully accomplish the task. As diversity of resources, processes or outputs increases, inter-process coordination requirements, uncertainty and system complexity all increase. As uncertainty increases, information-processing requirements increase. These changes yield incomplete management information, which requires more mutual adjustment and cooperation in the organizational system. Conversely with more homogeneous, predictable and independent tasks, management's ability to predict situations and plan for solutions increases. Thus standard operating procedures can be implemented and hierarchical control systems created to manage the organization effectively.

In our research we postulate that the environment-structure relationship outlined in the paragraphs above is also reflected in Software Systems designs, especially those utilizing intelligent agents. In previous research (Durrett, Burnell & Priest, 2000, 2001), we have developed, and tested, the following CT-based guidelines for creating MASs:

1. *Describe business activity and identify tasks*: Allow management and developers to refine the overall purpose of the software being designed.
2. *Determine task predictability*: Since a basic premise of CT is that the control structure of a business process must match the environment in which it operates, we must identify the predictability of each task.
3. *Assign tasks to employees*: Once the level of predictability has been estimated for each task, the granularity of the employees being created can be determined and component designs finalized.
4. *Group employees into teams*: As with human organizations, our employees can be grouped along any of several dimensions, including task, workflow, product, manager or communication requirements, as required by the operating environment.
5. *Identify communications needs*: Once teams are determined, the communication requirements of individual employees, and of teams, can be determined.
6. *Construct management groups*: In software systems operating in a dynamic environment, management is required only when employees are unable to handle events.

In the next section, we describe how we combine the IPT and MAS paradigms to create a virtual advisor system.

THE SARA VIRTUAL ADVISOR

The SARA Virtual Advisor is a smart MAS that is part of a planned Web-based information management system (a *knowledge portal*) to support traditional and distributed education. SARA is intended to deliver many advising services to students, such as degree planning, semester scheduling and course approval. Other components with which SARA will interact include those that perform transfer analysis, general information regarding types of degree plans and market outlook (types of jobs, location and pay). Moving beyond the common, inadequate strategy of making paper-based advising materials electronically available, we seek to provide a means by which a student (or potential student) may engage in a dialogue with a "virtual advisor." Students want to get answers quickly to specific questions, not spend hours looking through pages of online documents. An example scenario of what students need is shown below:

> Elton wants to graduate as quickly as possible, subject to the realities of his specific situation. He can only take online or night classes, since he works full time during the day. In the summer, he could take a morning class, but he would prefer not to. He does want to take Dr. Smith for his circuits class. He assumes that if the classes are not too hard, he could take 15 hours a semester. If he has one or more tough or really time-consuming classes, he should take only nine or 12 hours. He wants to get a COSC degree, but if he can graduate much sooner, he would like to consider a CISC degree.

One function of SARA is the graduation planner, which identifies a degree's requirements, compares it to a student's information, determines courses that need to be taken, and then develops a schedule based on these requirements and user preferences. A partial list of the user options is shown below:

- Graduation Plan
    - Preferred or absolute graduation date—user selected
    - System-suggested graduation date based on user selected number of hours, schedule and other limitations
    - Shortest path of the fewest number of semesters to graduate
    - Critical path of courses to meet graduation goal date (i.e., considering prerequisites—the order in which classes must be taken to meet desired graduation date)

- Class selection allowing student to select certain classes at certain times/semester and system then develops the plan around these selections
- Course Selection and Schedule
  - Absolute or preferred schedule limitations by semester or overall (no exceptions)—maximum number of hours per semester, limits including evening, day, M/W, Web, no class before 9:30, no class after 5:30, etc.
  - Average course difficulty rating over the remaining semesters (evenly distribute challenging courses over semesters)
  - Maximum difficulty rating to not exceed a set limit
  - Teacher preferences or teacher not-to-take list
- Course Information
  - Student comments, suggestions and reviews of curriculum available for perusal

In selecting a data representation scheme, a number of factors must be considered. The four most important are quantity, accessibility, quality and dynamicism. The planner function requires much data, some of which is imprecise or missing, and some of which is subject to frequent change. For example, planning a student's courses for Fall 2003 relies on many assumptions, including student performance and course offerings.

CT design guidelines tell us that domain policies must be specified declaratively and grouped according to predictability to minimize the impact of change. We use relational database tables to store raw data, downloaded from external systems. In our prototype system we allow database entry and retrieval based on university and department-level specifications. It is our intent in future versions to extend the database schema to include more generic metadata standards such as those specified in the CEN/ISSS workshop on learning technology standards (CEN/ISSS/WS-LT, 2000). These design choices isolate some of the more dynamic segments of the advising system, making changes to any component in SARA easier, and they also isolate legacy system interface tasks.

Another dynamic segment of SARA's task environment is the degree policies. With the increase and rapid change in special rules, exceptions and prerequisites used in universities today, it is easy to see that a system that is built by centralizing constraints will become obsolete within a matter of months after implementation. A useful advising system must be robust and readily configurable to allow for course exceptions or course requirements such as prerequisites, minimum grade point average or student standing.

Again, following IPT guidelines, domain policies are categorized and stored as rules. This part of the system is currently implemented in the Java Expert System Shell, JESS (Jess, 2002). The degree planner manager, written in Java, interfaces with the rules and internal database to provide a degree of isolation of policy and implementation. The degree planner manager controls the mechanics of supplying data to and storing data supplied by the degree planner rules. Thus, individual rule bases (which behave as employee specialists and are implemented as agents) are strictly focused on solving specific domain problems (such as creation of a degree plan based on student and university constraints). Managers handle the mundane tasks of acquiring and distributing resources (data) from the appropriate sources. A separate user interface again isolates domain policies and procedures from mechanics of implementation. The architecture for the system is shown in Figure 2 below.

Figure 2: Prototype Example

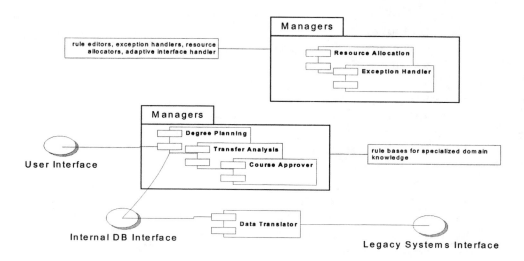

The first prototype developed was for the Industrial and Manufacturing Engineering Department at The University of Texas at Arlington. Their curriculum and degree requirements are typical for an undergraduate program.

For this graduation planner example, 47 rules and 65 data requirements were identified. The rules could be classified by owner such as university, college and department requirements or by functions such as transfer credit and minimum GPAs. An example rule (in JESS) that checks if a student can take a course is shown below:

```
(defrule can-take-course "check if student can take a course"
  ?goal2 <- (goal-is-to (action check-course) (argument-1 ?ID) (argument-2
?course))
  (course-prerequisites (dept ?Dept) (course ?course) (prereqs $?plist)
(coreqs $?))
  (passing-grade $?passing-grades)
  (not (transcript ?ID ?course ? ? ?grade&:(member$ ?grade $?passing-
grades)))
```

```
;; check if student has passed every pre-requisite
  (courses (studentID ?ID) (course-list $?passed))
  (test (subsetp $?plist $?passed)
  ?fact <- (can-take (studentID ?ID) (course-list $?courses)) ;
=>
  (printout t " ==> " ?course " prereqs are satisfied." crlf)
  (bind $?newcourses (insert$ $?courses 1 (create$ ?course))) ; add valid
course to list
  (assert (can-take (studentID ?ID) (course-list $?newcourses)))))
```

Many of the problems we found centered on 1) lack of data standardization, 2) data quality, 3) number of changes and 4) algorithm complexity. An example of a data standardization issue is shown in course naming schemes (e.g., IE3315 versus Math321). The largest data quality concern was missing data that was usually caused by an inability of the department to commit to a long-term schedule, e.g., instructor teaching assignments.

The dynamic nature of the data is the largest challenge to system maintainability. As already noted, change must be dealt with in any virtual advising system. The most common changes for each semester are faculty changes, especially for adjunct professors and instructors teaching lower level classes. Another major problem is catalog changes, that often occur every two years, in which all three organizational units (university, college and department) can change requirements. These changes affect many of the rules. Finally, dealing with rules interaction and interfacing with the wide variety of legacy systems negatively affects algorithm complexity.

We verified the selected architecture and its desired features by customizing the system for the Texas Christian University Computer Science Department. This extra step was crucial to testing the maintainability and robustness of the design.

FUTURE TRENDS

Given the expected increase in both purely online courses (eLearning) and traditional courses augmented with Web technologies, the importance of infrastructure systems such as the virtual advisor (SARA) described in this chapter will become increasingly important. In addition, if the current dominance of busy professionals (Symonds, 2001) in eLearning classes continues, those systems will need to be as flexible, easy to use and beneficial as other software available in the broadly defined domain of electronic commerce. To facilitate this continued shift in education, which parallels that of many other industries, future systems require technologies to support rapid, adaptable, distributed and shareable resources. To achieve these capabilities, enhancements are needed in Web services, intelligent systems engineering and educational metadata standards.

Web services provide an abstraction layer between the service and the service user. They are built using standard Internet technologies such as XML, HTTP and SOAP (Snell, Tidwell & Kulchenko, 2002). Use of these or their descendents supports the independent development and deployment of educational materials and tools that may be dynamically located, organized and used. For example, current systems such as SARA may be initially implemented as resource components within a monolithic, centralized system and later, through the use of standard distributed Web communication protocols, as a collection of independently accessible Web services. In doing so, we allow much more flexible reintegration of the individual agent "employees" of SARA into ad hoc software teams.

Efforts to engineer intelligent systems should address the needs of the entire life-cycle, from domain modeling and initial implementation, to maintenance. For example, graphical, domain-aware editors ease the task of maintaining intelligent systems. Business rule editors currently exist, and the extension of such editors to include structural analysis of rules and domain-specific knowledge using industry-adopted ontologies is an important area for future research. In addition to business rule editors, other computer-aided software engineering tool support is needed to locate existing components for reuse and integration, and to support Web-based development, visualization and secure deployment. Finally, better tools are needed for verification, validation and debugging.

Standardization efforts are needed to rapidly and broadly deploy the technologies described. Standardized course metadata, using standards such as CWA 14040 (CEN/ISSS/WS-LT, 2000), provides guidelines on categorization of learning resources used in a course along several levels of granularity. IEEE P1484 (IEEE Learning Technology Standards Committee, 2001) provides a draft standard of a schema for learning objects that can be used by students, instructors and software agents in finding or defining courses. The creation and use of such standards will greatly increase the utility and ease of construction of intelligent agent systems for education. The same is true for virtually any domain, from supply-chain management to medicine.

CONCLUSION

The SARA agent-based architecture was created by applying our contingency-theoretic guidelines to the analysis of the advising domain. By organizing rules according to unit (university, college and department), setting up a conflict resolution strategy via a manager agent to resolve rule conflicts between units, creating specialist agents to deal with connections to legacy systems and isolating the most dynamic data elements in the system, we have created a system that we believe will be adaptable to new advising situations, including those in virtual universities. Some of the special features of SARA include adaptability to changing requirements and new experiences via a knowledgebase of advisor policies and end-user customization for different departments and universities.

We expect to continue extending SARA, even as we move forward with integrating the system with other components necessary for virtual university support systems. Some of the specific enhancements we have planned include adding interactive personalities that adapt to different classes of users to provide specific answers to many common questions and exploring alternative representations of rules for the domain policies. These alternatives include case-based reasoning to capture exception handling, influence diagrams to reason about preferences and uncertainty, and machine learning capabilities using data mining methods to improve advice given by the system.

REFERENCES

Bellifemine, F., Poggi, A. & Rimassa, G. (2001). Developing multi agent systems with a FIPA-compliant agent framework. *Software - Practice And Experience, 31,* 103-128.

Butterfield, J., Cooprider, J.G. & Rathnam, S. (1994). *Resolving Cognitive Conflict in Requirements Definition: A Blackboard-Based Model and System Architecture.* Paper presented at the Computer Personnel Research Conference on Reinventing IS: Managing Information Technology in Changing Organizations, Alexandria, Virginia, March 24-26.

CEN/ISSS/WS-LT. (2000). *A Standardization Work Programme for "Learning and Training Technologies & Educational Multimedia Software."* European Committee for Standardization. Retrieved from the World Wide Web: http://www.cenorm.be/isss/cwa_download_area/cwa14040.pdf.

CHEA. (1999). *Distance Learning in Higher Education.* Council for Higher Education Accreditation, February.

Cost, R.S., Finin, T., Labrou, Y., Luan, X., Peng, Y., Soboroff, I., Mayfield, J. & Boughannam, A. (1998). *Jackal: A Java-Based Tool for Agent Development*: AAAI Technical Report.

Cyert, R.M. (1963). *Behavioral Theory of the Firm, A.* Englewood Cliffs, NJ: Prentice-Hall.

Dumont, R. (1996). Teaching and learning in Cyberspace. *IEEE Transactions on Professional Communication, 39*(4), 192-196.

Durrett, J.R. (2001). *Area Report on College and Departmental Advising* (Internal Area). Lubbock: Texas Tech University, College of Business.

Durrett, J.R., Burnell, L.J. & Priest, J.W. (2000). *Contingency Theoretic Methodology for Agent-Based, Web-Oriented Manufacturing Systems.* Paper presented at the SPIE: Photonics East 2000, Boston, Massachusetts, November 2-8.

Durrett, J.R., Burnell, L.J. & Priest, J.W. (2001). *Organizational Metaphors for Software Architectures.* Paper presented at the IERC-2001: 10th Annual Industrial Engineering Research Conference, Dallas, Texas, May 20-22.

Galbraith, J.R. (1973). *Designing Complex Organizations.* Reading, MA: Addison-Wesley.

Genesereth, M.R. & Ketchpel, S.P. (1994). Software agents. *Communications of the ACM, 37*(7), 48.

Graf, D.M. (2002. *E-Learning: Analysis, Design, Development, Implementation and Evaluation.* Paper presented at the 2002 Information Resources Management Association International Conference, Seattle, Washington, May 19-22.

Howell, K. & Lassila, K.S. (2002). *Guidelines for Development of an Online Baccalaureate Degree in Information Systems.* Paper presented at the 2002 Information Resources Management Association International Conference, Seattle, Washington, May 19-22.

IEEE Learning Technology Standards Committee. (2001). *Learning Object Metadata.* IEEE, May 3. Retrieved, from the World Wide Web: http://ltsc.ieee.org/doc/wg12/LOM_WD6-1_1.pdf.

Jeon, H., Petrie, C. & Cutkosky, M.R. (2000). JATLite: A Java agent infrastructure with message routing. *IEEE Internet Computing, 4*(2), 87-96.

Labrou, Y., Finin, T. & Peng, Y. (1999). The current landscape of agent communication languages. *Intelligent Systems, IEEE Computer Society, 14*(2), 45-52.

Scott, W.R. (1992). *Organizations: Chapter 1.* New York, NY: Prentice Hall.

Snell, J., Tidwell, D. & Kulchenko, P. (2002). *Programming Web Services with SOAP.* Sebastopol, CA: O'Reilly.

Symonds, W.C. (2001). Giving it the old online try. *Business Week,* (December 3), 76-80.

Van de Ven, R. (1985). The concept of fit in contingency theory. In Cummings, B. (Ed.), *Research in Organizational Behavior,* 7, 333-365. New York: JAI Press.

Part II

E-Collaboration

Chapter V

Identifying Key Factors of Motivation to Share and Re-Use Pedagogical Documents

Emmanuel Fernandes
HEC/Inforge, University of Lausanne, Switzerland

Fabrice Holzer
Centef, University of Lausanne, Switzerland

Maia Wentland Forte
HEC/Inforge, University of Lausanne, Switzerland

Bahram Zaerpour
Centef, University of Lausanne, Switzerland

ABSTRACT

Lots of efforts (ARIADNE, Dublin Core, IMS, eBioMED.ch, IEEE-LTSC, CEN-CENELEC, Medline Mesh tree, SCORM, etc.) have been invested in defining a proper indexation schema, resulting in an appropriate descriptor or header for describing pedagogical documents. The difficulty stems from the following paradox: the header should be as detailed as possible to get, when querying the knowledge pool, an adequate set of documents, and as light as possible to make sure that indexation will be performed. So whatever the international standard might be, it will achieve its aim of fostering share-and-reuse only if the majority of the involved persons accept to use it!

The question therefore is: "How do you convince an author to index a document?" To try and answer this question, we are investigating the key factors of motivation for an author.

INTRODUCTION

Computer-based training (CBT) and computer aided learning (CAL) applications have been around for more than 30 years. Conceived as rigid, integrated, stand-alone pieces of software, they never turned out a real success although they cost a huge amount of human and financial effort. Thanks to the dazzling deployment of information and communication technologies (ICTs) coupled with the tenfold increase of computer power, new and promising opportunities for open and distance education opened up. New paradigms were born, among which those of *knowledge pool, modularized pedagogical component, learning citizen* and *share-and-reuse* are worth mentioning. If properly taken into consideration, these concepts will influence greatly the way online teaching and training could be handled, in turn modifying the way the production of electronic documents for education and training will be dealt with.

In this chapter, because we firmly believe it to be one of the main issues, we will concentrate on the notion of share-and-reuse that in our mind is to prosper if: (i) a critical mass of pedagogical material is made available and (ii) efficient search mechanisms allow for retrieving at least the most relevant candidate resources according to the context of actual use. Lots of international joint efforts have already been invested in order to achieve this goal. An international standard1 for a proper metadata, providing for an adequate indexation scheme that in turn allows for a clear and interoperable description of pedagogical documents (the *header*), was approved on June 13, 2002.

The difficulty stems from the following paradox: the header should be: (i) as detailed as possible to facilitate getting, when querying a pedagogical repository (the so-called *knowledge pool*), an appropriate set of documents, and (ii) as light as possible to ensure that the indexation itself will be performed. Therefore, whatever the standard, it will achieve its aim of fostering share-and-reuse if, and only if, the majority of the involved persons accept to use it! The question therefore is: " What do you do to ensure document indexation?" To try and answer this question, we are investigating the key factors of motivation.

The work in progress, detailed hereafter, intends to detect: (i) what could motivate or impede authors from sharing and/or re-using educational documents, and (ii) what could be proposed to increase their willingness to do so. A hopefully representative panel of authors, belonging to the academic world, will be requested to answer a survey that should help determine these key factors. At this stage we exclude the professional world, although we assume that the underlying reluctance and/or motivation for share-and-reuse of these two distinct environments could feature some similarities (confidentiality or publication considerations, strategic information, institutional policies, fear of being plagiarized, etc.).

BACKGROUND

Should the pedagogical community dispose of—as it is the case in the ARIADNE Foundation (http://www.ariadne-eu.org)—its distributed knowledge pool system (cf., Figure 1), each of its members can query either the local, the regional or the international knowledge pool to check whether there exist some pedagogical documents that could be reused in the context of a specific course to be prepared and delivered.

Figure 1: The ARIADNE Knowledge Pool Distributed System

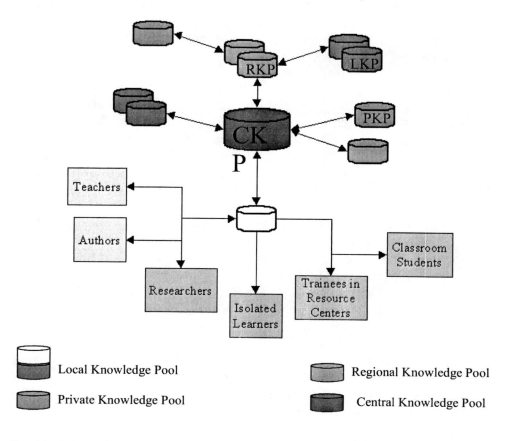

The greater the number of documents retrieved, the better their quality and the finer their level of granularity, the easier it becomes to make a document produced by someone else. Facilities should be provided to adapt the document, allowing for real appropriation and hence increasing the chances of renouncement to the well-known syndrome of the "not written by me."

RESEARCH ASSUMPTIONS AND OBJECTIVES

According to the already-mentioned context and target audience, it appears that authors'—persons involved in the production and drafting of electronic documents dedicated to the academic training—motivation to share, use and re-use documents is a determining factor when aiming at improving the quality of shared/sharable documents, thus contributing to increase their production. Our hope is that studying both the related variables, we will be able to deduce which of these endogenous and exogenous factors should be considered to help increase the authors' motivation.

The main endogenous factors retained so far are:

(i)   confidence in the quality of what is produced both by oneself and by others;
(ii)   trust in reciprocation, meaning that when one shares its production with others they, in turn, will do the same, defeating the belief that "I always give and never receive";
(iii)   the conviction that by feeding a cooperative database and contributing to it scaling up, the whole community will benefit from it;
(iv)   the wish to belong to a network, so that the combined efforts alleviate a burden that otherwise might be to heavy—investing efforts, time and money to rediscover what already exists;
(v)   the personal intention in sharing with third parties;
(vi)   the ability to consider its specific research and curricular field like forming part of a broader network of general disciplines.

Regarding the exogenous factors, we will consider:

(i)   the financial and temporal constraints;
(ii)   the institutional capacity to support transdisciplinarity;
(iii)   the increased visibility of the resulting curriculum;
(iv)   the possibility of developing new collaborations;
(v)   the reluctance towards technological constraints.

We thus propose to examine some dimensions intervening in the motivation process and to interpret them in the light of the variables of the here above mentioned. In order to justify a lack of cooperation, authors often mention exogenous factors; however, we believe that endogenous factors are likely to impact the tendency more strongly when being taken in to account in a cooperative model.

Endogenous factors of the first level (authors' intention) must be understood according to the model of coalition presented by Foray and Zimmermann (2001).

A population I is involved in producing pedagogical contents, of cardinal N, which can influence the individual decision of taking part or not in the collective efforts of sharing these contents. It is considered that these collective efforts generate, for each N individuals (authors) of I, an externality of use resulting from the improvements made to the first teaching step of production. We represent this externality in the *f(n)* function of the number of cooperating authors, where *f(n)* is increasing and strictly concave.

In a simplified way, we initially assume that the individual cost of participation per unit of time is uniform and is indicated by *CP*, as well as for the expected effects in terms of reputation and competence, indicated by *KR*. Thus we can derive that the cumulated profit for any individual author, for each unit of time, depends on whether he cooperates or not.

Regarding motivations of the authors in the step of use, sharing and re-use of electronic documents, a study about these motivations implies targeting the under-lying endogenous and exogenous factors (psychosocial perspective) acting in this

Figure 2

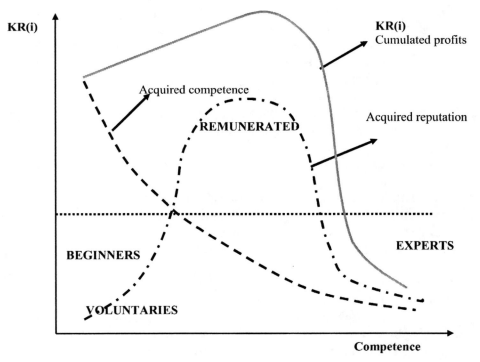

process. We assume that the cumulated profits (i.e., acquired competence and reputation), after a strong growth, decrease gracefully as authors become experts.

METHODOLOGICAL ASPECTS

It should be noted that the endogenous factors to study are divided into two dimensions: (i) dimension of intentionality (above mentioned) and (ii) social factors (gender and age). With regard to the exogenous factors, we subdivide them into three categories of dimension: (i) the institutional constraints (existing network, transdisciplinarity, etc.); (ii) the technological constraints (reluctance towards technology); and finally (iii) the academic and linguistic traditions to which belong the institutions in which authors are in function (Latin-speaking European, German-speaking European, English-speaking European and North American, etc.).

Experimental Conditions

Our experimental conditions will include:
1. design of a preliminary questionnaire in order to target a representative sample of population (authors involved in production and drafting of electronic documents dedicated to the academic training, independently of their motivations);
2. determination of the sample (determining the sample size for a factor or effect in an **AN**alysis **Of VA**riance between groups is usually difficult because of the need to specify all of the treatment means in order to calculate the non-centrality parameter of the F-distribution, on which power depends);
3. dividing this sample into equal and significant (F-distribution) groups (regarding to gender, age, language and academic tradition, etc.);
4. multivariate questionnaire suitable for informing us about all above-mentioned dimensions, factors and correlations between the studied variables;
5. factor analysis of correspondences—one-, two- and three-way interaction effect (ANOVA), correlations (multiple regression if necessary), etc.;
6. analyzing the results and offering a grid of interpretation.

QUESTIONNAIRE

Following Singly (1992), who advises to split questionnaires dealing with a practice or a set of practices into two parts, we have organized ours with Part I focusing on the "object of the survey" and part II focusing on the "social determinants."

In order to find indicators about the studied notion, we relied on Paul Lazarfeld's multiplicity principle (Schumann, 1993) which states as follows: "As the relation between each indicator and the fundamental concept is defined in terms of probabilities, a lot of indicators should be used." It is said that when creating a questionnaire, the best practice is to use both open questions and closed questions. A question is said to be closed when only one among a number of possible answers is to be selected, whereas when confronted with an open question, one can answer freely. Needless to say that all answers have to be carefully categorized before treatment in order to be computed correctly. On one hand, open questions offer a wider opportunity of expression and support the own perception by people of the social environment; on the other hand the information related to these answers seems to be useless because it is too dispersed or hard to compute.

As it is known, answers are often biased by the way the question is put, so some rules should be considered in order not to influence them as little as possible.

The general scheme of the first part of the questionnaire should provide for the detection of the sample's past and current practices: Do they share documents? Did they share documents in the past? Do they re-use documents produced by third parties? In which way? In which context? etc. The second part aims at detecting various dimensions of motivation underlying these:

- What factors can/could increase the motivation to share documents: visibility, recognition, altruism, practice imposed by the institution, the possibility to access "in return" documents produced by others, etc.?
- What are the inhibiting factors for document sharing: lack of recognition, loss of control on its own work, copyright and other legal problems, technical and organizational problems, lack of human and/or financial resources, lack of information, specificity of produced documents to a particular situation, etc.?
- What are the factors that justify the use of documents produced by others: time saving, lack of competences and/or resources to produce its own documents, the need to diversify resources placed at the disposal of learners, institutional policy, etc.?
- What are the factors inhibiting the re-use of documents produced by others (inadequacy with the needs, difficulties to find appropriate documents, poor quality of scientific content, technical problems, copyright problems, language and translation problems, price of the documents, the inappropriate granularity of the documents, impossibility to modify and adapt documents, the too large specificity of available material).

We suppose that the level of expertise has a deep impact on the practice of share and re-use. What are the independent variables, the dependant variables, and exogenous and endogenous factors?

1. Endogenous factors
    a. Independent variables

        i.   Number of years of practice of teaching
        ii.   Level of expertise
        iii.   Membership at a community of practice
        iv.   Knowledge of computer based tools
   b.   Dependant variables
        i.   type of practice: share, re-use, participation
2.   Exogenous factors
   a.   Independent variables
        i.   Age
        ii.   Sex
        iii.   Mother tongue
        iv.   Work methods
   b.   Dependant variables
        i.   type of practice : share, re-use, participation

The questionnaire should be anonymous, and try to show that as well as the level of expertise, the sex and mother tongue could impact on the practice.

Different Groups of Questions

Identifying the person
1.   Age:
2.   Sex: Female or Male
3.   Mother tongue:
4.   Continental origin:
5.   Country of work:
6.   Language used for work:

Identifying the practice
7.   Do you currently share your documents? Yes or no?
8.   If yes, what is the frequency during the last year?
   a.   1-10
   b.   10-20
   c.   20-50
   d.   50-100
   e.   more than 100
9.   If not, why?
10. Did you share documents in the past? Yes or no?
11. If yes, when?
   a.   Beginning of your career
   b.   Middle of your career
   c.   End of your career

12.   If yes, what is the frequency?
    a.   Give an average number of documents per year
13.   Do you think your practice has changed?
    a.   Why?
14.   With whom do you share your documents?
    a.   My offices' colleagues
    b.   My university colleagues
    c.   My institute colleagues
    d.   Within a network of universities
    e.   Within an international network
    f.   Other: explain
15.   Do you re-use document from others?
16.   What kind of documents?
    a.   Newspaper articles
    b.   Books
    c.   Internal publications
    d.   Academic reviews
    e.   Courses from other colleagues
    f.   Documents of unknown authors
    g.   Documents of known authors
    h.   CD-ROMs
    i.   Films
    j.   Photos
    k.   Cassettes
    l.   Animations
    m.   Images
    n.   Practical cases
    o.   Sound
    p.   Other
17.   What are your choosing criteria?
18.   Do you belong to a community of practice?

FUTURE TRENDS

This study will detect factors allowing share and re-use of the electronic documents for education. First of all we will categorize the population sample according to their present and past practices. Ability of sharing and re-using documents will constitute the two main dimensions used in order to extract this sample (those sharing documents, those re-using them, those doing both). We will then try to detect the motivations underlying each type of practice regarding the sharing and re-use of documents. The main factors highlighted by this inquiry will then be studied, more intensively, in a second article. Obviously the model is not strictly defined, and should be completed by including other factors like the relation between the number of documents re-used and the number of documents shared.

REFERENCES

Cardinaels, K., Hendrikx, K., Vervaet, E., Duval, E., Olivie, H., Haenni, F., Warkentyne, K., Wentland Forte, M. & Forte, E. (1998). A knowledge pool system of reusable pedagogical elements. *Proceedings of CALISCE'98,* Göteborg Sweden.

Copyleft, http://www.eff.org/IP/Open_licenses/open_alternatives.html.

David, P. (1997). Communication norms and the collective cognitive performance of invisible colleges. In Navaretti, G.B. (Ed.), *Creation and Transfer of Knowledge: Institutions and Incentives.* Physica Verlag.

David, P. & Foray, D. (1995). Accessing and expanding the science and technology knowledge base. *STIReview,* OCDE, Paris, 16, 13-68.

de Singly, F. (1992). *L'Enquête et ses Méthodes: Le Questionnaire.* Nathan Université.

Dublin Core, http://dublincore.org.

Duval, E., Vervaet, E., Verhoeven, B., Hendrikx, K., Cardinaels, K., Olivié, H., Forte, E., Haenni, F., Warkentyne, K., Wentland Forte, M. & Simillion, F. (2000). Managing digital educational resources with the ARIADNE metadata system. *Journal of Internet Cataloging.*

Foray, D. & Zimmermann, J.B. (2001). *L'Économie du Logiciel Libre: Organisation Coopérative et Incitation à L'Innovation.* Flash Informatique EPFL.

Ganagé, M. & Bonnet, R. (1998). Linux: L'explosion du phénomène des logiciels libres. *L'Ordinateur Individuel, 97.*

IEEE P1484.12 Learning Object Metadata Working Group, http://ltsc.ieee.org/wg12/index.html.

Opencontent Licence, http://opencontent.org/opl.shtml.

Salvador, J. (1986). L'ouvert et le fermé dans la pratique du questionnaire. *French Review of Sociology.*

Schumann, H. & Kalton, G. (1993). Context and contiguity in survey questionnaires. *Jacob Ludwig Public Opinion Quarterly.*

Schumann, H. & Presser, S. (1979). The open and closed questions. *American Sociological Review.*

SCORM, http://www.adlnet.org.

ENDNOTE

[1] Standard for Learning Object Metadata approved by the Standards Board of the IEEE Standards Association (IEE-LTSC); http://ltsc.ieee.org.

Chapter VI

EFT*Web*: A Model for the Enhanced Use of Educational Materials

Luís Borges Gouveia
CEREM, University Fernando Pessoa, Portugal

Joaquim Borges Gouveia
DEGEI, Aveiro University, Portugal

ABSTRACT

The EFTWeb is a model proposed for developing a World Wide Web based-system that allows the interaction between users and contents. The users can be students and teachers that place, modify and use available contents. Contents can be any type of digital education materials. The system provides the means to control security, intellectual property rights and billing issues, giving both types of users the necessary tools to access the system, prepare materials and use them.

One important facility associated with the system is its ability to create contexts. The creation of context is made possible by the combined use of thesaurus technology and referencing content by recurring to dynamic catalogues, providing different perspectives to exist at the same time.

The authors defend the importance that context may have to provide a usable environment to support education, learning and training activities, and to make available the associated concepts that help to support such a semantic approach to content reuse.

INTRODUCTION

The EFTWeb is a model proposed for developing a World Wide Web-based system that allows the interaction between users and contents. The users can be students and teachers that place, modify and use available contents. Contents can be any type of digital education materials. The system provides the means to control security, intellectual property rights (IPR) and billing issues, giving to the users the necessary tools to access the system, prepare materials and use them.

One important facility associated with the system is its ability to create contexts. The creation of context is made possible by the combined use of thesaurus technology and referencing content by recurring to dynamic catalogues.

The authors defend the importance that context may have when providing usable environments to support education, learning and training activities, and provide the associated concepts that help to support such a semantic approach to content reuse.

Based on a current project to support distributed education with strong coordination requirements, the authors developed a framework to assist education, learning and training needs using common available technologies like the World Wide Web and databases.

The framework is supported by an infrastructure that led to a novel propose of a value added chain for the education business, where teachers and students play an equal part on the system being considered both as producers and consumers. The system aim is to support with maximum flexibility both teachers and students, and treat them as clients that produce, share and consume contents organized by sequences that can be customized according to different situations regarding the context of education, learning and training.

The chapter presents the system with a focus on the creation of contexts and how they provide a real support for both teachers' and students' work. We will attempt to demonstrate the role that the use of context creation facility can have to structure information about a knowledge theme and thus provide users with a better service to support education, training and learning activities.

Motivation

The digital economy obeys very different paradigms from the traditional ones. Among interesting characteristics in the Society of Information is the possibility, with great easiness, to start from information picked up in the most varied sources and for the most forms, to store, to negotiate, to conceive, to produce, to reconfigure, to manage, to implement and to control the development of new products, including the opening of enormous opportunities in the field of the education, training and learning.

Rethinking education, training and learning is critical. From the EFTWeb point of view, it can be seen as a group of services, taking a perspective from demand to the offer, and conceiving it as a product that allows its easy transformation in a service and making it more useful to the students and professionals. It is important to state that the authors defend the perspective of students as customers who are information and knowledge buyers. But they also can be seen as knowledge builders!

CURRENT ISSUES ON EDUCATION, TRAINING AND LEARNING

Many of the current education, learning and training issues are related to the need of flexible independent learning in terms of time and place The available information and communication technologies (ICTs) also allow new opportunities to innovate and propose life-long learning (LLL), on-the-job training facilities, open and distance education (ODE) and new forms of knowledge delivery even for the more traditional teaching.

With the evolving change in the way we work and learn in the new economy age, there is also a strong demand for new paradigms of teaching and learning which focus on social interaction, as in the case of collaborative learning (Dillenbourg & Schneider, 1995). A great number of existent learning paradigms are based on constructivistic principles (Brown et al., 1989). As stated by Manderveld and Koper (2000), the new learning paradigms focus on the following concepts:

- education an training is learner centered (Kinzie, 1990);
- learning as an active, constructive and goal-directed process (Shull, 1988);
- individual differences of students are taken into account;
- the teacher or trainer is a facilitator and a coach (Wood & Wood, 1995)
- learning is embedded in a social context;
- emphasis on performance assessment methods.

Manderveld and Koper (2000) suggest that in order to support these new learning paradigms, learning environments need to be rich, flexible environments, and they must be available anytime and anyplace.

Taking these issues into account, a higher level of concern is introduced and new forms of doing are needed to engage an existing learning community into the use of ICTs and, in particular, to take advantage of the World Wide Web- (Web-) based environment as the one described in this chapter.

The Case of Web-Based Learning

McCormack and Jones proposed a broad definition for Web-based learning system in 1998. They considered it as an environment created on the World Wide Web in which students and educators can perform learning-related tasks. They add that it is not simply a mechanism for distributing information to students, but also performs tasks related to communication, assessment and class management.

One of the existing resources in the Web concerning Web-based learning is the *Web-based learning resources library* at *http://www.outreach.utk.edu/weblearning/*. There, Web-based learning is defined as a major subcomponent of the broader term "e-learning." Web-based learning is one of the tools with which education can be delivered. In traditional academic institutions, Web-based learning systems are generally housed administratively in a "distance education" department alongside other at-distance delivery methods such as correspondence, satellite broadcast, two-way videoconferencing, videotape and CD-ROM/DVD delivery systems. All such systems seek to serve learners at some distance from their learning source. Many such systems attempt to serve learners interacting with the learning source in an asynchronous mode (for example, e-mail). Distance education, then, is often referred to as those delivery modalities that seek to reduce the barriers of time and space to learning, thus the frequently used phrase "anytime, anywhere learning."

Walkden and Sharp (2000) propose that the most effective learning system will be hybrids, using conventional settings with a mixture of some virtual features.

A number of changes are required when paper-based learning resources are changed by the use of the electronic medium (Thompson & Boak, 2000). In particular they can:

- make available a range of items within a package;
- offer users diagnostic checklists, which the software can code and advise users, on the basis of their responses, which packages and which items within packages may be of most relevance to them;
- offer users choices from menus, so they can explore the packages and the items within packages: choose to ignore some, or to explore them in an order that reflects their own interests and priorities;
- invite users to write their own answers, suggestions, observations, into the package, and then quickly allow them to compare their contributions with system answers and suggestions;
- collate information that users provide in response to questions, and enable users to save it, print it or send it to a tutor using some Internet facility (such as e-mail);
- use media other than the printed word—illustrations, photograph, animations and sound.

These changes can provide an opportunity for innovation in education, learning and training. However, a proper environment other than technology must be available and developed for creating a true learning community. This chapter deals with the EFTWeb model, but a broader discussion must take place when implementing it in a real setting for a particular learning community that introduces human factors and the right information system to integrate people, technology and organization.

Innovation and Opportunities within Education, Training and Learning

Education, learning and training constitutes one of the areas of great potential for innovation. This enormous potential can promote modifications both in the processes and in the way that these activities are performed. It is currently accepted that education, training and learning will meet, in a close future, among economic activities of larger importance.

However, education, learning and training on move despite presential teaching has remained almost the same for the last four centuries (Puttnam, 1996). Even with current available information technologies and their impact, no relevant changes are in sight. Tension between what can be expected by students and current educational offers is greater as shown each day by new signs of the growing difference between what students want and what society needs and what institutions can provide. Even teachers seem lost somewhere by the pace of change and by the lack of interest among students to attend, discuss and produce work in a traditional education environment.

Opportunities to take advantage of information technologies in educational contexts are reported by several authors (Harasim, 1995; Papert, 1993). In particular, there is an opportunity to innovate by reinventing time and space constraints in educational settings (Gouveia, 1999) and introducing computer and network support on presence teaching (Gouveia, 1998).

However, the use of ICTs generally does not introduce innovation into educational practices although they offer tremendous opportunities for that (Goodyear, 1999). Among these ICT offerings are the use of laptop computers, PDAs, network support and the Internet itself.

Also, Semantic Web techniques provide an opportunity to support reusing content. Semantic Web is a mesh of information linked in such a way as to be easily processed by machines, on a global scale. Its aim is to provide an efficient way of representing data on the World Wide Web, or as a globally linked database. A number of those concerns lie within the Semantic Web concept such as metadata, formal annotations of Web information, information extraction, knowledge representation for the Web, integration of databases in the knowledge Web, interoperability of Web services at the semantic and pragmatic levels, content-based information retrieval, knowledge retrieval and tool environments, as is the case of the one proposed in this chapter.

EFT*WEB* SYSTEM PROPOSAL

Basic Model Concepts

The EFTWeb system proposes an innovation of the education, training and learning process, through the use of the Web by presenting a framework that bases teacher and student interaction on the materials and tasks to be accomplished. In the proposed model, content has the same importance as the means for classifying it (Gouveia et al., 2000).

The EFTWeb model was designed to support three main concepts for content structuring—unit, theme and content. A unit possesses themes and for them corresponds presential sessions or module units. Each theme has a group of contents that aids information and knowledge transmission. A *content* is an independent object of a given format, among the many multimedia formats supported by the Internet.

The organization scheme for user access, unit – theme – content, is given by the notion of a guide. A guide is a well-defined sequence of the referred elements associated to structure contents and gives the user a path to explore information (Borges Gouveia et al., 2000).

One of the underlying ideas for EFTWeb is to support with maximum flexibility content access by giving total permission to use available resources and facilities. This is implemented by assigning a particular profile to each user. To support it the model implements a credit-based system allowing each user the access to a given resource based on a cost for each unit retrieved. Each user receives a given amount of credits that can be used with some degree of freedom. The EFTWeb user can be a single user or a group of users like a class. A user can be any teacher or student.

An important model characteristic is considering each user a client. The model allows the necessary flexibility to consider users, regardless of if they are teachers or students, as potential consumers and producers. This way, the system provides support to organize students' works and integrate them in the content offering by appropriate control of author rights and content's versioning and certification. It also allows teachers to build, along with content, new or existing guides based on others' work. This can include, in all or in part, already existent guides. Each user can also introduce enhancements in the way content is classified.

Technology Support

The EFTWeb model is implemented with available widespread technology. To support content distribution, the World Wide Web becomes the natural solution. It has a lot of information available that needs to be mediated for being trusted. Also, its information can be searchable and exists in a digital format, in particular using a textual search engine. Web access is possible with a personal computer and its cost is acceptable.

To support content, database technology is used. This technology eases the storage and retrieval of contents and supports multiple and concurrent accesses supporting multimedia storage and activity logs. It also provides a proven mean for searching and to support the dynamic maintenance of contents and model data structures.

Figure 1: The Offer in the EFTWeb Model

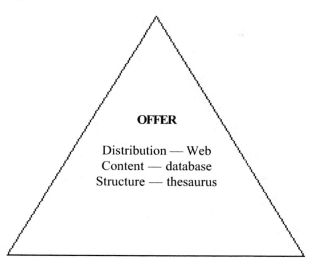

To support semantic structures, where relations between contents are of importance, thesaurus technology is used. This will provide the necessary flexibility to access content by using a set of ordered concepts that allow storage of, with each content, independent semantic and high-order relationships.

The combined use of the World Wide Web, databases and thesaurus technologies are designed as the support for the system offer—distribution plus content plus structure—and constitutes the system core added value. Figure 1 represents the model offer. A number of systems already take this approach, including some intranet models (Duncan, 2000) and education-specific models such as WebCT and others. A comparison of the EFTWeb with a number of education models (Aulanet, Classnet, Learning space, Live/Books, Serf, Virtual-U, WCB and WebCT) is made in Gouveia et al. (2000). One of EFTWeb's main distinctions is its reliance on thesaurus technology to introduce semantics to the model.

One of the more relevant features of this model is the use of thesaurus technology to structure content semantics. The thesaurus is used to describe a particular model of knowledge about a given area in terms of keywords and relations between these keywords. The system allows the creation of several different structures in the thesaurus, for different overlapping classification systems to use at the same time.

From the user perspective, the Web browser integrates system functionality by offering a common and easy-to-use hypermedia interface. This option allows for the technology integration without increasing user client complexity to configure and use. Its use also allows integration with Internet and intranet existent facilities.

Model Entities

EFTWeb model considers in its core some support for security and billing issues. The entities represent the interface with external issues like client, security and billing (Figure 2). These three entities were selected in order to provide a clear business orientation for the EFTWeb model.

- *Client*: includes teachers and students. The model allows a client to be a consumer and also a producer.
- *Security*: deals with the need of protecting client identification and client system use. Also, it includes allowed user operations and what can the user really do, modify, comment and add as content and context information.
- *Billing*: allows the necessary arrangements to use the system in a commercial way, where different types of promotions, paying education, learning and training programs, and fees can be applied.

Figure 2: The Entities in the EFTWeb

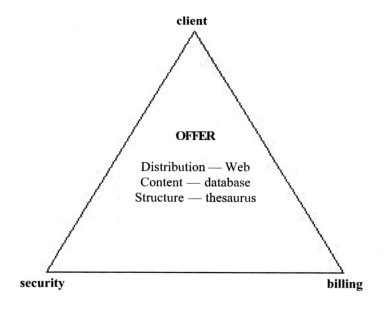

Model Mechanisms

The model mechanisms are used to interface the offer with the entities presented. The mechanisms receive the information from corresponding entities, and provide the processes and storage needs to deal with entity requirements in a flexible and independent way.

For each entity, the model offers a correspondent mechanism that acts like a system translator between each entity's requirements and the functioning for system offer integration. The model mechanisms are defined as (Figure 3):

- *Scripts*: having the distribution, content and structure as an organized and available offer, to each client can correspond a particular path that shows a set of selected offer.
- *Profiles*: corresponds to how each client can interact with the offer, by allowing different levels of functionality to take place. These levels are described as use, read, execute, comment, add, certify and evaluate.
- *Credits*: allows client interaction with the offer in a cost-based approach. Each action concerning content or each kind of interaction can have a particular cost or be rewarded with credits. Credits also allow system usage regulation by controlling accesses. The credits mechanism interacts with the billing by allowing an internal unifying cost for tracking usage and a commercial independent pricing.

EFTWeb User Types

Three types of users should be considered. The normal user can be a teacher or a student. The administrative users are responsible for the normal definition of the system offer and operation. There are two types of administrative users: the ones that

Figure 3: The Mechanisms in the EFTWeb Model

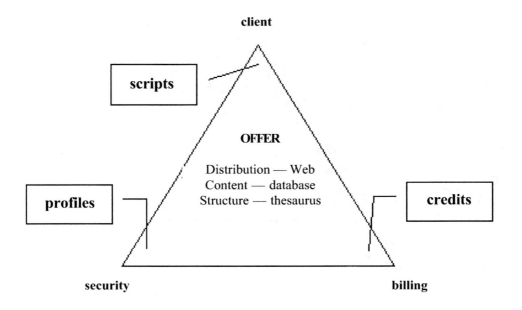

deal with the base offer definitions and the thesaurus administrative users that are responsible for maintaining multiple catalogues and thesaurus.

The model also proposes two types of services: administrative services that allow administrative users and thesaurus administrative users to enter the information necessary to the system operation, like user information, content and structure information. The administrative services are:

- *certifying and authoring*: certifying contents and authoring scripts;
- *version control*: promoting and maintaining related content collections;
- *catalogue creation*: complementing the thesaurus with additional information by introducing lists of available thesaurus keywords with correspondent weighting factors.

Notice that although these services were designed to be performed by different people, anyone can be part of each group and each group will not excludes members from the other groups. The three groups were devised in order to reinforce content quality and its categorization effort.

System Services

The system takes advantage of existent worldwide and low-cost Web facilities. It is based on a client/server architecture where the core content is stored in a database and all the interaction between the system and users is made by a Web browser using standard facilities (no plug-ins). This means that no additional plug-in for running EFTWeb is needed, although any format used for content support may require plug-ins to be presented. That's the case for, among others, content produced using Flash or VRML code.

The novelty is on the model used to create the database structure, where focus was directed to clients, security and cost supervision. In order to fill these requirements, some integration mechanisms have been developed. In the system core, contents classification (metadata) based on thesaurus technology is placed along with the contents, allowing great flexibility in the terms definition.

The EFTWeb can be used as broker to assist both teacher and students needs by providing content in context. Different educational contexts can be envisaged as resulting from presence education support, distance education and training or even instruction activities.

The current implementation of the EFTWeb model supports several services including the use of a recommender system and the support for cooperative work for document tracking and folder sharing (version management). These facilities, along with the more usual electronic mail, news, forum and chat, provide a set of services integrated with the content database and a thesaurus-based content classification for accessing and searching available content. Users can also trade content by using credits to buy and sell contents. Security issues are implemented in the base system in order to certify who is doing what with respect to a given content.

The implemented user services are (Borges Gouveia et al., 2000):

- *mail*: each client must have access to an e-mail address to send/receive messages;
- *dialog*: allows client chat in real time.

The service is organized in rooms that groups users by topic:

- *personal area*: works as a system portal, proposing a link collection;
- *personal folder*: the place where the client places his documents with the option to share them;
- *search engine*: available in two modes—textual search and thesaurus (by directory); and
- *guides*: this facility defines the content sequence—*"knowledge road"*—to be used. It groups other guides, units and content.

IMPACT ON EDUCATION, LEARNING AND TRAINING

Considering current education, learning and training processes, the ones that are proposed by EFTWeb favored content reuse by allowing its combination based on existing context creation facilities. These facilities are implemented by the creation of a thesaurus and its flexibility based on alternative catalogs for each context—thus allowing alternative models to user access content. These models can exist and be used at the same time for different users and be replaced at any time for each user, providing alternative contexts to access content. Four types of activities in the process of education, learning and training can be proposed as follows:

- *lecturing*: the activity of content transmission and facilitation;
- *certifying*: the activity of validating contents and education contexts;
- *evaluating*: the activity of validating and assessing client (both teachers and students) knowledge;
- *production*: the activity of content creation, methodology elaboration and technology selection.

Considering the above activities, three main education types are proposed:

- *lecturing*: actions that involve one individual responsible for knowledge transmission to an audience composed of a group of individuals that may have different goals;
- *training*: actions oriented to the content, where the intended audience has common and well-defined goals; and

- *instruction*: actions oriented to the context, where the intended audience has a well-known profile and a group of tasks to be executed.

From these definitions (activities and education types), two important issues arise. First, there is a need to deal with the available resources in a flexible way—especially the ones concerned with content. The second allows combining types and education activities for extending, and describes resources as contents and contexts in the EFTWeb perspective.

EFTWeb proposes a model to support the need to store, represent and maintain both contents and semantic of contents in order to allow contents relations in independent and not previous known ways. This characteristic allows context support along with contents and also with semantic support given by using thesaurus technology.

THE USE OF THESAURUS

The current proposal for using thesaurus technology allows for the provision of a high-level description of the context and meaning of specific works within the knowledge domain where the available model offer is to be used (distribution + content + structure).

As the use of thesaurus allows the specification of meanings for the more important words used for classification, it supports search and browse tactics (Baeza-Yates & Ribeiro-Neto, 1999). In conjunction with the use of catalogs, the thesaurus facility allows a group of users to construct and develop a context where they can both explore available content and create a high-level description of the knowledge domain to be used.

Such a system is integrated with the available content by the use of a textual search engine. It takes advantage of the specified thesaurus keywords and the provided catalog weights for these keywords, to build queries and to retrieve content that matches with these weighted keywords by using not an existing content classification, but the content description itself.

The use of thesaurus and catalogues allow students to reason not only for how to select content, but also to develop the context within those content is select and has a particular reasoning. It provides a way to organize available content and provide a tool for information management about a given knowledge domain.

Thesaurus and Catalogues in Practice

We can define a thesaurus for a given knowledge area or topic. It can be a broader topic such as *Informatics*, or a more specific one such as *Human Factors*

Figure 4: A Partial Thesaurus Example

```
Information
Technology
System
Enterprise
```

in HCI. For demonstration, Figure 4 presents a small example of a thesaurus for the *Information Systems* topic.

A catalog enhances a thesaurus by considering further detail about a given topic. For example, when considering a thesaurus about *Information Systems* (IS), several different catalogs can be proposed such as one considering an *IS Management* perspective (Figure 5) and another about an *IS Socio-Technological* perspective (Figure 6).

Note that both catalogs are about the *Information Systems* topic, but focus on different issues regarding the same knowledge theme. Thus the initial keywords associated with the thesaurus remain the same (the bold words), but the catalogue terms are different (the ones that follow each thesaurus keyword).

The use of the proposed "thesaurus and catalogue" solution provides both the possibility to classify content and characterize a given knowledge domain as a set of

Figure 5: A Catalogue Example

```
Information: value, data, process
Technology: office, production, productivity
System: model
Enterprise: value, added-value, profit
```

Figure 6: An Alternative Catalog Example

```
Information: data, knowledge
Technology: support, learning
System: human, process, ergonomic
Enterprise: work, system
```

keywords (terms) that can be used to inform search and content retrieval. In particular, this approach can be used to use a textual search engine to mine the content database, and to inform the inclusion of more classification keywords to each content occurrence.

An approach to use these facilities is to consider the use of the thesaurus to restrict available keywords and define a context, thus producing a high semantic level description to access content.

Also, the use of the catalog to define further detail and expand the thesaurus in a number of ways produces the following advantages:

- adding more semantics by feeding more keywords for each of the thesaurus entries;
- expanding the description level of the thesaurus, using the catalog as a strategy to search content, providing a tuning facility to classify the content itself (adding and deleting keywords associated with each content);
- allowing the use of specific keywords to refer to existing thesaurus entries. This will provide different perspective descriptions such as the client that can be a user within an enterprise context, and students within an academic context or an employee within the implementation of an ERM—*Employee Relationship Management*—system.

CONCLUSIONS

EFTWeb proposes a system that unifies content reuse for education, learning and training activities. The EFTWeb proposes content reuse from and by teachers taking advantage of students' work. It provides a structured approach to store educational materials. This will allow content classification as an ongoing activity using EFTWeb, and its thesaurus and catalog facilities.

Content retrieval can be made by taking advantage of both a textual search engine and a combined thesaurus and catalog search, allowing the use of more restrictive conditions to be followed to find relevant content within the available content database.

The use of thesaurus facilities allows for the creation of alternative contexts where same contents can be used and referred within different perspectives, produced as additional catalogs to use taking into account a given thesaurus. Traditional ways of content classification offer a limited perspective based on the content's aim at creation time and focused on content rather than taking into account the content plus context.

If we can, based on learning needs, specify a given knowledge topic using a high abstract level description instead of relying on same previous content classification, a much wider potential use for available content can be expected and thus take a semantic approach to content management.

EFT*Web* also provides the support for education, learning and training activities based on the following advantages:

- *flexibility*: concerning the production process; the production includes contents, thesaurus and guides;
- *diversification*: by means of reusing existent content in new guides (contexts) and upgrading them both with new contents or by improving existent ones;
- *differentiation*: at the product level, by offering content and guides for satisfying each client's needs.

EFTWeb can be of help in the emerging of new approaches to the education business, not only by supporting but also for packaging contents and facilitate its management. Central to EFTWeb use is the creation of thesaurus and guides, which turn out easy context descriptions for client needs fulfillment. These contexts allow taking advantage of existing content in different perspectives with different goals and within various activities.

The creation of multiple catalogs to be used with each thesaurus definition provides an even richer context description by allowing the use of the language and each area glossary to be integrated with EFTWeb facilities to browse available content. Beyond content and its reuse is the context offering to support education, learning and training activities.

REFERENCES

Baeza-Yates, R. & Ribeiro-Neto, B. (1999). *Modern Information Retrieval.* Addison-Wesley.

Borges Gouveia, J., Gouveia, L. & Restivo, F. (2000). Proposing a knowledge network to assist education, training and learning. *Proceedings of ITS'2000 XIII Biennial Conference.* July 2-5, Buenos Aires, Argentina.

Brown, J., Collins, A. & Duguid, P. (1989). Situated cognition and the culture of learning. *Educational Researcher,* 18(1), 32-42.

Dillenbourg, P. & Schneider, D. (1995). Mediating the mechanisms which make collaborative learning sometimes effective. *International Journal of Educational Telecommunications,* 1, 131-146.

Duncan, N. (2000). *The Case of the Volunteer Infrastructure.* Ohio University Press.

Goodyear, P. (1999). New technology in higher education: Understanding the innovation process. In Eurelings, A. et al (Eds.), *Integrating Information & Communication Technology in Higher Education.* Kluwer-Deventer, 107-136.

Gouveia, L. (1998). The NetLab experience. Moving the action to electronic learning environments. *Proceedings of BITE International Conference,* March 25-27, Maastricht, The Netherlands, 395-405.

Gouveia, L. (1999). On education, learning and training: Bring windows where just walls exist. *UFP Journal,* 3(May), 223-227.

Gouveia, L., Borges Gouveia, J. & Restivo, F. (2000). EFTWeb: A working model to support education, learning and training. In Tavares, L. & Pereira, M. (Eds.), *New Economy and Information Technologies.* Universidade Católica Editora, 400-410.

Gouveia, L., Borges Gouveia, J. & Restivo, F. (2000). EFTWeb: An application to support skills trading within education, learning and training environments. *Proceedings of the First World Conference on Production and Operations Management (POM Sevilla 2000),* August 26-30, Sevilla, Spain.

Harasim, L. (1995). *Learning Networks.* Boston, MA: The MIT Press.

Kinzie, M. (1990). Requirements and benefits of interactive instruction: Learner control, self-regulation, and continuing motivation. *Educational Technology Research and Development,* 38(1), 5-21.

Manderveld, J. & Koper, R. (2000). Edubox, a platform for new generation learning environments. *Proceedings of the European Conference Web-Based Learning Environments,* June 5-6, Porto, Portugal, 38-41.

Papert, S. (1993). *The Children's Machine.* City: Basic Books.

Puttnam, D. (1996). *Communication and Education.* The Ninth Colin Cherry Lecture, Imperial College, London, June.

Shull, T. (1988). The role of the student in learning from instruction. *Contemporary Educational Psychology,* 13, 276-295.

Thompson, D. & Boak, G. (2000). Experiences of producing Web resources that can be integrated with learning activities for coherent and planned learning. *Proceedings of the Bolton International Conference Towards the E-Learning Community: Challenges for Business and Education.* October 19-20, Bolton, UK, 207-222.

Walkden, F. & Sharp, J. (2000). Issues related to the co-development of a virtual environment. *Proceedings of the Bolton International Conference Towards the E-Learning Community: Challenges for Business and Education.* October 19-20, Bolton, UK, 42-50.

Wood, D. & Wood, H. (1996). Vygotsky, tutoring and learning. *Oxford Review of Education,* 22(1), 5-10.

Chapter VII

Group Support Systems and the Removal of Barriers to Creative Idea Generation within Small Groups: The Inhibition of Normative Influence

Esther E. Klein
Hofstra University, USA

ABSTRACT

This chapter explores the use of group support systems (GSSs) with anonymous interaction capability as a means of enhancing creativity in small groups by inhibiting normative influence. GSS anonymity provides an environment in which social cues (e.g., social presence, status, gender, seniority) are masked, thus ensuring merit-based evaluation of ideas and equalizing participation rates. The central argument of this chapter is that anonymity-featured GSSs inhibit the exertion of normative influence on lower-status, junior, shy or female members and thereby removes barriers to creative idea generation. The author applies this argument to organizational small task-oriented groups, focus groups and classrooms, where GSSs have the potential for encouraging all participants to propose creative ideas by allowing all participants an equal voice.

INTRODUCTION

Creativity and innovation are the lifeblood of organizations and, as such, are central concerns of management. In today's competitive business environment, managers are frequently required to generate creative ideas as solutions to business problems (see Taggar, 2002). The generation of creative solutions is a vital organizational task as successful businesses are likely to be innovators, "produc[ing] ideas or products that have changed their industries" ("Fear of the Unknown," 1999, p. 61). Organizational scholars and management have long recognized that creativity can lead to innovative and novel solutions to highly complex and intractable problems (Paper & Johnson, 1997). As such, creativity is essential for organizational small task-oriented groups as well as for focus groups and classrooms. Focus group participants are encouraged to produce creative ideas, which have the potential of being transformed into useful products. Similarly, teachers in classrooms challenge students to generate creative ideas so as to foster independent thinking.

The objectives of this chapter[1] are to explore normative influence as a barrier to creative idea generation that is present in small groups[2] and to suggest information technology (IT)-based solutions to remove such barriers. The chapter considers three types of small groups—organizational task-oriented groups, focus groups and classrooms, and the effect of one technology—group support systems (GSSs), also referred to as groupware—on creativity within these groups.

BACKGROUND
Group Interaction: Advantages and Disadvantages

Group interaction has a number of advantages, encapsulated by Paulus, Laurey, and Dzindolet (2001, p. 319) as follows:

> Group activities can build cohesiveness or team spirit, which in turn may be related to increased job motivation and morale. The shared decision making and responsibility of a team-based organization may lead to greater support or endorsement of organizational initiatives or programs. Groups can also take advantage of the shared expertise of the members. This may be particularly useful both in generating novel approaches and avoiding costly mistakes.

However, group interaction has some drawbacks, including limited amount of time for presenting individual ideas (air fragmentation), domination by one member, reluctance to express ideas due to fear of public speaking or due to evaluation apprehension, "groupthink" (the pressure on group members in decision-making groups to achieve consensus at the expense of objective analysis of the facts (see

Janis, 1972) and, of special relevance to this chapter, normative influence. (For fuller treatments of group interaction disadvantages, see Klein & Dologite, 2000, pp. 115-116; Nunamaker, Dennis, Valacich, Vogel & George, 1993, pp. 128-129; Paulus et al., 2001, pp. 321-323; Napier & Gershenfeld, 1999.) Its shortcomings notwithstanding, groups and teamwork are preferred over the individual in many situations and for many tasks. Hackman and Kaplan (1974, p. 461) captured the reason for this partiality toward groups thus:

> Despite all the evidence that group process can and does significantly impair group effectiveness in many cases, it remains unavoidably true that groups do [italics in original] have more resources than do single individuals, and therefore the potential for highly effective performance is very much present in most groups.

Normative Influence

A significant barrier to creativity within organizational small task-oriented groups, focus groups and classrooms is normative influence, which is defined as the "influence to conform to the expectations of others" (Kaplan & Wilke, 2001, p. 410; Cialdini & Trost, 1998; Deutsch & Gerard, 1955; Moscovici, 1985; Myers, 2002, p. 229). Normative influence deters the free expression of ideas by individual group members, such as when the latter are reluctant to propose ideas because of the perception that these ideas run counter to those of higher status members (see Tan, Wei, Warson & Walczuch, 1998) or because of the fear that their contributions will be devalued or rejected when evaluated by others (see Herschel, 1994; Klein & Dologite, 2000).[3] Idea generation, brainstorming, decision making, problem solving and other interactions in small groups frequently result in the exertion of normative influence by some group members on others. Normative influence hinders the equal participation of all group members, constraining the creativity of lower-status, junior, shy or female members. Kaplan and Wilke (2001) argued that normative influence "may inhibit the processing of information in breadth" (p. 423), thereby inhibiting the generation of creative ideas and instead promoting the generation of merely conventional ideas.

Group Support Systems

Nunamaker, Briggs, Mittleman and Vogel (1996/1997, p. 164) defined GSS as "interactive computer-based environments which support concerted and coordinated team effort towards completion of joint tasks. Besides supporting information access, GSSs can radically change the dynamics of group interactions by improving communication, by structuring and focusing problem solving efforts ...." According to Davison and Vogel (2000, p. 3), GSSs:

...are networked, computer-based systems designed to facilitate structured, interactive discussion in a group of people communicating face to face or remotely, synchronously [at the same time] or asynchronously [at different times]. Group members type their contributions into the system, which immediately makes each contribution available to all other participants. Thus, nobody forgets what they want to say while waiting for a turn to speak.

GSS have anonymous interaction capability, which allows group members to participate without being identified. According to Dennis, Tyran, Vogel and Nunamaker (1997, p. 159): "Anonymity may reduce evaluation apprehension—the fear of negative evaluation that can cause individuals to withhold ideas and opinions...It may also reduce the pressure to conform to the opinions of others, whether the pressure is intentional or not."

In the last two decades, GSSs have emerged as important end-user[4] support tools in computer-mediated communication (CMC) (Vreede & Bruijn, 1999; Vreede, Jones & Mgaya, 1998/1999) as "the GSS field [has become] a rapidly growing research area" (Zigurs, 1993, p. 115; see also Briggs, Nunamaker & Sprague, 1997/1998; Davison & Vogel, 2000; Kline & McGrath, 1999). Scholars and researchers within IS and related disciplines have suggested that creative idea generation may be enhanced in anonymity-featured GSS-supported groups (e.g., see Hender, Dean, Rodgers & Nunamaker, 2001; Klein & Dologite, 2000; Nunamaker, Applegate & Konsynski, 1987; Siau, 1996). The present chapter argues that the anonymity provided by GSSs inhibits normative influence within groups and thereby enhances creativity, and applies this argument to three contexts: organizational small task-oriented groups, focus groups and classrooms.

Creativity and Innovation

Creativity and innovation are difficult to define and to distinguish. In fact, the study of creativity and innovation is marked by definitional diversity and imprecision (e.g., see Bruner, 1968; Keil, 1987; Miller, 1987; Mumford & Gustafson, 1988; Parnes, 1967, 1992; Torrance, 1988). Guilford (1967) and Kris (1952) defined creativity in terms of the generation of novel ideas, whereas Cattell (1971) considered creativity as a kind of problem-solving ability. Further refining the concept of creativity, Rhodes (1961) classified definitions of creativity on the basis of four factors: person, product, process and press (or environment) (see also Woodman, Sawyer & Griffin, 1993). Despite their differences, virtually all definitions of creativity involve "a combination of originality and usefulness" (Bostrom & Nagasundaram, 1998, p.2). (For a recent history of creativity research, see Albert & Runco, 1999.) Often the terms "creativity" and "innovation" are used synonymously. However, according to Couger, Higgins and McIntyre (1990, 1993), Frame

(1989) and Rickards (1988), innovation is the process whereby new creative ideas are put into practice (see also Woodman et al., 1993). This definition of innovation is consistent with Amabile (1988), who held that creativity is a prerequisite for innovation.

The success of businesses, both large and small, often depends, in large part, upon the development of new ideas (Paulus et al., 2001, p. 319). Under pressure to have their companies operate more efficiently and profitably, managers often call upon groups to generate creative ideas to assist in product development, business strategy, problem solving and decision making. Creativity, then, is a prerequisite for innovation, which has been defined by some organizational scholars as "the adoption of an idea or behavior that is new to the organization adopting it" (Daft, 1978, p. 197). Frequently, but not always, innovations concern "the organizational initiation, adoption and/or implementation of one or more emerging technologies" (Fichman, 2001, p. 429).

Empirical support exists for the intuitive notion that innovation is crucial for the success of businesses (Brown & Eisenhardt, 1995; Eisenhardt & Tabrizi, 1995; Bean & Radford, 2001; Eisenhardt, Schoonhoven & Lyman, 2001). In a study of computer companies, Eisenhardt and Tabrizi (1995) found that "a rapid flow of innovative products" is critical to firm performance (Eisenhardt, Schoonhoven & Lyman, 2001, p. 339). In fact, innovation is vital to the economy as well as to the individual firm. "Economic growth depends on the ability of companies to do existing tasks more efficiently and the willingness of entrepreneurs to create innovative businesses and products" (Mandel, 2001, pp. 30-31). "Innovative activity," then, is an economy's engine of growth (Baumol, 2002)[5], in addition to being a goal of commercial enterprises, focus groups and classrooms.

NORMATIVE INFLUENCE AS A BARRIER TO CREATIVE IDEA GENERATION

Normative influence as a barrier to creative idea generation is a problem present in various small group settings. In mixed status groups having brainstorming sessions or otherwise involved in generating creative solutions, lower-status members may be influenced by higher-status members (Walker, Ilardi, McMahon & Fennell, 1996; Tan et al., 1998). This finding is in line with research that indicates that in face-to-face groups, higher-status individuals talk more than those of lower status (Garton & Wellman, 1995). Shy group members are frequently inhibited by other group members (see Utz, 2000), thereby participating less in group discussion and thus generating fewer creative ideas along with fewer creative solutions.

Moreover, gender-based differences concerning interaction behaviors in mixed gender groups create a normative-influence-as-a-barrier-to-creativity problem in middle management when women members of small task-oriented groups participate in idea generation, brainstorming and decision-making sessions. Specifically, in these mixed gender groups, women are more likely to stifle their ideas (Craig & Sherif, 1986), with evaluation apprehension playing a role (see Meeker & Weitzel-O'Neill, 1977). Smith-Lovin and Brody (1989) reported that in mixed gender groups, men interrupt women more frequently than they do other men, thereby chilling unrestrained discussions (see also Tannen, 1994, pp. 53-83). Moreover, men tend to speak more often and participate more than women in these settings, thereby dominating the decision-making process (Herschel, 1994; Klein & Dologite, 2000; Leaper, 1998; Wood, 1994). As women comprise half of middle management (Conlin & Zellner, 1999), the unequal participation of women in groups poses a serious challenge to upper management, which is deprived of creative, unconventional or controversial ideas.

Status characteristics theory, a branch of the more general expectation states theory (Berger, Webster, Ridgeway & Rosenholtz, 1986; Berger & Zelditch, 1998; Wagner & Berger, 1997; Kasof, 1995; Okamoto & Smith-Lovin, 2001; Shelly & Troyer, 2001) originating within the disciplines of sociology and social psychology, has been used to explain the inhibition of creative idea generation in mixed status and mixed gender groups. These theories suggest that group members tend to evaluate other group members on the basis of stereotypical performance expectations, which are shaped by external status characteristics. Thus, the ideas put forth by higher-status group members will be ranked as more valuable than the ideas contributed by lower-status members, even when, objectively viewed, the ideas of the former are no better, or are worse, than those of the latter.

When gender is considered as a status characteristic, the status characteristics and expectation states theories predict that because society regards men as having higher status than women, the ideas contributed by the men in a mixed gender group will be regarded as more valuable than the ideas presented by women, even when, in fact, the ideas contributed by the men are poorer than those proposed by women members (Lockheed & Hall, 1976; Meeker & Weitzel-O'Neill, 1977; Sell, 1997; Klein, 2000; Klein & Dologite, 2000). Consistent with status characteristics and expectation states theories, Tannen (1995) reported the attribution of ideas to a male member of a focus group when, in fact, the original contributor was a female member, with the male member merely picking up on the idea and lending it support in the deliberations with the group.

In an age when businesses desire to ascertain what consumers want, the normative influence problem is faced by focus groups—interactive discussion groups led by a moderator, which are frequently used in market research—where the opinions and creative contributions of shy and reserved members may be suppressed by group interaction dominated by more vocal individuals (Riley, 1999, p. 6; see also Albrecht, Johnson & Walther, 1993, p. 57). In addition, the ideas generated by higher-status focus group members tend to dominate the discussion and thus discourage lower-status members from speaking (Stewart & Shamdasani,

1990, pp. 45-46). Moreover, men in focus groups tend to speak more often and with greater authority than women ("peacock effect"), a situation that is a potential source of irritation to women (Krueger, 1994, p. 78) and one that may inhibit women from generating creative ideas, voicing their opinions, and otherwise participating fully in group discussions and deliberations. In line with the above-mentioned barriers to participation and creativity that plague focus groups, Fern (1982) reported that more ideas are generated in individual depth interviews than in focus groups.

In classrooms, from elementary to graduate schools, the reluctance of shy students to express themselves and make creative contributions during class discussions, "where the loudest and boldest often hold sway" (Sullivan, 1998, p. 3), leads to uneven participation and consequently to uneven creative idea generation. This point was well made by Hacohen (2000, p. 527) in describing the philosopher Karl Popper's "(in)famous" seminar at the London School of Economics: "[T]he atmosphere did not encourage free debate. Insecure or timid students found it difficult to contribute…." Not only will shy students tend to participate less, but also they may be subject to conformance pressures (e.g., see LaForge, 1999, p. 4). In fact, some teenage students "worry excessively about conformity and being accepted" (Shyness Centre, n.d., p. 8). This chapter suggests that shy students will participate less and will not contribute creative or controversial ideas because they are subject to the normative influence of dominant group members. (For a study on the generation of controversial ideas, see Cooper, Gallupe, Pollard & Cadsby, 1998.)

This disparity in participation rates of non-shy and shy students is in addition to a persistent gender gap, whereby girls have lower rates of participation across the entire curriculum (see American Association of University Women Educational Foundation, 1998; see also Fredericksen, 2000). According to Benbunan-Fich and Hiltz (2002, p. 3): "Studies of gender inequity in traditional face-to-face classes tend to indicate that class participation is male dominated…However, with asynchronous computer-mediated communication, the tendency is toward more equal participation."

ANONYMITY IN GROUP SUPPORT SYSTEMS

CMC, a tool in the arsenal of IT, offers a solution to the problem of normative influence as a barrier to creative idea generation in small groups. Specifically, GSSs, which allow for anonymous interaction, provide an environment in which social cues (e.g., social presence, status, gender, seniority) are absent (see Adrianson, 2001; see also Kiesler, Siegel & McGuire, 1984; Tan, Wei & Watson, 1999), thereby ensuring that the contributions of each group member are judged solely on merit and not on the external characteristics of the contributor (see Boiney, 1998; Herschel, 1994; Klein & Dologite, 2000).

GSSs are interactive computer-based information systems that support and structure group interaction, including idea generation and problem solving (e.g., see Huber, Valacich & Jessup, 1993; Poole & DeSanctis, 1990; see also Aiken & Carlisle 1992; Fjermerstad & Hiltz, 2000; Nunamaker, 1997), and encourage divergence from customary modes of thinking (Reinig, Briggs & Nunamaker, 1997/1998). GSSs, then, can be used to enhance creativity by assisting in the idea generation process.

Hayne and Rice (1997) summarized the literature on GSS and anonymity thus: "Efforts by many researchers…have generally found an increase in production and satisfaction when anonymous group brainstorming is used. Other advantages of anonymous participation include decreased evaluation apprehension, decreased member domination, decreased conformance pressure and decreased status competition, which can lead to increased exploration of alternatives and surfacing of assumptions" (p. 431). According to Salisbury, Reeves, Chin, Bell and Gopal (1997, p. 576), "[o]ne of the earliest assertions of the importance of GSS technology is that it could be designed in such a way as to reduce conformity to social psychological pressures of the group…by providing anonymity (Dennis, George, Jessup, Nunamaker & Vogel, 1988)." Thus, GSSs, with their anonymity feature, promote increases in participation, creativity and productivity, and fosters the expression of diverse opinions. The central argument of this chapter is that, by inhibiting normative influence, anonymity-featured GSSs remove barriers to creative idea generation.

Organizational Small Task-Oriented Groups

As group support tools, GSSs may be helpful to organizations, which rely on small task-oriented groups for activities such as idea generation, brainstorming and decision making. These groups are critical to the organization's survival and growth. For example, such groups generate ideas for new products and services, thereby allowing the organization to stay competitive. Despite the reliance on groups by the business world, women in management operate at a particular disadvantage (Martin & Shanahan, 1983) and have their input devalued because of gender stereotyping (Gopal, Miranda, Robichaux & Bostrom, 1997). By having the anonymity-featured GSSs assist these groups in their tasks, the organizations foster the equal participation of all group members and, in turn, benefit from the resultant divergent viewpoints and creative contributions.

There is empirical support for the notion that, in providing an environment that masks the external characteristics of group members, GSSs ensure that the contributions of each group member will be judged solely on merit (Klein & Dologite, 2000). In an experimental study, Klein and Dologite showed that mixed gender groups using GSS generated ideas that were as innovative as the ideas generated by all-male or all-female groups using GSS. Explaining their findings by reference to expectation states theory, Klein and Dologite suggested that the anonymity feature of GSSs eliminates gender as a status characteristic and thus equalizes participation by allowing for the merit-based evaluation of ideas.

In a similar vein, the anonymity afforded by GSSs should increase the participation and creative idea generation of shy group members. In a study on the anonymity of the Internet, Utz (2000) argued that this is so because shy group members "cannot be judged primarily by their appearance [and] they do not have to fear any consequences offline...." In another study on anonymous online communication, Roberts, Smith and Pollock (1997, p. 2) found that "individuals who self-identified as shy reported that they were less inhibited and less conservative in online environments." Along the same lines, the anonymity made possible by GSS is expected to increase the participation of shy persons and thereby facilitate the generation of creative ideas.

Boiney (1998, p. 330) developed a conceptual framework for the study of GSSs, including their effect on creative idea generation, and made this observation: "Anonymous input of ideas via personal computer is intended to eliminate individuals' awareness of the source of ideas, thereby lessening inhibition, evaluation apprehension and fear of reprisal. The goal is to encourage merit-based evaluation of ideas and fuller, more equal, participation; this can lead to more honest and creative input by decreasing conformity pressure." According to Dennis et al. (1997, p. 159), the anonymity in a GSS may "reduce the pressure to conform to the opinions of others, whether the pressure is intentional or not."

Focus Groups

Within the realm of marketing research, the use of GSSs to assist focus groups will encourage increased participation by all members, resulting in the generation of more—and more creative—ideas. In a study in which GSS-supported focus groups were compared with traditional focus groups, Parent, Gallupe, Salisbury and Handelman (2000) reported that focus groups using GSSs generated a greater number of ideas and had better quality of ideas. Explaining their findings, Parent et al. (2000) suggested that GSSs allow all focus group members to have an equal voice, with the dominant personalities losing their dominance. With respect to female group members, the implementation of GSSs in focus groups may eliminate the "peacock effect," whereby male group members participate with greater frequency and more authority (see above), thereby ensuring equal male-female participation rates and facilitating creative contributions from all members of the group.

Advocating the use of GSS in focus groups because of its anonymous interaction capability and the attendant masking of social cues, Clapper and Massey (1996, p. 47) posited that GSS would reduce or remove normative influence while increasing informational influence, resulting in the merit-based consideration of ideas by the focus group participants:[6]

Normative influence is the process leading to conforming to the expectations of others, while informational influence implies that the members are influenced by the merit of the ideas being examined. Technology would seem to make it less likely that participants are swayed by normative influence. This should increase the likelihood that ideas will be evaluated based on their merit. Thus, it would seem that a role for technology in facilitating group interaction would be to aid the session moderator in encouraging the sharing of views potentially different from the group position while minimizing the negative results to the people who suggest these new ideas.

In providing an environment where normative influence is minimized and where each participant can have an equal voice, a GSS-supported focus group can potentially enhance the quality and quantity of ideas contributed and thus foster creative idea generation.

Classrooms

Amid the increase in group meetings using CMC (Valacich, Sarker, Pratt & Groomer, 2002), the past few years have witnessed "a surge of interest" in GSS-supported collaborative learning (Khalifa, Kwok & Davison, 2001, p. 1; see also Benbunan-Fich, 2002; Feather, 1999; Gros & Dobson, 2001; Palo Verde High Magnet School, 2002). Although GSSs were originally designed for use in industry (Reinig et al., 1997/1998; Nunamaker, Dennis, Valacich & Vogel, 1991; Nunamaker, Dennis, Valacich, Vogel & George, 1991; Vreede & Bruijn, 1999), their employment in schools "can improve the classroom experience" (Reinig et al., 1997/1998, p. 45; see also Alavi, 1994; Brandt & Lonsdale, 1996; Khalifa et al., 2001; Kwok, Ma, Vogel & Zhou, 2001; Money, 1995/1996; Parent, Neufeld & Gallupe, 2002; Tullar, Kaiser & Balthazard, 1998). In an exploratory study of GSS use in a case method classroom, Parent et al. (2002, p. 1) found: "Overall, participation increased significantly as students became more comfortable and adept with the technology. The GSS appeared to provide marginalized students with a 'voice' in the classroom, and allowed prolific participators an additional outlet."

The use of GSSs in the classroom has the potential of drawing students, including female students and students of both genders who are shy, into class discussions and encouraging them to make creative contributions. Benbunan-Fich, Hiltz and Turoff (2001) reported that computer-mediated groups using an Asynchronous Learning Network (ALN) had broader discussions than face-to-face groups. Although the cost of implementing most GSS packages in the classroom is at present prohibitive, there are some less expensive GSS packages that may be appropriate for school use in achieving broader student participation and creative idea generation. Advocating electronic study forums—where students can use a popular groupware package such as Lotus Notes—which offer anonymity, Kleiber, Holt and Swenson (n.d., pp. 6-7) list among its advantages fuller participation and no domination by individuals. These very advantages may result in greater involvement of, and more creative contributions by, students who are female or shy.

FUTURE AND EMERGING TRENDS

GSSs are increasingly being deployed in organizational small task-oriented groups, focus groups and classrooms. According to Valacich et al. (2002, p. 1), "[g]roup meetings using computer-mediated communication systems are on the rise" as organizations recognize the importance of collaboration and creative idea generation for problem solving and are increasingly adopting GSSs to assist in intellectual teamwork (see Hender et al., 2001; Nagasundaram & Bostrom, 1994/1995; Satzinger, Garfield & Nagasundaram, 1999). At the same time, computer-mediated focus groups, many using GSSs, are receiving growing commercial, as well as academic, attention (e.g., see Veverka, 2001; Walston & Lissitz, 2000). Moreover, "[t]he use of information technology (IT) to support teaching and learning in formal education settings is increasing at a dramatic rate" (Parent et al., 2002, p. 1), with the past few years experiencing a "surge of interest in [GSS] usage to support collaborative learning" (Khalifa et al., 2002, p. 1).

The convergence of these above-mentioned trends provides an opportune time to empirically investigate the impact of normative influence on creative idea generation within GSS-supported groups. The current body of research on the effects of GSSs on creative idea generation, although marked by considerable progress, is still in its formative stages and thus is not well developed. The pioneering studies that have been conducted to date have yielded mixed results (for a comprehensive literature review, see Bostrom & Nagasundaram, 1998; for a recent paper, see Klein & Dologite, 2000), while some theoretical papers have proposed various conceptual frameworks (e.g., see Bostrom & Nagasundaram, 1998; Couger, 1996; Fellers & Bostrom, 1993). Accordingly, further experimental studies are required to confirm the suggested relationship between the use of GSS and creative idea generation. Such investigations are worthwhile as their findings will have significant implications for businesses and schools.

A CAVEAT:
LIMITATIONS OF ANONYMITY-FEATURED GSS

Anonymity is a double-edged sword. Along with its advantages (see above), anonymity may also have negative effects for some GSS-supported groups. Potential disadvantages include social loafing (e.g., free riding) and flaming (Jessup & George, 1997). Moreover, although a GSS can aid in "getting a group of experts to work together efficiently and effectively" (Hender et al., 2002, p. 1), there is anecdotal evidence suggesting that in groups consisting of true experts and pseudo-experts (non-experts), use of anonymity-featured GSSs may result in prolonging the time required to achieve consensus, apparently because of the increased time needed for the former to convince the latter. Thus, the anonymity afforded by GSSs may not be helpful in all circumstances. It is suggested that future studies examine under what conditions anonymity-featured GSSs are most effective. Such scholarship holds the promise of greatly contributing to the ever-growing fund of theoretical and applied knowledge concerning GSSs.

CONCLUSION

This chapter has explored how GSSs can assist intellectual collaborative work by fostering the production of creative ideas. Given the scholarly literature, it is expected that the use of anonymity-featured GSSs will inhibit the distorting effects of status, seniority, shyness and gender in group interactions and thereby will remove the barriers to participation and creative idea generation.

The anonymous interaction capability of GSSs allows group members to assess ideas solely on merit and not on the basis of the external characteristics of the originator, thereby counteracting the reluctance of group members to contribute their ideas. The normative influence problem, then, will be eliminated and a barrier to creative idea generation will be removed. In equalizing participation rates, GSS anonymity has the potential for increasing the number of creative ideas proposed in organizational small task-oriented groups, focus groups and classrooms.

REFERENCES

Adrianson, L. (2001). Gender and computer-mediated communication: Group processes in problem solving. *Computers in Human Behavior, 17*, 71-94.

Aiken, M. & Carlisle, J. (1992). An automated idea consolidation tool for computer supported cooperative work. *Information & Management, 23*, 373-382.

Alavi, M. (1994). Computer-mediated collaborative learning: An empirical evaluation. *MIS Quarterly, 18*(2), 159-174.

Albert, R.S. & Runco, M.A. (1999). A history of research on creativity. In Sternberg, R.L. (Ed.), *Handbook of Creativity* (pp. 16-31). Cambridge, England: Cambridge University Press.

Albrecht, T.L, Johnson, G.M. & Walther, J.B. (1993). Understanding communication processes in focus groups. In Morgan, D.L. (Ed.), *Successful Focus Groups: Advancing the State of the Art* (pp. 51-64). Newbury Park, CA: Sage.

Amabile, T.M. (1988). A model of creativity and innovation in organizations In Staw, B. & Cummings, L.L. (Eds.), *Research in Organizational Behavior* (pp. 123-167). Greenwich, CT: JAI Press.

American Association of University Women Educational Foundation. (1998). *Gender Gaps: Where Schools Still Fail Our Children*. Washington, DC.

Baumol, W.J.J. (2002). *The Free-Market Innovation Machine: Analyzing the Growth Miracle of Capitalism*. Princeton, NJ: Princeton University Press.

Bean, R. & Radford, R. (2001). *The Business of Innovation: Managing the Corporate Imagination for Maximum Results*. New York: Amacom.

Benbunan-Fich, R. (2002). Improving education and training with IT. *Communications of the ACM, 45*(6), 94-99.

Benbunan-Fich, R. & Hiltz, S.R. (2002). Correlates of effectiveness of learning networks: The effects of course level, course type, and gender on outcomes. *Proceedings of the Thirty-Fifth Annual Hawaii International Conference on System Sciences*. Retrieved May 28, 2002, from http://www.computer.org/proceedings/hicss/1435/1435toc.htm.

Benbunan-Fich, R., Hiltz, S. & Turoff, M. (2001). A comparative content analysis of face-to-face vs. ALN-mediated teamwork. *Proceedings of the Thirty-Fourth Annual Hawaii International Conference on System Sciences*. Retrieved May 29, 2002, from http://www.computer.org/proceedings/hicss/0981/0981toc.htm.

Berger, J. & Zelditch, M. (1998). Theoretical research programs: A reformulation. In Berger, J. & Zelditch, M. (Eds.), *Status, Power, and Legitimacy: Strategies and Theories* (pp. 71-93). New Brunswick, NJ: Transaction Publishers.

Berger, J., Webster, M., Ridgeway, C. & Rosenholtz, S.J. (1986). Status cues, expectations, and behavior. In Lawler, E.J. (Ed.), *Advances in Group Processes* (Vol. 3, pp. 1-22). Greenwich, CT: JAI Press.

Boiney, L.G. (1998). Reaping the benefits of information technology in organizations: A framework guiding appropriation of group support systems. *Journal of Applied Behavioral Science, 34*(3), 327-346.

Bostrom, R.P. & Nagasundaram, M. (1998). Research in creativity and GSS. *Proceedings of the Thirty-First Annual Hawaii International Conference on System Sciences*. Retrieved May 29, 2002, from http://www.computer.org/proceedings/hicss/8233/8233toc.htm.

Brancheau, J.C. & Wetherbe, J.C. (1990). The adoption of spreadsheet software: Testing innovation diffusion theory in the context of end-user computing. *Information Systems Research, 1*(2), 115-143.

Brandt, S.A. & Lonsdale, M. (1996). Technology-supported cooperative learning in secondary education. *Proceedings of the Twenty-Ninth Annual Hawaii International Conference on System Sciences*, 313-322.

Briggs, R.O., Nunamaker, J.F. Jr. & Sprague, R.H. Jr. (1997/1998). 1001 unanswered research questions in GSS. *Journal of Management Information Systems, 14*(3), 3-21.

Brown, S. & Eisenhardt, K. (1995). Product development: Past research, present findings, and future directions. *Academy of Management Review, 14*, 234-249.

Bruner, J. (1968). The conditions of creativity. In Gruber, H.E., Terrel, G. & Wertheimer, M. (Eds.), *Contemporary Approaches to Creativity*. New York: Atherton.

Cattell, R.B. (1971). *Abilities: Their Structure, Growth and Action*. Boston, MA: Houghton Mifflin.

Cialdini, R.B. & Trost, M.R. (1998). Social influence: Social norms, conformity, and compliance. In Gilbert, D.T., Fiske, S.T. & Lindzey, G. (Eds.), *The Handbook of Social Psychology: Volume II* (4th ed., pp. 151-192). Boston: McGraw-Hill.

Clapper, D.L. & Massey, A.P. (1996). Electronic focus groups: A framework for exploration. *Information & Management, 30*, 43-50.

Conlin, M. & Zellner, W. (1999). The CEO still wears wingtips: Jobs that lead to the top remain overwhelmingly female-free. *Business Week*, (November 22), 82.

Cooper, W.H., Gallupe, R.B., Pollard, S. & Cadsby, J. (1998). Some liberating effects of anonymous electronic brainstorming. *Small Group Research, 29*(2), 147-178.

Couger, J.D. (1996). A framework for research on creativity/innovation in IS organizations. *Proceedings of the Twenty-Ninth Annual Hawaiian International Conference on System Sciences*. Retrieved June 2, 2002, from http://www.computer.org/proceedings/hicss/7333/7333toc.htm.

Couger, J.D., Higgins, L.F. & McIntyre, S.C. (1990). Differentiating creativity, innovation, entrepreneurship, intrapreneurship, copyright and patenting for IS products/processes. *Proceedings of the Twenty-Third Annual Hawaiian International Conference on System Sciences*, 370-379.

Couger, J.D., Higgins, L.F. & McIntyre, S.C. (1993). (Un)structured creativity in information systems organizations. *MIS Quarterly, 17*(4), 375-397.

Craig, J.M. & Sherif, C.W. (1986). The effectiveness of men and women in problem-solving groups as a function of group gender composition. *Sex Roles, 14*, 453-466.

Daft, R.L. (1978). A dual-core model of organizational innovation. *Academy of Management Journal, 21*(2), 193-210.

Davison, R. & Vogel, D. (2000). Group support systems in Hong Kong: An action research project. *Information Systems Journal, 10*, 3-20.

Dennis, A.R., George, J.F., Jessup, L.M., Nunamaker, J.F. Jr. & Vogel, D.R. (1988). Information technology to support electronic meetings. *MIS Quarterly, 12*(4), 591-624.

Dennis, A.R., Tyran, C.K., Vogel, D.R. & Nunamaker, J.F. Jr. (1997). Group support systems for strategic planning. *Journal of Management Information Systems, 14*(1), 155-184.

Deutsch, M. & Gerard, H.B. (1955). A study of normative and informational social influence upon individual judgment. *Journal of Abnormal and Social Psychology, 51*, 629-636.

Eisenhardt, K. & Tabrizi, B. (1995). Accelerating adaptive processes: Product innovation in the global computing industry. *Administrative Science Quarterly, 40*, 84-110.

Eisenhardt, K.M., Schoonhoven, C.B. & Lyman, K. (2001). Effects of top management teams on the organization of innovation through alternative types of strategic alliances. In Turner, M.E. (Ed.), *Groups at Work: Theory and Research* (pp.339-367). Mahwah, NJ: Erlbaum.

Fear of the unknown. (1999). *The Economist*, (December 4), 61-62.

Feather, S.R. (1999). The impact of group support systems on collaborative learning groups' stages of development. *Information Technology, Learning, and Performance Journal, 17*(2), 23-34.

Fellers, J.W. & Bostrom, R.P. (1993). Application of group support systems to promote creativity in information systems organizations. *Proceedings of the Twenty-Sixth Annual Hawaiian International Conference on System Sciences*, 332-341.

Fern, E.F. (1982). The use of focus groups for idea generation: The effects of group size, acquaintanceship, and moderator on response quantity and quality. *Journal of Marketing Research, 19* (February), 1-13.

Fichman, R.G. (2001). The role of aggregation in the measurement of IT-related organizational innovation. *MIS Quarterly, 25*, 427-453.

Fjermestad, J. & Hiltz, S.R. (2000). Case and field studies of group support systems: An empirical assessment. *Proceedings of the Thirty-Third Annual Hawaii International Conference on System Sciences*. Retrieved May 29, 2002, from http://www.computer.org/proceedings/hicss/0493/0493toc.htm.

Florida, R.L. (2002). *The Rise of the Creative Class: And How It's Transforming Work, Leisure, Community and Everyday Life*. New York: Basic Books.

Frame, J.D. (1989). Stimulating high technology innovations. In Whiting, B.G. & Solomon, G.T. (Eds.), *Key Issues in Creativity, Innovation and Entrepreneurship*. Buffalo, NY: Bearly Limited.

Fredericksen, E. (2000). Muted colors: Gender and classroom silence. *Language Arts, 77*(4), 301-308.

Garton, L.E. & Wellman, B. (1995). Social impacts of electronic mail in organizations: A review of the research literature. Communication Yearbook, 18, 434-453.

Gopal, A., Miranda, S.M., Robichaux, B.P. & Bostrom, R.P. (1997). Leveraging diversity with information technology: Gender, attitude, and intervening influences in the use of group support systems. *Small Group Research, 28*(1), 29-71.

Gros, B. & Dobson, M. (Eds.). (2001). Computer supported collaborative learning [Special issue]. *Computers in Human Behavior, 17*(5-6).

Guilford, J.P. (1967). *The Nature of Human Intelligence*. New York: McGraw-Hill.

Hackman, J.R. & Kaplan, R.E. (1974). Interventions into group process: An approach to improving the effectiveness of groups. *Decision Sciences, 5,* 459-480.

Hacohen, M.H. (2000). *Karl Popper—The Formative Years, 1902-1945: Politics and Philosophy in Interwar Vienna*. Cambridge, England: Cambridge University Press.

Hare, A.P. (1994). Introduction. In Hare, A.P., Blumberg, H.H., Davies, M.F. & Kent, M.V. (Eds.), *Small Group Research: A Handbook* (pp. 1-7). Norwood, NJ: Ablex.

Hayne, S.C. & Rice, R.E. (1997). Attribution accuracy when using anonymity in group support systems. *International Journal of Human-Computer Studies, 47,* 429-452.

Hender, J.M., Dean, D.L., Rodgers, T.L. & Nunamaker, J.F. Jr. (2001). Improving group creativity: Brainstorming versus non-brainstorming techniques in a GSS environment. *Proceedings of the Thirty-Fourth Hawaii International Conference on System Science*. Retrieved May 29, 2002, from http://www.computer.org/proceedings/hicss/0981/0981toc.htm.

Herschel, R.T. (1994). The impact of varying gender composition on group brainstorming performance in a GSS environment. *Computers in Human Behavior, 10,* 209-222.

Huber, G.P., Valacich, J.S. & Jessup, L.M. (1993). A theory of the effects of group support systems on an organization's nature and decisions. In Jessup, L.M. & Valacich, J.S. (Eds.), *Group Support Systems: New Perspectives* (pp. 255-269). New York: Macmillan.

Janis, I.L. (1972). *Victims of Groupthink: A Psychological Study of Foreign-Policy Decisions and Fiascoes*. Boston: Houghton Mifflin.

Jessup, L.M. & George, J.F. (1997). Theoretical and methodological issues in group support systems research: Learning from groups gone awry. *Small Group Research, 28*(3), 394-413.

Kaplan, M.F. & Wilke, H. (2001). Cognitive and social motivation in group decision making. In Forgas, J.P., Williams, K.D. & Wheeler, L. (Eds.), *The Social Mind: Cognitive and Motivational Aspects of Interpersonal Behavior* (pp. 406-428). Cambridge, England: Cambridge University Press.

Kasof, J. (1995). Social determinants of creativity: Status expectations and the evaluation of original products. In Lawler, E.J. (Series Ed.) & Markovsky, B., Heimer, K. & O'Brien, J. (Vol. Eds.), *Advances in Group Processes* (pp. 167-220). Greenwich, CT: JAI Press.

Keil, J.M. (1987). *The Creative Corporation*. Homewood, IL: Dow Jones-Irwin.

Khalifa, M., Kwok, R. & Davison, R. (2001). GSS facilitation restrictiveness in collaborative learning. *Proceedings of the Thirty-Fourth Hawaii International Conference on System Science*. Retrieved May 28, 2002, from http://www.computer.org/proceedings/hicss/0981/0981toc.htm.

Kiesler, S., Siegel, J. & McGuire, T.W. (1984). Social psychological aspects of computer-mediated communication. *American Psychologist, 39*(10), 1123-1134.

Kleiber, P.B., Holt, M.E. & Swenson, J.D. (n.d.). *The Electronic Forum Handbook: Study Circles in Cyberspace*. Retrieved May 27, 2002, from http://www.empowermentzone.com/eforum.txt.

Klein, E.E. (2000). The impact of information technology on leadership opportunities for women: The leveling of the playing field. *Journal of Leadership Studies, 7*(3), 88-98.

Klein, E.E. & Dologite, D.G. (2000). The role of computer support tools and gender in innovative information system idea generation by small groups. *Computers in Human Behavior, 16*, 111-139.

Kline, T.J.B. & McGrath, J. (1999). A review of the groupware literature: Theories, methodologies, and a research agenda. *Canadian Psychology, 40*(3), 265-271.

Kris, E. (1952). *Psychoanalytic Explorations in Art*. New York: International Universities Press.

Krueger, R.A. (1994). *Focus Groups: A Practical Guide for Applied Research* (2nd ed.). Thousand Oaks, CA: Sage.

Kwok, R.C.W., Ma, J., Vogel, D. & Zhou, D. (2001). Collaborative assessment in education: An application of a fuzzy GSS. *Information & Management, 39*, 243-253.

LaForge, A.E. (1999). *Defiance at School*. Retrieved June 11, 2002, from http://www.scholastic.com/smartparenting/schoolsuccess/devmilestones/4_defiance.htm.

Leaper, C. (1998). Decision-making processes between friends: Speaker and partner gender effects. *Sex Roles, 39*(1), 125-133.

Lockheed, M.E. & Hall, K.P. (1976). Conceptualizing sex as a status characteristic: Applications to leadership training strategies. *Journal of Social Issues, 32*, 111-124.

Mandel, M.J. (2001). A slow road to recovery. *Business Week*, (December 10), 30-32.

Martin, P.Y. & Shanahan, K. (1983). Transcending the effects of gender composition in small groups. *Social Work with Groups, 6*, 19-32.

Meeker, B.F. & Weitzel-O'Neill, P. (1977). Sex roles and interpersonal behavior in task-oriented groups. *American Sociological Review, 42*, 91-105.

Miller, W.C. (1987). *The Creative Edge: Fostering Innovation Where You Work.* Reading, MA: Addison-Wesley.

Money, W.H. (1995/1996). Applying group support systems to classroom settings: A social cognitive learning theory explanation. *Journal of Management Information Systems, 12*(3), 65-80.

Moscovici, S. (1985). Social influence and conformity. In Lindzey, G. & Aronson, E. (Eds.), *Handbook of Social Psychology: Volume II* (3rd ed., pp. 347-412). New York: Random House.

Mumford, M.D. & Gustafson, S.B. (1988). Creativity syndrome: Integration, application, and innovation. *Psychological Bulletin, 103*(1), 27-43.

Myers, D.G. (2002). *Social Psychology* (7th ed.). Boston: McGraw-Hill.

Nagasundaram, M. & Bostrom, R.P. (1994/1995). The structuring of creative processes using GSS: A framework for research. *Journal of Management Information Systems, 11*(3), 87-114.

Napier, R.W. & Gershenfeld, M.K. (1999). *Groups: Theory and Experience* (6th ed.). Boston: Houghton Mifflin.

Nunamaker, J.F. Jr. (1997). Future research in group support systems: Needs, some questions and possible directions. *International Journal of Human-Computer Studies, 47*, 357-385.

Nunamaker, J.F. Jr., Applegate, L.M. & Konsynski, B.R. (1987). Facilitating group creativity: Experience with a group decision support system. *Journal of Management Information Systems, 3*(4), 5-19.

Nunamaker, J.F. Jr., Briggs, R.O., Mittleman, D.D. & Vogel, D.R. (1996/1997). Lesson from a dozen years of group support systems research: A discussion of lab and field findings. *Journal of Management Information Systems, 13*(3), 163-207.

Nunamaker, J.F. Jr., Dennis, A.R., Valacich, J.S. & Vogel, D.R. (1991). Information technology for negotiating groups: Generating options for mutual gain. *Management Science, 17*(10), 1325-1346.

Nunamaker, J.F. Jr., Dennis, A.R., Valacich, J.S., Vogel, D.R. & George, J.F. (1991). Electronic meeting systems to support group work. *Communications of the ACM, 34*(7), 60-61.

Nunamaker, J.F. Jr., Dennis, A.R., Valacich, J.S., Vogel, D.R. & George, J.F. (1993). Group support systems research: Experience from the lab and field. In Jessup, L.M. & Valacich, J.S. (Eds.), *Group Support Systems: New Perspectives* (pp. 125-145). New York: Macmillan.

Okamoto, D.G. & Smith-Lovin, L. (2001). Changing the subject: Gender, status, and the dynamics of topic change. *American Sociological Review, 66*, 852-873.

Palo Verde High Magnet School. (2002). *Applying Group Support Systems to the Classroom.* Retrieved June 10, 2002, from http://www.cmi.arizona.edu/research/PastResearch/tsl/palo.htm.

Paper, D.J. & Johnson, J.J. (1997). A theoretical framework linking creativity, empowerment, and organizational memory. *Creativity and Innovation Management,* 6(March), 32-44.

Parent, M., Gallupe, R.B., Salisbury, W.D. & Handelman, J.M. (2000). Knowledge creation in focus groups: Can group technologies help? *Information & Management,* 38(1), 47-58.

Parent, M., Neufeld, D.J. & Gallupe, R.B. (2002). A longitudinal analysis of GSS use in the case method classroom. *Proceedings of the Thirty-Fifth Annual Hawaii International Conference on System Sciences.* Retrieved May 28, 2002, from http://www.computer.org/proceedings/hicss/1435/1435toc.htm.

Parnes, S.J. (1967). *Creative Behavior Handbook.* New York: Scribner.

Parnes, S.J. (Ed.) (1992). *Source Book for Creative Problem Solving.* Buffalo, NY: Creative Foundation Press.

Paulus, P.B., Larey, T.S. & Dzindolet, M.T. (2001). Creativity in groups and teams. In Turner, M.E. (Ed.), *Groups at Work: Theory and Research* (pp. 319-338). Mahwah, NJ: Erlbaum.

Poole, M.S. & DeSanctis, G. (1990). Understanding the use of group decision support systems: The theory of adaptive structuration. In Steinfeld, C.W. & Fulk, J. (Eds.), *Organizations and Communication Technology* (pp. 173-193). Newbury Park, CA: Sage.

Rainer, R.K. Jr. & Harrison, A.W. (1993). Toward development of the end user computing construct in a university setting. *Decision Sciences, 24,* 1187-1202.

Reinig, B.A., Briggs, R.O. & Nunamaker, J.F. Jr. (1997/1998). Flaming in the electronic classroom. *Journal of Management Information Systems, 14*(3), 45-59.

Rhodes, M. (1961). An analysis of creativity. *Phi Delta Kappan, 42,* 305-310.

Rickards, T. (1988). *Creativity at Work.* Aldershot, England: Gower.

Riley, S. (1999). *Use of Focus Groups in Qualitative Research Methods in Psychology.* Retrieved May 26, 2002, from http://staff.bath.ac.uk/psssr/courses/69focusgroupOHs.html.

Roberts, L.D., Smith, L.M. & Pollock, C. (1997). 'u r a lot bolder on the net': The social use of text-based virtual environments by shy individuals. Paper presented at the *International Conference on Shyness and Self-Consciousness.*

Salisbury, W.D., Reeves, W.J., Chin, W.W., Bell, M. & Gopal, A. (1997). Robbing Peter to pay Paul: The other side of group support systems. *Proceedings of the Third AIS Americas Conference on Information Systems,* 575-577.

Satzinger, J.W., Garfield, M.J. & Nagasundaram, M. (1999). The creative process: The effects of group memory on individual idea generation. *Journal of Management Information Systems, 15*(4), 143-160.

Sell, J. (1997). Gender, strategies, and contributions to public goods. *Social Psychology Quarterly, 60*(3), 252-265.

Shelly, R.K. & Troyer, L. (2001). Emergence and completion of structure in initially undefined and partially defined groups. *Social Psychology Quarterly, 64,* 318-332.

Shyness Centre. (n.d.). *Children, Adolescents & Families.* Toronto. Retrieved June 11, 2002, from http://www.shyhelp.on.ca/children_families.html.

Siau, K.L. (1996). Electronic creativity techniques for organizational innovation. *The Journal of Creative Behavior, 30*(4), 283-293.

Smith-Lovin, L. & Brody, C. (1989). Interruptions in group discussions. *American Sociological Review, 54,* 424-435.

Stewart, D.W. & Shamdasani, P.N. (1990). *Focus Groups: Theory and Practice.* Newbury Park, CA: Sage.

Sullivan, P. (1998). Gender issues and the on-line classroom. Paper presented at *Third Annual TCC Conference, Online Instruction: Trends and Issues II,* Honolulu, HI. Retrieved May 27, 2002, from http://leahi.kcc.hawaii.edu/org/tcon98/paper/sullivan.html.

Taggar, S. (2002). Individual creativity and group ability to utilize individual creative Resources: A multilevel model. *Academy of Management Journal, 45*(2), 315-330.

Tan, B.C.Y., Wei, K.K. & Watson, R.T. (1999). The equalizing impact of a group support system on status differentials. *ACM Transactions on Information Systems, 17*(1), 77-100.

Tan, B.C.Y., Wei, K.K., Watson, R.T. & Walczuch, R.M. (1998). Reducing status effects with computer-mediated communication: Evidence from two distinct cultures. *Journal of Management Information Systems, 15*(1), 119-141.

Tannen, D. (1994). *Gender and Discourse.* New York: Oxford University Press.

Tannen, D. (1995). The power of talk: Who gets heard and why. *Harvard Business Review,* (September/October), 138-148.

Torrance, E.P. (1988). The nature of creativity as it manifests in its testing. In Sternberg, R.J. (Ed.), *The Nature of Creativity: Contemporary Psychological Perspectives* (pp. 43–75). New York: Cambridge University Press.

Tullar, W.L., Kaiser, P.R. & Balthazard, P.A. (1998). Group work and electronic meeting systems: From boardroom to classroom. *Business Communication Quarterly, 41*(4), 53-65.

Utz, S. (2000). Social information processing in MUDs: The development of friendships in virtual worlds. *Journal of Online Behavior, 1*(1). Retrieved May 27, 2002, from http://www.behavior.net/JOB/v1n1/utz.html.

Valacich, J.S., Sarker, S., Pratt, J. & Groomer, M. (2002). Computer-mediated and face-to-face groups: Who makes riskier decisions? *Proceedings of the Thirty-Fifth Hawaii International Conference on System Science.* Retrieved May 28, 2002, from http://www.computer.org/proceedings/hicss/1435/1435toc.htm.

Veverka, M. (2001). The real dot.coms: The companies of the Dow 30 are delivering on the vast promise of the Internet. *Barrons*, (December 24), 19-21.

Vreede, G.J. de & Bruijn, H. de (1999). Exploring the boundaries of successful GSS application: Supporting inter-organizational policy networks. *Data Base for Advances in Information Systems,30*(3/4), 111-130.

Vreede, G.J. de, Jones, N. & Mgaya, R.J. (1998/1999). Exploring the application and acceptance of group support systems in Africa. *Journal of Management Information Systems, 15*(3), 197-234.

Wagner, D.G. & Berger, J. (1997). Gender and interpersonal task behaviors: Status expectation accounts. *Sociological Perspectives, 40*(1), 1-32.

Walker, H.A., Ilardi, B.C., McMahon, A.M. & Fennell, M.L. (1996). Gender, interaction, and leadership. *Social Psychology Quarterly, 59*(3), 255-272.

Walston, J.T. & Lissitz, R.W. (2000). Computer-mediated focus groups. *Evaluation Review, 24*(5), 457-483.

Wood, J.T. (1994). *Gendered Lives: Communication, Gender, and Culture.* Belmont, CA: Wadsworth.

Woodman, R.W., Sawyer, J.E. & Griffin, R.W. (1993). Toward a theory of organizational creativity. *Academy of Management Review, 18*(2), 293-321.

Zigurs, I. (1993). Methodological and measurement issues in group support systems research. In Jessup, L.M. & Valacich, J.S. (Eds.), *Group Support Systems: New Perspectives*, (pp. 112-122). New York: Macmillan.

ENDNOTES

[1] This chapter has its genesis in an IRMA 2002 conference paper, "Group Support Systems as Handmaidens of Innovation: The Removal of Barriers to Creative Idea Generation Within Small Groups," which served as a skeletal and rudimentary draft as well as a springboard for new ideas and fresh material developed in this chapter. In building on and expanding upon the conference paper, this chapter, *inter alia*, extends to classrooms the conference paper's main thesis—that, by inhibiting normative influence, GSS with anonymous interaction capability removes barriers to creative idea generation.

[2] Hare (1994, p. 1) defined a small group as one having between two and 30 members.

[3] This problem is an ancient one. For example, over 2000 years ago, the junior judges of the *Sanhedrin*, a judicial and legislative body, stated their opinions first, followed by the more senior members. This procedure was instituted in order to allow the junior jurists to freely express themselves and not be subject to the normative influence of jurists with greater seniority (Babylonian Talmud, Tractate Sanhedrin 32a).

[4] End user computing is defined as "the autonomous use of information technology by knowledge workers outside the information systems department" (Brancheau & Wetherbe, 1990, p. 115). See also Rainer and Harrison (1993, p. 1188).

[5] For a recent work on the importance of creativity to the economy, see Florida, 2002.

[6] Building on the work of Deutsch and Gerard (1955), Clapper and Massey (1996) employed the normative influence-informational influence distinction. See also Kaplan and Wilke (2001).

Chapter VIII

E-Business Modeling

Tomaso Forzi
Aachen University, Germany

Peter Laing
Aachen University, Germany

ABSTRACT

This chapter introduces a meta-method for e-business modeling. As a matter of fact, the Internet and Web-based e-business solutions nowadays play a crucial enabling role for the design and implementation of new business models. This implies high chances, but also remarkable risks for enterprises that choose to pursue a new business model striving to exploit new technology potentials. In fact, the implementation of a strategically not appropriate business model would critically undermine the long-term success of a company. Hence there is a clear need for action in the field of methodical business modeling. We present a new approach for a customer-oriented e-business modeling, with specific attention on inter-organizational cooperative networks and re-intermediation, as well as on information management within distributed manufacturing networks. The approach has been validated in the case of the information service intermediary of a collaboration network in the German manufacturing industry.

THE IMPACT OF E-BUSINESS ON ORGANIZATIONAL STRUCTURES

During the past few years, the fast development of new information and communication technologies (ICTs) has been revolutionizing the market arena, has extended the horizon of competition and has caused radical changes in all business sectors (Afuah & Tucci, 2001; Bensaou, 1997; Brynjolfsson & Kahin, 2000; Filos, 2001; Gebauer & Buxmann, 1999; Hagel & Singer, 1999; Holland & Lockett, 1994; Kornelius, 1999; Picot et al., 2001; Porter, 2001; Rentmeister & Klein, 2001; Schoder, 2000; Timmers, 2000; Wirtz, 2000). Among others, the effects of the introduction of new ICTs and of the related e-business solutions were an enhanced globalization process, an even more uncertain and dynamic economic environment and a technology-driven development of new capabilities, products and services as well as new businesses (Evans & Wurster, 2000; Hagel & Singer, 1999; Kremar, 2000; Mooney, 1996; Pietsch, 1999; Ruohonen, 1996; Teubner, 1999).

Currently, there are different and not always concordant definitions of the term electronic business (e-business), e.g., according to Afuah and Tucci (2001), Brynjolfsson and Kahin (2000), Forzi and Luczak (2002), Evans and Wurster (2000), Hoeck and Bleck (2001), Porter (2001), Rayport (1999), Rentmeister and Klein (2001), Timmers (2000) and Wirtz (2000). *E-business* will be here defined according to Forzi and Luczak (2002) as the "holistic ICT-based support of (dynamic) inter-organizational and intra-organizational processes and transactions" (p. 494). E-business hence implies the *modification of existing business relationships* and might thus lead to the *development of new or modified business models.* Furthermore, we define *e-business engineering* according to Luczak et al. (2002a) as "all the methods and procedures that support companies of different industrial sectors to systematically develop, implement and run e-business solutions" (p. 223). E-business engineering is hence the systematic design and implementation of e-business solutions and models.

Transactions (i.e., the transfer of goods among the different economic subjects) and the related costs represent a basic element of economic analysis (Coase, 1937; Williamson, 1975). Transaction costs vary in function of the specificity of the involved good or job. Furthermore, the management of transactions may take place in the *market* (under various contractual forms), within a *hierarchy* (i.e., an organization in which transactions are regulated by hierarchical relationships) or within intermediate forms of transaction governance (so-called *hybrids*) (Coase, 1937; Mintzberg, 1979; Williamson, 1975). One of the most significant effects caused by new ICTs and the related e-business solutions is the decrease of transaction costs for all coordination instances (as shown in Figure 1), which might eventually lead to a change of the transaction governance (Forzi & Luczak, 2002; Malone et al., 1987; Picot et al., 2001).

In fact, ICT-based e-business solutions allow enterprises to design leaner *intra-organizational* processes, with the result of enhancing higher efficiency and productivity within a hierarchy (Davenport & Short, 1990; Fine, 1998). Besides that, ICTs can also strongly influence *inter-organizational* processes (hybrids up to market-like), by supporting cooperation within entrepreneurial networks as well as by enabling their coordination—by means of Internet-based business collaboration infrastructures (BCIs), such as e-marketplaces or collaboration platforms (Biggiero,

Figure 1: ICTs and Transaction Costs (Source: Picot et al., 2001)

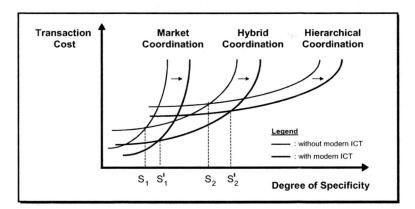

1999; Davidow & Malone, 1993; Gebauer & Buxmann, 1999; Hoeck & Bleck, 2001; Klein, 1995; Luczak et al., 2002; Schoder, 2000).

On the other hand, during the past years it often happened that e-business solutions were simply and hastily embedded into the existing business processes and organizational structures (Beyer et al., 2002; Bleck et al., 2001; Luczak et al., 2002b; Porter, 2001; Tan, 2001). As a result, e-business projects often did not reach the striven targets or even failed, with the consequently growing lack of trust towards ICTs and the related solutions. Because of our experience with reorganization projects, we are convinced that, instead of a partial one, a holistic approach has to be followed (Beyer et al., 2002; Bleck et al., 2001; Luczak et al., 2002a). Such an approach can enable planners and decision makers to identify and manage causal relationships between the strategic planning, the management of technology, the engineering of new organizational structures and the related controlling.

Because of the high complexity and multi-disciplinarity of projects related to the development and deployment of e-business solutions, several established methods from the fields of business organization, product and service engineering, and computer science (e.g., methods of business modeling, service engineering, product design, process and system design, monitoring and planning of technology) can be really helpful. On the other hand, in order to fulfill the new modeling and organizational requirements triggered by the potentials of new ICTs and of the related solutions, such modeling, design or engineering methods have to be adapted and appropriately integrated. Interesting integration approaches to support such a process can be found, e.g., in the works of Andrade and Clausing (1995), Beyer et al. (2002), Bleck et al. (2001), Clausing and Witter (1992) and Luczak et al. (2002a).

On the one side, the trend towards a tightly inter-connected economy seems to be nowadays unquestionable (Brynjolfsson & Kahin, 2000; Filos, 2001; Gebauer &

Buxmann, 1999; Tan, 2001; Timmers, 2000). On the other side, the development process towards a dynamically networked economy has just recently started and it is a path full of a variety of different obstacles. In order to be successful within a networked economy, enterprises will thus have to undergo a deep transformation process in their organizational philosophy, in their structure and also in their methodical approach. The objective of this chapter is to present a new approach for customer-oriented e-business modeling, with specific attention on inter-organizational cooperative networks and re-intermediation. The approach has been developed with the above-mentioned integration objective; furthermore, the method has been validated within the design process of an information service intermediary, whose objective is the support of a collaboration network in the German manufacturing industry.

STRATEGY AND BUSINESS MODELING
From Strategy Definition to Business Controlling

In the previous section we showed how ICTs can strongly influence both intra-organizational and inter-organizational processes. As a result, Web-based ICT solutions play a crucial *enabling role* both for new business models and for those models that, until now, had a higher value on a theoretical than on a practical level, such as virtual organizations or economic webs (Forzi & Luczak, 2002; Franz, 2002; Picot et al., 2001). Companies, in order to face the quick-paced globalization process, tend nowadays to concentrate on their own core competencies, before starting to cooperate within global networks of enterprises (Davidow & Malone, 1993; Kornelius, 1999; Molina et al., 1998; Parolini, 1999). This transformation process is increasingly crucial for the success of the company's business (Filos, 2001; Hagel & Singer, 1999; Klein, 1995; Picot et al., 2001; Wirtz, 2000). Therefore, before making a crucial decision regarding the participation to a cooperation network, the management of an enterprise has to define a (new) *entrepreneurial strategy* and hence take into consideration a wide set of aspects, such as the entrepreneurial organization, the own core competencies, the category of products or services to deal with (as well as the substitutes), all strong players (suppliers, customers and possible competitors) in the considered market, the readiness of the potential partners to cooperate, and the availability of the needed technologies and tools (Andrade & Clausing, 1995; Evans & Wurster, 2000; Hagel & Singer, 1999; Hinterhuber 1992; Porter, 1985; Porter, 2001; Timmers, 2000). Possible approaches that can be used during the strategy definition are, e.g., Porter's *five forces* (Porter, 1985, 2001) or Parolini's *value net* (Parolini, 1999).

As a result, in order to deploy innovative network-oriented cooperation structures, managers of firms tend to design new network-oriented *business models* that strive the achievement of sustainable turnovers and profits (Afuah & Tucci, 2001;

Osterwalder & Pigneur, 2002; Rayport, 1999; Rentmeister & Klein, 2001; Timmers, 2000; Wirtz & Kleinecken, 2000). The design process of new business models in a networked economy as well as the definition and assessment of e-business scenarios are major issues that enterprises cannot underestimate, as the "dot.com" crisis of the recent past made clear to everybody in the entrepreneurial world. Among other aspects, the processes of intermediation and disintermediation are relevant phenomena in this context (Rose, 1998; Klein, 1995; Ruohonen, 1996; Schoder, 2000).

When the business model in question is defined, managers have to concentrate their efforts on its successful implementation both in the organization and in the business processes (Afuah & Tucci, 2001; Hinterhuber 1997; Rayport, 1999; Rentmeister & Klein, 2001; Timmers, 2000; Wirtz & Kleinecken, 2000; Wirtz, 2000). As a matter of fact, the *organization* has to be adapted to the new alignment, this fact implying that the whole entrepreneurial structure might undergo deeper changes to be able to deal with the (new) organizational requirements of the identified business model (Davidow & Malone, 1993; Mintzberg 1979; Parolini, 1999; Picot et al., 2001). Furthermore, because of the fact that both inter-organizational and intra-organizational activities and processes can be heavily supported by ICTs, another crucial issue is that also the business *processes* might have to be (re-)engineered to enable the company to integrate ICTs in the organization and hence achieve the striven performances (Davenport & Short, 1990; Kornelius, 1999; Picot & Rippenberger, 1996; Ramaswamy, 1996).

Last but not least, the management of the company has to build up an appropriate *controlling* system that enables a suitable *management* of both organization and processes. The scheme of Figure 2 sums up the above-mentioned steps within the described entrepreneurial dimensions.

In the next section, our contribution will focus on the first two layers pictured in Figure 2, namely *strategy* and *business model*.

Figure 2: Entrepreneurial Dimensions

State-of-the-Art in Business Modeling and Need for Action

In the management literature there are different and discrepant definitions of the term *"business model"* (see, e.g., Afuah & Tucci, 2001; Brynjolfsson & Kahin, 2000; Evans & Wurster, 2000; Hagel & Singer, 1999; Osterwalder & Pigneur, 2002; Porter, 2001; Rayport, 1999; Rentmeister & Klein, 2001; Timmers, 2000; Wirtz & Kleinecken, 2000). Furthermore, e-business models can be classified according to the most different criteria, such as the degree of innovation and functional integration, the collaboration focus or the involved actors (Afuah & Tucci, 2001; Rentmeister & Klein, 2001; Timmers, 2000; Wirtz & Kleinecken, 2000).

The core objective of each company is a long-term creation of *added value* (see, e.g., Hinterhuber, 1992; Porter, 1985, 2001). The entrepreneurial strategy defines how such a target has to be fulfilled. A *successful strategic* positioning is achieved through a sustained profitability, an own value proposition, a distinctive value chain, an entrepreneurial fit and continuity of strategic direction (Porter, 1985, 2001).

According to our understanding, *a business model is an instantiation of an entrepreneurial strategy related to a specific business* and it encompasses six different sub-models (see Figure 3): *(1) Market model:* definition of the market(s) of action (targeted customers as well as potential competitors); *(2) Output model:* definition of the output requirements and design of the *outputs* (products or services); *(3) Revenue model:* estimation and calculation of the expected revenues; *(4) Production design:* design of how the performances have to be deployed; *(5) Network and information model:* partner selection and configuration of the network, as well as configuration and management of the (distributed) information; and *(6) Financing model:* scenario-based definition of risks and expected profits to search for investors or to persuade the stockholders.

Figure 3: Strategy, Business Model and Creation of Added Value

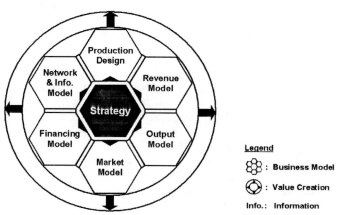

In the new ICT era, companies strive to exploit the advantages of the networked economy. Lately, business models tend to involve different (networked) enterprises with the goal of bringing higher profits to each of the participants (Brynjolfsson & Kahin, 2000; Davidow & Malone, 1993; Evans & Wurster, 2000; Gebauer & Buxmann, 1999; Hagel & Singer, 1999; Hirschhorn & Gilmore, 1992; Malone et al., 1987; Molina et al., 1998; Osterwalder & Pigneur, 2002; Picot et al., 2001; Wirtz, 2000).

The modeling of such cooperative e-business models represents a significant challenge, both because of the problem complexity and because of the lack of appropriate methods to tackle systematically such a modeling issue. As a matter of fact, until now the development and adjustment of business models has been performed by companies mostly in a creative way (Afuah & Tucci, 2001; Evans & Wurster, 2000; Laing & Forzi, 2001; Osterwalder & Pigneur, 2002; Porter, 2001; Rayport, 1999; Rentmeister & Klein, 2001; Timmers, 2000; Wirtz & Kleinecken, 2000). This was also confirmed by the "dot.com" crisis, in which weak or improvised business models led both single enterprises and networks to unrecoverable bankruptcies (Forzi & Luczak, 2002). Hence, companies do need a methodical and holistic approach to develop new business models. Furthermore, due to globalization, the growing transparency of the markets and the resulting increased competition, enterprises have to focus more and more on their customers (Balakrishnan, 1996; Kleinaltenkamp & Dahlke, 1998; Pelham, 2000; Webb et al., 2000). This implies that the fulfillment of the customers' needs is an essential precondition to be competitive in the market arena and hence generate turnover. As a result, enterprises have to take this aspect into consideration when shaping new business models.

In the next section we will present a business modeling approach that focuses explicitly on the solution of the above-mentioned open issues.

BUSINESS MODELING FOR E-COLLABORATION NETWORKS

A New Approach for Customer-Oriented Business Modeling

As noted above, due to globalization, the growing transparency of the markets and the resulting increased competition, enterprises have to focus more and more on their customers. As a matter of fact, the fulfillment of the customers' needs is an essential precondition to generate turnover for a sustainable profitability. This means that enterprises have to take this aspect into deep consideration and must consequently shape business models that reflect the customers' needs (Balakrishnan, 1996; Forzi & Laing, 2002; Kleinaltenkamp & Dahlke, 1998; Pelham, 2000; Ramaswamy, 1996; Webb et al., 2000).

As pointed out above, until now the development and adjustment of business models has been performed by companies mostly in a creative way (Afuah & Tucci, 200; Rayport, 1999; Timmers, 2000). Furthermore, in the state of the art, there is hardly any available methodical and holistic support (Afuah & Tucci, 2001; Evans & Wurster, 2000; Porter, 2001; Rayport, 1999; Rentmeister & Klein, 2001; Timmers, 2000; Wirtz & Kleinecken, 2000). A successful approach to tackle this methodical lack must be based on a strategic focus on the *customers' needs*.

Within a running research project funded by the German Federal Ministry of Economy and Technology (project name: Z-Online, grant number: VI B 4 – 00 30 60/ 35), we developed the *House of Value Creation (HVC),* a method to design customer-oriented and sustainable business models (see Figure 4). The HVC is a meta-method, since it consists of *three logical pillars* (input, method and output) and of *six process layers* (each of the process steps requires a suitable method). The method suits explicitly the design of Internet-based business collaboration infrastructures.

Because of our understanding of the term business model and because of the fact that the ultimate goal of a company is long-term value creation, the design of a business model has to be definitely based upon the entrepreneurial strategy.

Figure 4: The House of Value Creation

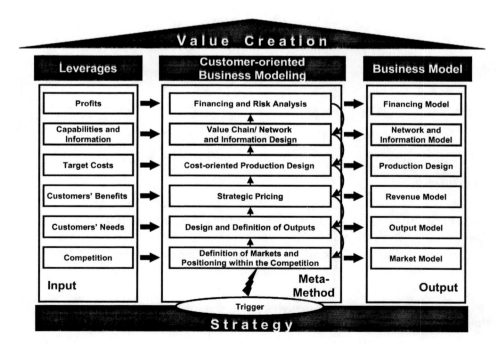

Therefore, if not already done, the first step within a business modeling process is to define the rough entrepreneurial strategy, on which the business model will be based. The meta-method of the House of Value Creation illustrates the correlation between a set of significant leverages (first pillar of the HVC), the customer-oriented business modeling process (second pillar) and the resulting business model (third pillar). As previously hinted, our business modeling approach encompasses six layers that correspond to the six steps of the method. The first HVC phase is triggered either by the inside or by the outside of the company—through a new idea, invention, innovation or modifications of the economical environment. The six steps of the method are:

1. **Definition of the markets and positioning within the competition.** The initial decision regards the category of products or services to deal with. Hence, a consequent monitoring of all strong players (suppliers, customers and possible competitors) has to be done. This phase deals with the branch profitability and with the rivalry among existing and potential competitors. Phase output: *market model*, with a clear identification of the key players, customers and competitors.

2. **Definition and design of the outputs.** In the product design, a well-proven method is the *quality function deployment* (QFD) (Akao, 1990; Pfeiffer, 1993; Warnecke et al., 1995; Hoffmann, 1997). With this approach, a customer-oriented product development can be successfully realized. Therefore, after defining markets and identifying core customers and competitors, the outputs (physical products or services) have to be shaped in order to maximize the customers' benefit according to a QFD-like method. Phase output: *output model*, with a detailed customer-oriented design of the outputs.

3. **Strategic pricing.** The identification of prices for the planned outputs should be more the result of a strategic positioning than of a cost-oriented approach (Laing & Forzi, 2002b; Hagel & Singer, 1999). The price calculation should take into consideration the customers' surplus constraint as well as the strength of the competition (existing barriers of entry, such as patents, industry property rights, etc.) (Kim & Mauborgne, 2000). Phase output: *revenue model*, with a detailed description of how earnings can be achieved.

4. **Cost-oriented production design.** According to the guidelines of the revenue model, the target costs for the output model will be calculated (as the upper bound for direct costs). Hence, the requirements to the value chain will be detailed. Phase output: *production design*, with a detailed description of how the performances have to be achieved.

5. **Partners, network and information.** In this phase, starting from the requirements on performances of the value chain, the capabilities (core competencies, capacities, available modules and components, ICT infrastructure) of the own performance structure and of the potential partners will be thoroughly scanned. Phase output: *network model*, selection of the partners

within a specific instantiation of the value chain and network configuration, as well as *information model*, i.e., the approach according to which the information management issue has to be tackled.

6. **Financing and risk analysis.** Eventually, based upon the expected profits and a suitable scenario analysis, the risk-level as well as the need for working capital must be calculated to start the search for investors (Fink et al., 2000). Phase output: *financing model*.

At each step of the HVC, the corresponding targets must be fulfilled. If one step is not fulfilled, then the process should go back to a prior phase as long as the issue is tackled—with an iterative approach.

In the following section, our contribution will focus on a specific level of our HVC, namely the one regarding *network* and *information model*. Specific attention will be paid to the necessity to manage information, information flows and ICTs within distributed manufacturing networks

The Design of Information Models in a Networked Economy

In the fifth phase of the HVC customer-oriented business modeling, starting from the requirements on performances of the value chain, the state of the art and the capabilities of the own performance, information structures and ICTs, as well as of the ones of the potential partners, will be thoroughly scanned. The striven value chain will be designed and a specific network will be instantiated (see Figure 5).

As stated previously, before making a strategic decision regarding the creation of a cooperation network, the management of an enterprise has to take into consideration a wide set of aspects, such as the entrepreneurial organization, the own core competencies and the ones of the partners, and the available technology. The gathering of all information regarding the potential network participants represents what we define as *capabilities and information*. According to the requirements previously identified within the *production design* (output of Phase 4 of the HVC),

Figure 5: The Fifth Level of the House of Value Creation

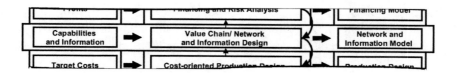

a cross-check with the capabilities of all potential partners helps to define a set of suitable partners. This process can be supported, e.g., by the use of specific intermediaries such as vertical e-portals. The data about the entrepreneurial capabilities must regard the own performances, the ICT capabilities as well as the maturity of the involved technologies (Krcmar, 2000; Picot et al., 2001). As a result, the instantiation of a *specific network configuration* can be identified. Furthermore, the definition of inter-organizational blue prints and branch-specific process standards is necessary to enable lean and efficient *inter-organizational processes and workflows*. The result is the *network model* (see Figure 6). The most relevant aspect for the following phase is that the inter-organizational processes determine the *sources* and the *sinks* of distributed information.

The *information design* focuses on the management of the information within such entrepreneurial networks and inter-organizational value chains (see Figure 6).

Within the modeling of an inter-organizational information management model, we distinguish three different layers:

1. **Inter-organizational information flows.** Starting from the sources and sinks of distributed information, the inter-organizational information flows can be derived and consequently defined (Gebauer & Buxmann, 1999; Levitan, 1982; Krcmar, 2000; Picot et al., 2001). Within this process, several different aspects have to be taken into consideration (Laing & Forzi, 2002a): *direction* (e.g., one-way or bi-directional information flow), involved *actors* (broker, network

Figure 6: Inter-Organizational Network and Information Models

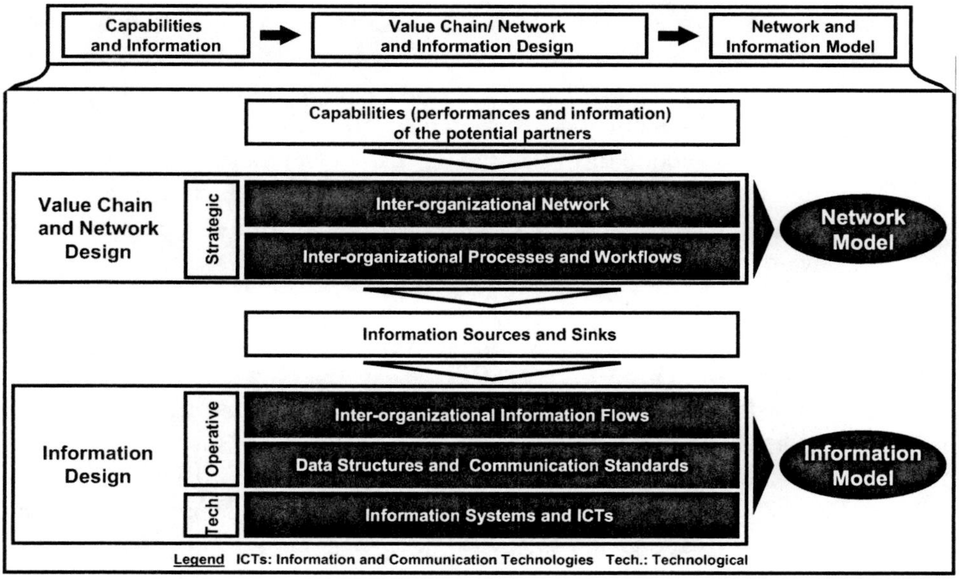

members and related intelligent agents), involved *systems* (e.g., knowledge management, distributed database information sources) and *relationship* (e.g., 1:1, 1:n, m:n). Furthermore, information flows encompass two other major dimensions: *information width*, which sets the different degrees of information broadcasting and transparency within the network; and *information depth*, which defines the scope, aggregation level and content of the information flow.

2.   **Inter-organizational data structures, communication standards.** A crucial issue is the development of an inter-organizational *data model* to ensure the consistency, quality and transparency of the data. A data model also encompasses the aggregation levels for management support systems (e.g., data warehousing and data mining) (Krcmar, 2000). Furthermore, the branch-specific development of *shared communication standards* (e.g., based on XML) is essential to achieve and ensure a fast exchange of information and data through inter-organizational networks, as well as the integration of different ERP systems within an Internet-based BCI (Bray et al., 2000; Picot et al., 2001). The identification of the most appropriate technology standards is important also to deploy a back-end integration in each of the involved enterprises. Eventually, an appropriate solution for the *security issue* has to be identified.

3.   **Information systems and ICTs.** Enterprises have to weigh a set of crucial success factors in the field of technology management. The analysis of the potentials of new technologies as well as their diffusion and maturity can help enterprises to select the most suitable technologies to face challenges in the context of new collaborative businesses. For instance, the technical support of information flows in relation to complexity of the considered job and to the media richness (regarding, e.g., real-time or asynchronous response) can be done according to the *Media Richness Theory* (Daft & Lengel, 1984). As a matter of fact, a proper *technology and innovation management* is important to plan the development of the entrepreneurial core businesses in coordination with a strategic technology planning (Bleck & Quadt, 2002; Bullinger, 1994; Krcmar, 2000). Last but not least, a *make or buy* decision has to be taken, e.g., between the exploitation of the services of an application service provider and the development of an own platform.

Integrated Planning of Network and ICTs

Within the definition of information systems and ICTs, one of the most crucial issues is the identification of the most appropriate ICTs, out of the set of all suitable technologies, that might suit the striven target (Bensaou, 1997; Bleck et al., 2002; Bleck & Quadt, 2002; Bullinger, 1994; Daft & Lengel, 1984; Gebauer & Buxmann, 1999; Krcmar, 2000; Mooney, 1996; Pietsch, 1999; Teubner, 1999). In order to meet this particular challenge, we outline an ad-hoc developed planning approach that incorporates the interdependencies between inter-organizational processes and ICTs. As a matter of fact, the adequate identification, selection and management of suitable information systems and ICTs is a great challenge because of several different aspects. In fact, there might be many different, often even partly competing network partners, whose different needs must be considered when selecting and assessing ICTs and electronic services to support the network (Bensaou, 1997; Bleck & Quadt, 2002; Gebauer & Buxmann, 1999; Rose, 1998; Schoder, 2000). Within our research, we observed that various ICTs are capable of supporting the different inter-organizational processes and workflows. In order to guarantee smooth inter-organizational processes, the selected ICTs must therefore be integrated seamlessly. Furthermore, the high pace of technical development requires a planning process that considers both currently available and also future ICT solutions (Bleck & Quadt, 2002; Bullinger, 1994; Krcmar, 2000; Teubner, 1999). Finally, new ICT solutions influence the network structure, so that the business relations between participating companies may change (Gebauer & Buxmann, 1999; Rose, 1998; Ruohonen, 1996; Schoder, 2000). Therefore, potential impacts on the network must be considered and evaluated when *selecting* and *assessing* specific information systems and ICTs as network infrastructure (Bleck et al., 2002). This is what we define as *integrated planning and management of networks and of information technology*. Because of the complexity related to this planning task, we are convinced that a suitable description model is fundamental for a successful planning. As a matter of fact, such a model must describe all characteristics of potential networks, the different parameters of ICTs, as well as the complex links between these two clusters. Furthermore, this approach has to enable the full and sustainable exploitation of technologies over the time and herewith the implementation of new and unique network structures. For this reason an *integrated description model* to identify and highlight the interdependencies between different network instantiations

Figure 7: Integrated Description Model for the Planning of Information Systems and ICTs

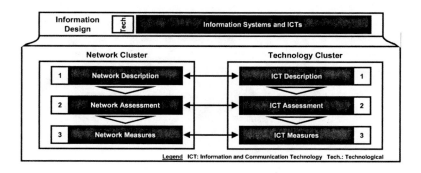

and the underlying technologies has to be developed (Bleck et al., 2002; see also Davenport, 1993). The description model (see Figure 7) fulfills all the above-mentioned requirements.

The description model consists of three layers for each of the two clusters. These layers correspond to three different steps within the planning and management process. The first layer is a crucial step within the model, and it aims at the description of networks and ICTs as well as their matching. In Figure 7, the matching is represented by the arrows. The description and matching of the network and ICTs is a complex task, because of the existence of several interdependencies between the two clusters. More details about this phase can be found in Bleck et al. (2002). In the second layer all relevant factors for the assessment of the feasibility as well as the sustainable cost effectiveness are collected and compared. Eventually, in the third layer the necessary measures to deploy a specific network as well as to develop and exploit the appropriate ICT infrastructure are derived. Within this last step particular attention is paid to temporal constraints. This fact will be highlighted within the case study later in this chapter (see also Figure 10).

In the next section we will show, with the help of a case study, how the potential of our HVC meta-method can be exploited in practice.

CASE STUDY

Each industrial sector has its own peculiarities; therefore, it is necessary to develop approaches and solutions that take into account such specific requirements. Our institution has a proven experience with German SMEs of the manufacturing and machinery industry. Since we identified a remarkable *need for "e-action"* in this traditional and static industrial branch, we therefore decided to develop *customized business models* and *e-business solutions* with a high impact on this industrial sector. In this context we developed the case study for the present contribution.

Figure 8: Supply Chain of the Metal Industry

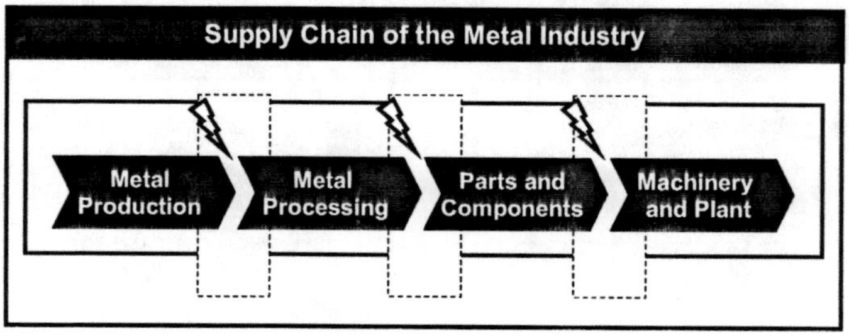

The case study has been conducted in the field of *manufacturing networks for metallic material* with 10 German SMEs (Figure 8 shows the structure of the supply chain of the metal industry). As a matter of fact, the generation and mailing of so-called *paper-based test reports* for metallic material, which document and guarantee to the buyer specific material properties, is nowadays accompanied by several serious problems. For instance, the open issues concern the archiving of reports, the specification check of corresponding material standards or norms referenced in a test report (DIN, 1990).

The innovative *trigger* for this case study is the worldwide dissemination and acceptance of the Internet as communication and information channel as well as the idea to exchange material test reports electronically. This makes the development of new intermediary services for the efficient transmission and storage of material test reports based on an electronic business collaboration infrastructure feasible (see Figure 9). Based upon the innovative idea of exchanging *electronic material reports* on a collaborative Internet platform, we proposed a business model—the result of the use of the House of Value Creation.

We are now going to present the results obtained within the business modeling process.

1. **Market model.** After a thorough market analysis, we identified similar solutions to manage and exchange material reports (e.g., document management systems, DMSs), but we realized that none of them fulfills all relevant requirements. Hence, in the resulting market model, there are no *direct competitors* because of the fact that the planned service is innovative and therefore it is not offered in the market yet. Furthermore, the *potential customers* are all the manufacturing enterprises that exchange metallic products—i.e., both ferrous metals (all sorts of steel) and non-ferrous metals (such as tin, copper and brass)—with specified and guaranteed properties, as well the different testing and inspection organizations (such as TÜV or Dekra

Figure 9: Business Collaboration Infrastructure for the Metal Industry

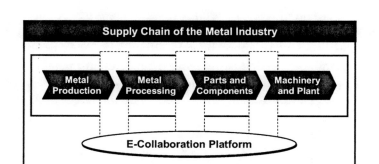

in Germany, Det Norske Veritas in Norway, BSI or ITS in Great Britain, UL in USA, SGS in Switzlerland, Bureau Veritas in France).

2.   **Output model.** We conducted several workshops with the involved SMEs and thus we gathered all the requirements related to the exchange of electronic material test reports in the manufacturing field. We distinguish two kinds of groups of services required by the potential customers of the platform:

- *Basic service*, e.g., storage, remote access and archiving of electronic material test reports over the Internet.
- *Value-added services*, e.g., assessment and evaluation of the suppliers, nominal/actual value comparison of measures certified in a test report, batch management, offering of detailed information about material-related quality.

Other general requirements on the overall performances of the platform are: a high operating efficiency and flexibility, specific security requirements (e.g., transmission and privacy), a 24/7 system availability, a suitable multi-user concept with different and adjustable levels of authorizations, support of surveyors of independent testing and inspection organizations.

3.   **Revenue model.** After an analysis of the customers' benefit, we used the two-step *price corridor method* of Kim and Mauborgne (2000) for the strategic pricing, in order to share for shaping a revenue model:

a)   *Identification of the price corridor of the mass*, i.e., search for the price corridor that the majority of the customers is willing to bear. According to the market model, there are no direct competitors, but only some possible substitutes, i.e., providers of DMSs, whose products, though, do not fulfill all relevant customers' requirements. We observed that the innovative services of the planned intermediary service infrastructure might therefore crucially change the power balance in the market of tools for the management and exchange of material test reports. The current cost to process a single material report amounts up to about US$50, which clearly represents an upper bound for the price model. Since the process cost for an electronic test report drops drastically by the use of the intermediary service infrastructure, the decision was to pursue a *low* price corridor strategy to target a high number of customers.

b)   *Specification of a level within the price corridor*, i.e., identification of an appropriate price level within the chosen low price corridor. A detailed analysis of the customers' benefit of the DMSs underlined that none of them can fulfill all industrial requirements. Therefore, the intermediary service infrastructure with its innovative customer-oriented services has realistic chances to be widely accepted by the target group and thus to penetrate successfully the market. In order to conquer the market and achieve the striven critical mass in terms of traffic (reports/period of time), it was furthermore decided to choose a lower pricing level within the chosen low price corridor. High traffic, though, does not yet guarantee long-term success, because second-movers might come up with similar solutions and quickly gain market share. Hence, the price should be maintained very low until the critical mass in terms of branch members is also reached. With the achievement of this goal, the developed *format for electronic test reports* will be widely disseminated, and hence it will have a good chance to be accepted and adopted as a branch-specific standard. At this stage, barriers for market entry for possible competitors will be significant. The deployment of a mid- or upper-level pricing within the selected price corridor might be then possible without risking to lose market share. A potential cash cow for the business is represented by the portfolio of attractive value-added services.

4. **Production design.** According to the guidelines of the revenue model, the target costs for the output model will be calculated within the *cost-oriented production design,* i.e., design of the electronic transmission, management and storage of material reports. In the case of the "production" design for the transmission of material reports, the attention was paid to the fixed costs (i.e., target costs for the infrastructure) since direct costs (i.e., cost for the report transmission) tend to be zero. Hence, the result is a platform with a targeted low fixed cost (e.g., hardware, software and mainly personnel costs). The lower the fixed costs are, the sooner the critical mass in terms of participants and transactions will be reached.

    As far as concerns the design of the platform, we identified the need for the following capabilities: management and archiving of material test reports with a Web-based database, material science know-how, trust management and information content for value-added services.

5. **Network and information model.** In this phase, starting from the requirements on performances and from the capabilities, core competencies and IT infrastructure of the involved potential partners, a specific performance network as well as an information and technology framework were defined. The targeted market consists of a multitude of SMEs, of which none of them is dominating the market. It is important that all enterprises that take part in the platform must trust and be able to rely on the carrier. Hence, the managing institution of the transaction platform for electronic test reports must be an independent company. It was thus decided that the collaboration platform should *not* be managed by one of the manufacturers of metallic material, but by a neutral intermediary with material science know-how as well as ICT competence (e.g., database management and archiving). As a matter of fact, the system management and value-added services that require particular material science know-how will be performed by the intermediary, who will outsource the other competencies to two different partners: one partner was identified to deal with trust management and another to provide information content for the value-added services.

Within the analysis of the information infrastructure, the crucial issue was the modeling of processes and the management of shared information to enable the *inter*-organizational and *intra*-organizational workflow capabilities of the planned ICT system. Furthermore, some of the other most interesting aspects that were dealt with are the definition of *process standards* for inter-organizational processes and workflows, the development of an appropriate and flexible interface to deploy a *back-end integration* in each of the involved enterprises and the branch-specific development of a *shared standard* for electronic test reports. Such standards ensure a fast exchange of the required information through inter-organizational networks, as well as the integration of different ERP systems. Last but not least, as far as *ICT planning and management* is concerned, an important part was the assessment and availability verification of the technologies that were previously selected to support the intermediary service processes. As mentioned in the previous section, suitable measures (i.e., further evaluation, acceptance and implementation, further development or rejection) had to be derived for each of the selected technologies. Within the assessment phase, in order to cope with the different requirements and the need to identify the necessary measures for each partner, the use of a technology calendar proved to be helpful to visualize critical temporal constraints (see Figure 10).

6. **Financing model.** Because of clear privacy reasons, we are at the moment not allowed to distribute information about the financing model.

Figure 10: Integrated Planning of Intermediary Services and ICTs

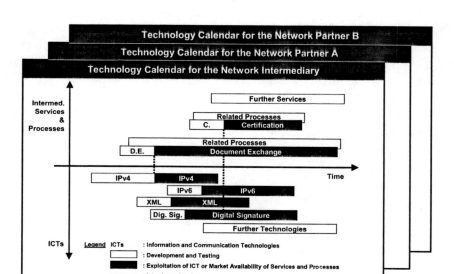

PERSPECTIVES OF E-BUSINESS MODELS AND ORGANIZATIONAL TRENDS

Nowadays, the evolution of economic systems is gradually leading to a progressive blurring of the company borders, to a reduction of physical and information barriers among enterprises, and to a consequent generation of continuity between internal and external aspects of an organization (Davidow & Malone, 1993, Hirschhorn & Gilmore, 1992; Picot et al., 1996, Wirtz, 2000). As we highlighted at the beginning of the chapter, transaction costs diminish and governance instances hence gradually shift from hierarchical to market-like structures (Biggiero, 1999; Picot et al., 2001; Williamson, 1975). These facts lead to a trend towards networked organizations which, along with high potentials, bears also remarkable challenges. In fact, even if companies remain the fundamental decision-making bodies, they must increasingly come to terms with the general increase in inter-organizational relationships (Bensaou, 1997; Filos, 2001; Gebauer & Buxmann, 1999; Hagel & Singer, 1999; Klein, 1995; Molina et al., 1998). The growing inter-relationships between functions of different companies are forcing enterprises to remove their own internal barriers, and the growing interactions with other economic players are forcing companies to deal with a structural instability and a closer interdependence with other economic players (Brynjolfsson & Kahin, 2000; Kornelius, 1999; Parolini, 1999; Wirtz, 2000). This implies that enterprises are bound to develop new business models and hence deploy a flexible and reactive organization in order to be able to deal with the modified and furthermore dynamically changing requirements of flexible business relationships (Evans & Wurster, 2000; Franz, 2002; Fine, 1998; Hagel & Singer, 1999). Before starting to cooperate within global networks of enterprises and hence deploy inter-organizational business models, companies tend thus to design a streamlined and lean entrepreneurial organization, to concentrate on their own core competencies, as well as to deploy the divestiture of non-core functions (Davidow & Malone, 1993; Hagel & Singer, 1999; Picot et al., 1996). This transformation process is crucial for the success of the company's business: the definition of their own core competence(-ies), the internal leanness and flexibility represent the precondition for a company to achieve the striven external organizational flexibility (Filos, 2001; Forzi & Luczak, 2002; Franz, 2002; Malone et al., 1987; Parolini, 1999).

ICTs and e-business solutions play—within the above-mentioned development process towards networked and flexible organizations—an important enabling role, by giving enterprises concrete and efficient tools to inter-connect and to integrate their performance and information systems. Thus, it can be stated that the "e" of e-business (namely the use of ICT-based solutions) is a means that promises higher integration and efficiency, lower costs, profitability and sustainable growth. Though e-business and the ICT-driven new business models are not a revolution, they are another (effective) way of doing business, an enabler that helps to integrate (inter and intra-organizational) performance processes and to make them more efficient. Companies may fail, but not because of the "e" in their business. More likely, the ones that failed after the hype of 1999 did so, among other reasons, because of a too hastily excitement-driven embedding of e-business solutions into the own organization and ICT infrastructure.

We are convinced that the path towards an inter-connected and dynamic economy is a way of no return. As a matter of fact, the business activities of the future are likely to be carried out across dynamic webs of companies (Filos, 2001; Franz, 2002; Parolini, 1999). There are different possible definitions of this vision of dynamic, inter-networked, Internet-based, flexible, hybrid or even market-like, knowledge-driven, agile and Web-oriented organizational paradigms: value-creating systems, smart organizations, economic webs, value nets or dynamic Internet-enabled supply networks, to mention just a few (Bergner et al., 2000; Filos, 2001; Forzi & Luczak, 2002; Franz, 2002; Hagel & Singer, 1999; Klein, 1995; Kleinaltenkamp & Dahlke, 1998; Kornelius, 1999; Parolini, 1999; Picot et al., 2001; Rentmeister & Klein, 2001; Timmers, 2000; Wirtz, 2000). In Figure 11, which shows the development trend, all such paradigms were clustered under the definition "Value Nets."

Within a decade, both academics and managers might not mention the "e" related to businesses anymore. This will not mean that e-business and all the ICT-driven business models will have failed; on the contrary, the thorough embedding

Figure 11: ICTs and the Development of Organizational Approaches

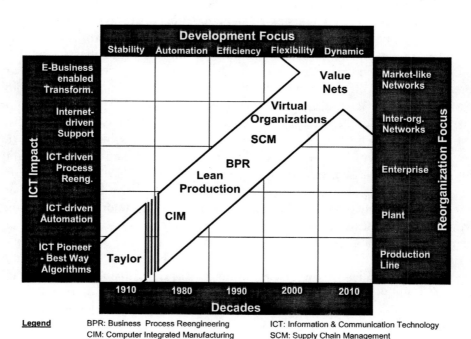

Legend
BPR: Business Process Reengineering   ICT: Information & Communication Technology
CIM: Computer Integrated Manufacturing   SCM: Supply Chain Management

process will have come to its conclusion, and the inter-organizational integration, probably even "back-end to back-end" (Filos, 2001), will be a common and accepted reality in the entrepreneurial world.

CONCLUSION

Until now, the development and adjustment of business models have been performed by companies mostly in a creative way. This was also confirmed by the "dot.com" crisis, in which weak or improvised business models led both single enterprises to unrecoverable bankruptcies and networks to failure. A suitable approach to design business models for a networked economy is the House of Value Creation (HVC), a meta-method to design customer-oriented and sustainable business models. The meta-method was validated in a specific case, namely in the case of the information service intermediary of a collaboration network in the manufacturing industry. We are convinced that the HVC is also a promising approach *for the development of business models in the case of inter-firm networks*. Hence, in order to verify such a fact, we plan to test its validity also in other cases and for other branches, such as IT and logistics.

Another interesting aspect is that the House of Value Creation can be also used to check the feasibility of existing business models as well as to improve and further develop business models.

As far as the project of the case study is concerned, the first step was the development of the prototypic BCI solution. Nowadays, a commercial business pilot is being deployed with the participation of all the 10 enterprises of the consortium; the objective is to gather precious information about the feasibility of the developed business model as well as about the acceptance of the BCI as an efficient means to exchange material test reports. The next phase will be a commercial rollout, initially in the German market and, if the sustainability will be confirmed, on European level.

To conclude, the trend towards a tightly inter-connected economy seems to be nowadays unquestionable. On the other side, the development process towards a dynamically networked economy has just recently started. We strongly believe that, in order to be successful within a networked economy, enterprises will thus have to undergo a deep transformation process in their organizational philosophy, in their structure, in the used methods as well as in their approach to interact with external organizations. We are convinced that, in order to face the challenges of such a dynamic and insecure business context, an appropriate business modeling approach is helpful to plan sustainable businesses.

REFERENCES

Afuah, A. & Tucci, C.L. (2001). *Internet Business Models and Strategies: Text and Cases.* New York: McGraw-Hill/Irwin.

Akao, Y. (1990). *Quality Function Deployment: Integrating Customer Requirements into Product Design.* Portland, OR: Productivity Press.

Andrade, R. & Clausing, D.P. (1995). *Strategic Information of Product, Technologies and Core Competencies with Support of Planned Reusabilitiy.* Working paper. Boston: MIT.

Balakrishnan, S. (1996). Benefits of customer and competitive orientations in industrial markets. *Industrial Marketing Management,* 25(4), 257-269.

Bensaou, M.(1997). Interorganizational cooperation—The role of information technology: An empirical comparison of U.S. and Japanese supplier relations. *Information Systems Research,* 8(2), 107-124.

Bergner, K., Deifel, B., Jacobi, C., Kellerer, W., Rausch, A., Sabbah, A., Schätz, B., Sihling, M., Vilbig, A. & Vogel, S. (2000). *The Future of Information Technology—An Interdisciplinary, Scenario-Based Approach.* Report of the Technical University of München, Institut für Informatik, München.

Beyer, M., Quadt, A. & Bleck, S. (2002). The FIR e-business engineering integration model. *Proceedings of the 18th International Conference on CAD/DAM, Robotics and Factories of the Future (CARs&FOF'2002),* Porto (P), July 3-5, 451-457.

Biggiero, L. (1999). Markets, hierarchies, networks, districts: A cybernetic approach. *Human Systems Management,* 18, 71-86.

Bleck, S. & Quadt, A. (2002). Planning and employment of information and communication technologies in the field of intermediary services. *Proceedings of the 6th International Conference on Work With Display Units (WWDU 2002) "World Wide Work,"* Berchtesgaden, May 22-25, 500-502.

Bleck, S., Beyer, M. & Laing, P. (2001). Methodeneinsatz bei der erschließung des e-business—Ergebnisse einer studie. *Industrie Management,* 1, 21-26.

Bleck, S., Forzi, T., Laing., P. & Stich, V. (2002). The path from business modeling to technology management. *Proceedings of the International Conference on Advanced Production Management Systems (APMS 2002),* Eindhoven (NL), September 8-13, pp. 34-46.

Bray, T., Paoli, J., Sperberg-McQueen, C.M. & Maler, E. (2000). *Extensible Markup Language (XML) 1.0 (Second Edition), WRC Recommendations, 2000.* Retrieved on March 5, 2002, from: http://www.w3.org/TR/2000/REC-xml-20001006.pdf.

Brynjolfsson, E. & Kahin, B. (2000). *Understanding the Digital Economy.* Boston: MIT Press.

Bullinger, H.J. (Ed.). (1994). *Einführung in das Technologiemanagement.* Stuttgart: B.G. Teubner Verlag.

Clausing, D.P.& Witter, J.H. (1992). *Integration of Reusability and Interface Management into Enhanced Quality Function Deployment Methods.* Working paper. Boston: MIT.

Coase, R.H. (1937). The nature of the firm. *Economica,* 4, 386-405.

Daft, R. & Lengel, R. (1984). Information richness: A new approach to managerial behaviour and organization design. *Research in Organizational Behaviour,* 6, 191-233.

Davenport, T.H. & Short, J.E. (1990). The new industrial engineering: Information technology and business process redesign. *Sloan Management Review,* (Summer), 11-27.

Davidow, W. & Malone, M. (1993). *Das virtuelle Unternehmen.* Frankfurt am Main, New York: Campus Verlag.

DIN. (Ed.). (1990). *DIN 10 204—Metallic Products—Types of Inspection Documents.* (German version). Berlin: Beuth Verlag.

Evans, P. & Wurster, T. (2000). *Blown to Bits—How the New Economies of Information Transforms Strategy.* Boston: Harvard Business School Press.

Filos, E. (2001). The impact of the eEconomy on the supply chain—The perspective of the EU research programmes. *Proceedings of Supply-Chain World-Europe 2001,* Berlin, October 1-3.

Fine, C.H. (1998). *Clockspeed—Winning Industry Control in the Age of Temporary Advantage.* MA: Perseus Books.

Fink, A., Schlake, O. & Siebe, A. (2000). Wie sie mit szenarien die zukunft vorausdenken. *Harvard Business Manager,* 2, 34-47.

Forzi, T. & Laing, P. (2002). Business modeling for e-collaboration networks. *Proceedings of the 2002 Information Resources Management Association International Conference (IRMA 2002),* Seattle, WA (USA), May 19–22, 961-963.

Forzi, T. & Luczak, H. (2002). E-business: Status quo and perspectives. In Luczak, H., Cakir, A.E. & Cakir, G. (Eds.), *Proceedings of the 6th International Conference on Work With Display Units (WWDU 2002) "World Wide Work,"* Berchtesgaden, May 22-25, 494-496.

Franz, A. (2002). The management of business webs. In Luczak, H., Cakir, A.E. & Cakir, G. (Eds.), *Proceedings of the 6th International Conference on Work With Display Units (WWDU 2002) "World Wide Work,"* Berchtesgaden, May 22-25, 506-508.

Gebauer, J. & Buxmann, P. (1999). Assessing the value of interorganizational systems to support business transactions. *Proceedings of the 32nd Hawaii International Conference on Systems Sciences (HICSS-32),* Maui.

Hagel III, J. & Singer, M. (1999). Unbundling the corporation. *Harvard Business Review,* 77(2), 133-141.

Hinterhuber, H.H. (1992). *Strategische Unternehmungsführung—I Strategisches Denken* (5th edition). Berlin, New York: Walter de Gruyer.

Hinterhuber, H.H. (1997). *Strategische Unternehmungsführung—II Strategisches Handeln* (6th edition). Berlin, New York: Walter de Gruyer.

Hirschhorn, L. &Gilmore, T. (1992). The new boundaries of the "boundaryless" company. *Harvard Business Review,* (May-June), 104-115.

Hoeck, H. & Bleck, S. (2001). Electronic markets for services. In Stanford-Smith, B. & Chiozza, E. (Eds.), *E-Work and E-Commerce, Volume 1.* Amsterdam: IOS Press, 458-464.

Hoffmann, J. (1996). *Entwicklung eines QFD-gestützten Verfahrens zur Produktplanung und -Entwicklung für kleine und mittlere Unternehmen.* Dissertation, University of Stuttgart.

Holland, C.P. & Lockett, G. (1994). Strategic choice and inter-organisational information systems. *Proceedings of the 27th Hawaii International Conference on Systems Sciences (HICSS-27).* Los Alamitos: IEEE Computer Society Press, 4, 405-416.

Kim, C. & Mauborgne, R. (2000). Knowing a winning business idea when you see one. *Harvard Business Review,* 78(5), 129-138.

Klein, S. (1995). *Interorganisationssysteme und Unternehmensnetzwerke— Wechselwirkungen zwischen organisatorischer und informationstech nischer Entwicklung.* Habilitationsschrift, University of St. Gallen.

Kleinaltenkamp, M. & Dahlke, B. (1998). Market orientation and customer orientation of industrial companies. *THEXIS,* 15(4), 32-37.

Kornelius, L.(1999). *Inter-Organisational Infrastructure for Competitive Advantage: Strategic Alignment in Virtual Corporations.* Doctoral Thesis, Technical University of Eindhoven.

Krcmar, H. (2000). *Informationsmanagement* (2nd edition). Berlin, New York: Springer Verlag.

Laing P. & Forzi, T. (2001). E-business and entrepreneurial cooperation. *Proceedings of the 1st International Conference on Electronic Business (ICEB 2001),* Hong Kong, December 19-21, 7-9.

Laing, P. & Forzi, T. (2002a). Management of shared information within manufacturing networks. *Proceedings of the 18th International Conference on CAD/DAM, Robotics and Factories of the Future (CARs&FOF'2002),* Porto (P), July 3-5, 459-466.

Laing, P. & Forzi, T. (2002b). Challenges for business modeling in the new communication era. *Proceedings of the 31st Annual Meeting of the Western Decision Sciences Institute (WDSI 2002),* April 2-5, Las Vegas, NV (USA), 434-436.

Levitan, K.B. (1982). Information resources as "goods" in the life cycle of information production. *Journal of the American Society for Information Science,* 33, 44-54.

Luczak, H., Bleck, S. & Hoeck, H. (2002b). Elektronische marktplätze— Voraussetzungen und erfolgsfaktoren für den elektronischen Handel mit Cdienstleistungen. In Stauss, B. & Bruhn, M. (Eds.), *Jahrbuch Dienstleistungsmanagement 2002.* Wiesbaden: Gabler Verlag, 149-176.

Luczak, H., Bleck, S., Forzi, T. & Laing, P. (2002a). *A Holistic Approach for E-Business Engineering.* In *Proceedings of the 2nd International Conference on Electronic Business (ICEB 2002)*, Taipei, December 10-13, pp. 222-224.

Malone, T., Yates, J. & Benjamin, R. (1987). Electronic markets and electronic hierarchies: Effects of information technology on market structure and corporate strategies. *Communications of the ACM,* 30(6), 484-497.

Mintzberg, H. (1979). *The Structuring of Organizations.* Englewood Cliffs, NJ: Prentice-Hall.

Molina, A., Ponguta, S., Bremer, C.F. & Eversheim, W. (1998). Framework for global virtual business. *Agility & Global Competition,* 2(3), 56-69.

Mooney, J.G. (1996). *The Productivity and Business Value Impacts of Information Technology: Economic and Organizational Analyses.* Dissertation, University of California Irvine.

Osterwalder, A. & Pigneur, Y. (2002). An e-business model ontology for modeling e-business. *Proceedings of the 15th Electronic Commerce Conference "e-Reality: Constructing the e-Economy,"* Bled (SLO), June 17-19.

Parolini, C. (1999). *The Value Net: A Tool for Competitive Strategy.* New York: John Wiley & Sons.

Pelham, A.M. (2000). Market orientation and other potential influences on performance in small and medium-sized manufacturing firms. *Journal of Small Business Management,* 38(1), 48-67.

Pfeiffer, T. (1993). *Qualitätsmanagement: Strategien, Methoden, Techniken.* Munich: Hanser Verlag.

Picot, A., Reichwald, R. & Wigand, R.T. (2001). *Die grenzenlose Unternehmung* (4th edition). Wiesbaden: Gabler Verlag.

Picot, A., Rippenberger, T. & Wolf, B. (1996). The fading boundaries of the firm: The role of information and communication technology. *Journal of Institutional and Theoretical Economics,* 152(1), 65-79.

Pietsch, T. (1999). Bewertung von informations und kommunikationssystemen. *Einvergleich Betriebswirtschaftlicher Verfahren.* Berlin: Erich Schmidt Verlag.

Porter, M.E. (1985). *Competitive Advantage—Creating and Sustaining Superior Performance.* New York: The Free Press.

Porter, M.E. (2001). Strategy and the Internet. *Harvard Business Review,* 79(3), 63-68.

Ramaswamy, R. (1996). *Design and Management of Service Processes—Keeping Customers for Life.* City: Addison-Wesley.

Rayport, J.F. (1999). *The Truth About Internet Business Models.* Retrieved on September 27, 2001, from www.strategy-Business.com/briefs/99301/page1.html.

Rentmeister, J. & Klein, S. (2001). Geschäftsmodelle in der new economy. *Das Wirtschaftsstudium,* 30(3), 354-361.

Rose, F. (1998). *The Economics, Concept, and Design of Information Intermediaries; A Theoretic Approach.* Dissertation, University of Frankfurt, Germany.

Ruohonen, M. (1996). *Information Technology Mediated Activities in Organizational Contexts—A Case of Strategic Information Systems Planning.* TUCS Technical Report No 3, Turku Centre for Computer Science, Turku.

Schoder, D. (2000). *Die Ökonomische Bedeutung von Intermediären im Electronic Commerce.* Habilitation, University of Freiburg.

Tan, B.F. (2001). Trends in global electronic commerce. *Proceedings of the 1st International Conference on Electronic Business (ICEB 2001),* Hong Kong, December 19-21.

Teubner, R.A. (1999). *Organisations und Informationssystemgestaltung: Theoretische Grundlagen und integrierte Methoden.* Dissertation, University of Münster. Wiesbaden: Gabler Verlag.

Timmers, P. (2000). *Electronic Commerce.* New York: John Wiley & Sons.

Warnecke, H.J., Melchior, K.W. & Kring, J. (1995). *Handbuch Qualitätstechnik: Methoden und Geräte zur effizienten Qualitätssicherung.* Landsberg/Lech: Verlag Moderne Industrie.

Webb, D., Webster, C. & Krepapa, A. (2000). An exploration of the meaning and outcomes of a customer-defined market orientation. *Journal of Business Research,* 48(2), 101-112.

Williamson, O.E. (1975). *Markets and Hierarchies: Analysis and Anti-Trust Implications.* New York: The Free Press.

Wirtz, B.W. (2000). *Electronic Business.* Wiesbaden: Gabler Verlag.

Wirtz, B.W. & Kleinecken, A. (2000). Geschäftsmodelltypologien im Internet. *Das Wirtschaftsstudium,* 29(11), 628-635.

Part III

Web-Based Learning & Teaching

Chapter IX

Preparation for E-Learning: An Australian Study (2001)

Andrew Stein
Victoria University of Technology, Australia

ABSTRACT

University students require considerable computer literacy to enter and then succeed at their studies. Many courses, whether technology focused or not, are using advanced Web technology to deliver digital content via e-learning. This chapter explores the changing nature of information and communication technology (ICT) literacy of university students and explores whether gender and age factors affect student's ICT literacy and Web usage. The primary focus of this chapter is to ascertain if transition or freshman students are prepared for the e-learning regimes they will encounter in higher education. Main findings show that there is a significant difference in how females and males use the Web and first-year (transition) students come to university with advanced ICT and Web literacy.

INTRODUCTION

Are transition students entering university with enhanced ICT and Web skills and are these students leading the e-learning curriculum within university courses? Do university students change in their patterns of Web usage? Does gender have an impact upon the patterns of Web usage? Are transition students ready for "e-learning" and can universities rely upon the incoming students having superior ICT and Web literacy? This chapter seeks to add to the dialogue by presenting the latest results in a study looking at the changing ICT and Web skills of university students.

This study is part of a longitudinal project that tracks the changes in the ICT profile of university business students within the Victoria University of Technology.

BACKGROUND
ICT and Web Literacy

The OECD commissioned the PISA (2001) project to report and track the reading, mathematical and science literacy of students leaving K-12 schools. The PISA project seeks to explore:

> "... the increasing role of science, mathematics and technology in modern life, the objectives of personal fulfillment, employment and full participation in society increasingly require an adult population which is not only able to read and write, but also [are] mathematically, scientifically and technologically literate."

The PISA project has focused on reading literacy in the 2000 survey and will focus on mathematical and technological literacy in 2003 and scientific literacy in 2006. The International Adult Literacy Survey (IALS) (ISR 122, 1999) studied the literacy patterns of the OECD countries in 1994 and 1995. The 1995 report commented:

> "While most people can read, the real question is whether their reading and writing skills meet the challenge of living and working in today's information-rich and knowledge-intensive society and economy."

The IALS report identified gaps in the "knowledge society" where re-skilling the workforce tends to narrow the pool of highly skilled workers rather than increasing the spread of skilled workers. The report went further and placed Australia in the bottom rank of OECD countries when looking at basic reading, teamwork, problem solving and ICT skills. In 1999 the Adult Literacy and Lifeskill Survey (ALLS, 1999) formed the information and communication technology (ICT) team to further develop the ICT component of the International Life Skills Survey (ILSS). The ICT team incorporated Brinkley's framework (ALLS, 1999) and incorporated five ICT areas:
- general use of ICT;
- computer use and skills;
- use in specific contexts;
- benefits of computer use;
- receptivity of computer use among non-users.

The IALS and PISA project are part of the significant research on computer literacy that was carried out with a variety of target groups. These groups included cross-cultural surveys (Collis & Andersen, 1994), TOEFL students (Kirsch, Jamieson & Taylor, 1997), adult populations (Oderkirk, 1996; Lowe, 1997) and student populations (Miller & Varma, 1994). These studies used the Technology Acceptance Model (TAM) (Davis, 1989) and the Computer Experience Questionnaire (CEQ) (Lee, 1986) as a basis for survey design. The Alberta Education Foundation (Alberta, 1997) developed a survey that describes the skills, knowledge and attitudes that are applied in a variety of learning and work settings. Most of the research describes computer literacy as including:

- incidence of computer use;
- frequency of use;
- location of use;
- complexity of use;
- adaptability of use and methods of skill development.

While we can measure computer use under various circumstances, there are also sets of factors that influence use. These include education and occupation, gender (Sacks et al., 1993), age (Linden & Adams, 1992), location (Oderkirk, 1996) and cognitive ability (Authur & Hart, 1990). This raises the question, to what extent are university students developing these skills and do university students reflect patterns of use from the wider community? To be able to best meet the students' needs, university departments must first recognize the need for computer literacy and second be able to measure the information knowledge of students. Many studies, (NCES 1999-011; ILSSL 1997; NCES 1999-017; Wenglinsky, 1998; Russell, 1996; Oliver, 1993) both in Australia and overseas have charted the ICT skills of university students. These studies all yielded results that showed that ICT skills of university students had increased significantly and anticipated that the ICT skills of students would always be escalating, matching the general trend within society. A recent comprehensive report (Meredith, 1999) reported on the ICT skills of years 6 and 10 students in Australian schools. This report found a developing divide between ICT "have" and "have-nots." The report recommends that students should be encouraged to develop ICT skills and further explore their own investigative, creative, problem-solving and communication activities when using ICT.

Definitions

We can define the term ICT literacy as referring to the ability to use and comprehend information and communications technologies. This chapter defines students emerging from K-12 into college or university as transition students or freshman students.

E-Learning

The advent of the Internet and WWW technology has created a whirlpool in the business community with organizations trying to develop business models to take advantage of "anywhere, anytime, anyhow" access. The rise and collapse of feted business models in the dot.com crash has shown that the business world is struggling to come to terms with the new technology. This uncertainty is mirrored in the educational field when we see educational bodies, institutions, technologists and practitioners struggling with the concept of e-learning. In 1996 the U.S. Department of Education released the National Educational Technology Plan (OEdTech, 1996) that developed goals in three broad areas; students and teacher access to technology, necessity for research into educational applications, and the move to transform teaching and learning through digital content. These early reports hinted at the potential power of e-learning, but recognized the legal, technological, pedagogical and management hurdles with the new technology. The move to e-learning has been the subject of many conferences here in Australia and around the world. There are many facets of e-learning that need to be researched (USDoE, 2000); the technology for delivering e-learning, the management of delivering digital content, the platforms needed for e-learning, matching learning styles to e-learning, equality and quality of access, ethical dimensions of e-learning, and the need to prepare educators and students to move to e-learning. There is evidence (Healy, 1999) that policy making in e-learning is lagging the practice and as a result there is no accepted view of what constitutes good e-learning practice.

Any Time, Any Place, Any Path, Any Pace

The factors driving e-learning span several fields; they include the nature of individual learning to the dispersal of Internet technologies and to the change in our work and societal lives (Carroll, 2000). Carroll suggests that e-learning will come about as a "fait accompli." Learners have unlimited access to technologies, the home has the potential to become an enhanced learning environment and lastly "The Kids Get It!" This focus on the learner is important as much research focuses on technology and management issues. The importance of the learning approach is best summed by the national School Boards Association in the USA (NASBE, 1998) when they propose that e-learning allows students to be; engaged, involved, empowered, individualized and challenged by higher-order thinking skills. It is very important not to lose sight of the learning focus of e-learning. When considering this learning focus, a crucial question needs to be asked: are all learners prepared for the e-learning environment?

The New Divides?

In Australia the adoption of Internet technologies in the home and by children and teenagers has been steep (ABS 8153, 2001). Similarly, about 50% of U.S. households have Internet access, rising to 62% for households with children under 18 (Evans, 2002). European data shows that about 45% of households have Internet access (Eurydice, 2001). The results from the Evans survey also show some divides opening up in Internet access. Income, location and race seem to have a significant effect upon the rate and type of Internet access. The U.S. government has poured resources into programs to alleviate the digital divide (The New Divide, 2001), but variances of access and use still exist. The concept of the digital divide starts to have a more important impact if universities are moving to e-learning. The NASBE (2001) reported the need to ensure students' access to technology in and out of the learning place, the importance of well-resourced universities and academic staff, the recognition of the needs of special needs students and lastly the need for "Universal Design for Learning" standards for all educational material. The concept of standards means we need to have an idea of what is quality e-learning.

Internet-Toybox or Toolbox

A report by the NTIA and ESA (Evans, 2002) showed an analysis of the major categories of use of the Internet by under 25-year-olds in the USA. The five categories included: schoolwork, e-mail, games, radio/movies and chatrooms. We can further aggregate these five categories into:

- Research—schoolwork
- Communication—e-mail/chat
- Entertainment—games/radio/movies

There are many other areas of research that could encompass e-learning. The next section of the chapter formalizes the questions raised from the literature.

E-Learning Questions

Two areas of ICT usage are proposed. ICT literacy looked at the availability and students' self-assessed literacy. These included home access, usage at home, number of home computers, previous information systems courses studied, computer knowledge, computer confidence and comparability. ICT usage referred to the use of ICTs. This included the familiar word processing, spreadsheet and database as well as the Internet, chat, e-mail and multimedia packages. The general research question for this study involves ascertaining the ICT skills/practices of university students. More specifically there are four questions: What is the self-assessed ICT and Web literacy of university students? How do university students use the Web? Does gender affect ICT literacy, ICT usage and Web usage? Are transition or freshman students prepared for "e-learning"?

METHODOLOGY

Data was gathered through a survey to all first-year commencing business undergraduate students on all five undergraduate campuses of the university. Students were surveyed in either the orientation week or the first week of classes at VUT. Questionnaires were distributed and collected in lectures. From a possible 1,000 students, 627 completed the survey. There were 598 useable surveys, giving a response rate of 60% with 351 first-year or freshman students.

The Questionnaire

The questionnaire comprised two sections. The first section gathered information concerning each student. This included campus, study mode, student/parent birthplace, languages spoken at home, family history of participation in higher education and course studied. The second section gathered information on ICT issues and skill levels. This included home use of computer, student self-perception of computer knowledge and confidence, previous experience in the use of computers and ICT packages. Karsten and Roth (1998) demonstrated the use of computer self-efficacy as a viable measure of student computer knowledge. The question relating to their use of ICT packages and ICT literacy required the student to select their weekly use of packages from None, < 2 hours and > 2 hours. This question sought a more quantifiable measure of student's use of technology. For each question students responded to either pre-selected options or a five-point Likert scale together with an option for additional comment. The student use of the Internet looked at the degree and type of use. Results were tested by time series comparative frequencies, mean m, standard deviation s and cross-tabulation frequency.

Demography

The proportion of female students (47%) is slightly lower than the proportion of females in the first-year undergraduate population as a whole (50%). Students born overseas accounted for 28% of the cohort, with higher proportions coming from families whose parents were born overseas: mother—64%, father—68%. These figures have been consistent with previous surveys (Stein & Craig, 2000). These figures should be considered together with the number of students who speak a language other than English at home (50%). First-year students accounted for 59% of the cohort with 25% being second year. The remaining were a mixture of TAFE articulators. Students who have university-qualified parents account for 40% of the cohort, and students with siblings who have studied at university account for 46%. These "university family" figures are important, as Victoria University would be identified as being populated by first-generation university students.

RESULTS

ICT Literacy: Computer Access, Knowledge, Confidence and Comparability

The PC home market has boomed and a high proportion of the student cohort (94%) had access to a home PC (Table 2); this was consistent with previous results (Stein & Craig; 2000, 1999, 1998). Home access to the Internet was 84% compared with 65% (2000), 45% (1999) and 33% (1998). The mean for computer knowledge (Table 1) was 3.00 with a tight standard deviation of 0.92; this was in line with results for previous surveys. The cohort indicated that 19% felt they had low confidence with 44% of average confidence and 37% having high levels of confidence. The mean value for computer confidence was slightly higher than knowledge at 3.19 with a standard deviation of .95. When compared with previous surveys, both knowledge and confidence while stable seem to be trending down. Comparability (m=3.16) is a

Table 1: Self-Assessed Computer Knowledge, Confidence and Comparison %

	2001 1st Year N=351	2000 1st Year N=369 (Stein, 2001)	1999 1st Year N=389 (Stein, 2000)	1998 1st Year N=521 (Stein, 1999)
Low Knowledge	22	26	24	21
Avg. Knowledge	53	47	42	48
High Knowledge	25	27	34	31
Knowledge - μ	3.00	3.01	3.10	3.07
Knowledge - σ	.92	.94	.97	.92
Low Confidence	19	27	19	19
Avg. Confidence	44	35	35	40
High Confidence	37	38	46	41
Confidence - μ	3.19	3.13	3.34	3.30
Confidence - σ	.95	1.08	1.05	1.05
Less Than Peers	19	na	na	na
About Same	48	na	na	na
More Than Peers	33	na	na	na
Comparison - μ	3.16	na	na	na
Comparison - σ	1.04	na	na	na

Table 2: Computer Background by Year of Study %

	2001 1st Year N=351	2000 1st Year N=369 (Stein, 2001)	1999 1st Year N=389 (Stein, 2000)	1998 1st Year N=521 (Stein, 1999)
Own Laptop	19	14	14	na
Computer at Home	96	96	95	83
Internet at Home	84	65	45	33

new construct measuring the student's self-assessed comparison with their peers and is to be used in future studies.

ICT Background

The 2001 first-year student showed laptop ownership trending up, home access to a computer pervasive and access to Internet at home rapidly increasing when

Table 3: Computer Background by Gender % (N=351)

		2001 1st Year N=351	2001 Male Cohort	2001 Female Cohort
Use Laptop		19	18	20
Computer at Home		96	94	95
Internet at Home		84	83	85
>1 computers at Home		42	37	40
Comp Hours at Home	0	7	11	8
	<2	37	30	44
	>2	56	59	47
Games Hours Play	0	56	49	67
	<2	33	36	28
	>2	11	15	5
Play Internet Games		13	16	7

compared to previous studies. In Table 3 there is no gender bias in laptop, home access, Internet access or number of computers at home.

There is a significant gender bias in games play as well as the female cohort being more likely to be a moderate user of the computer at home (44% vs. 30% <2hrs) but far less likely to be heavy users of the home computer (47% vs. 59% >2hrs). This could also be tied up with the male bias in games play. The male cohort rules the use of Internet games; this trend is explored further in Table 4.

Table 4: WEB Usage Patterns by Gender % (N=351)

		2001 1st Year N=351	2001 Male Cohort	2001 Female Cohort
Have E-Mail, e.g., Hotmail		89	90	87
Have Own Web Page		15	16	13
Used HTML Code		37	30	27
Shopped on Web		26	32	22
Use Web for Research	Low	57	64	49
	Mod	29	24	34
	High	14	12	17
Use Web for Entertainment	Low	51	41	70
	Mod	28	41	28
	High	11	17	2
Use Web for Communication, e.g., E-Mail	Low	45	49	39
	Mod	39	39	35
	High	16	12	26

ICT Usage

Several trends are evident in Table 4. Males (32% vs. 22%) are more likely to have shopped on the Web. Future surveys should try to distinguish between shopping and purchasing. There are significant differences in how males and females use the Web. Females are more likely to use the Web for research over males, while the reverse is true for using the Web for entertainment. Communication is more likely to be the purpose of Web usage for females. Using the Web for entertainment is almost a male domain; the figures show that almost no females say they are heavy users of the Web (2% vs. 17%) for entertainment. Both males and females use Web tools like e-mail and Web pages equally.

Students were then asked to report use of common ICT applications with the hours of use as reported in Table 5. The "big 3" applications showed variable results, with word processing being stable and spreadsheets and database trending down in usage. The "Internet" applications—Internet (90% vs. 72%), chat (58% vs. 42%) and e-mail (91% vs. 71%)—showed dramatic increases in usage; games showed a trend down in usage. The only gender bias in use of applications was for games (51% vs. 33%) with males the heavier users.

Table 5: Use of ICT (%) Applications [Combined <2&2+ Hours] by Year of Study

	2001 1st Year N=351	2000 1st Year N=369 (Stein, 2001)	1999 1st Year N=389 (Stein, 2000)	1998 1st Year N=521 (Stein, 1999)
Word Processing	89	83	90	84
Spreadsheet	49	46	64	60
Database	23	31	48	39
Internet	90	72	56	34
Chat	58	42	34	19
Music	79	na	na	Na
E-Mail	91	71	51	27
Programming	20	14	20	22
Slideshows	21	16	18	14
Games	44	44	50	47

Table 6: Use of ICT (%) Applications [Combined <2&2+ Hours] by Gender

	2001 1st Year N=351	2001 Male Cohort	2001 Female Cohort
Word Processing	89	84	89
Spreadsheet	49	48	49
Database	23	31	38
Internet	90	87	88
Chat	58	54	52
Music	79	73	67
E-Mail	91	88	93
Programming	20	21	16
Slideshows	21	21	21
Laptop	17	17	17
Games	44	51	33

DISCUSSION
Self-Assessed ICT Literacy

There is considerable evidence to suggest that the ICT practices and skills of university students are continuing to change. Home access continues to climb, indicating that the majority of university students possess access to a computer away from the university. The access rate to the Internet by first-year students (84% home Internet and 89% "Hotmail" e-mail) compares with the 77% rate for 18-24-year-olds in the wider Australian community (ABS 8147, 2000). The continuing rapid growth of the Internet applications and Web technology is evident in the home access to the Internet. This figure has increased 52% over the 1998-2001 period, from 33% to 84% for the cohort. The growth in home Internet usage outstrips the 56% of homes that have Internet access in the wider Australian population (ABS 4901, 2001), the U.S.

(Evans, 2002) and the EEC (Eurydice, 2001). The transition or "freshman" university student is a Web "Have." Advanced access, connection to the Internet and coverage of a wide variety of ICT packages is a hallmark of the 2001 transition student.

Web Usage Trends

The rapid growth in the university student's use of Internet applications is fortuitous given that many university schools and faculties are exploring Web delivery for subject material. An interesting feature is the far greater number of first-year students reporting use of HTML and Web pages over previous surveys. First-year students also are greater users of all Internet applications, e-mail, chat and games. This may seem to indicate an emerging surge of students coming into universities with advanced Internet skills, a Web "Have" generation. This surge of Web-savvy students will pose many questions for universities, not only the obvious one about course content. Will universities change delivery platforms to make them Web enabled? Will the Web "Haves" lead the move of universities to become Web enabled? Will university course designers harness the computer literacy of the incoming students? Much of the published research concerning "e-learning" comes from technical and educational analysis. The results from this survey show that the target of "e-learning" is very well positioned to explore the online classroom.

Gender Effects

As in previous surveys (Stein & Craig, 2000), gender differences are marked in several areas. Males prefer to use the Web for entertainment, whereas females prefer research and then communication. This "Toystore vs. Toolbox" comparison was coined by Margolis, Fisher and Miller (2000) and reinforces the findings that show that there is no difference in level or degree of use and no difference in computer knowledge or confidence between the genders. The difference lies in the type of use, entertainment versus communication and research. This trend is also evident in the wider Australian community where 84% of teenage boys use computer games as opposed to 53% of teenage girls (ABS 4901, 2001). U.S. data shows that the 18-24-year-old cohort uses the Web for research and communication in preference to entertainment (Evans, 2002). For university courses and the delivery of course content, this is important as the male students may need additional work on developing Web communications, specially if course content has heavy components of e-mail or group decision making via chat and e-mail. This difference in how the genders use the Web is not to be downplayed. Online learning environments rely heavily on communications, and any students that are loath to check their e-mail or loathe to engage in online chat will be at a disadvantage.

Prepared for "E-Learning"

A fundamental question that must be asked concerns the ability of universities to lead change in adopting "e-learning" environments. At Victoria University course Web pages range from the simple "brochure" type course site, where students only download course material, to the "fully interactive" decision support type site, where students engage each other in course outcomes. This research proposes that the students who are the recipients of "e-learning" are ready willing and able to thrive in online environments. They have access to the Internet, advanced Web practices in e-mail and chat, knowledge and confidence in using the technology and a widespread coverage of other Web practices. It is to be hoped that as "e-learning" advances, it will take into account the sophisticated ICT and Web literacy on the student cohort.

CONCLUSION

So one cog in the e-learning machine is in place, the learner is prepared to engage. What of the other cogs, that is, learning facilitators and learning institutions? As the technology moves to mobile communications and instant messaging and the next wave of communication technologies, the learners will again need to be asked if they are ready to engage. A more important question to ponder is, do designers of e-learning environments take into account the changing nature and mode of information access and learning that university students are adopting? It is proposed that richer analysis of how the Web is used by learners will be undertaken in coming surveys. With any study that is based in one faculty of one university, the question of generalizability is raised. This study is a longitudinal analysis of the students at Victoria University. It is proposed that further studies allowing for a broader view of university students should be carried out to see if the trends raised and discussed in this chapter could be extrapolated to other cohorts.

REFERENCES

ABS 4901. (2001). *Catalogue No. 4901.0—What Kids Get Up To*. Australia. Retrieved May 2001 from the Australian Bureau of Statistics website: http://www.abs.gov.au/.

ABS 8147. (2000). *Catalogue No. 8147.0—Use of the Internet by Householders*. Australia. Retrieved June 2000 from the Australian Bureau of Statistics website: http://www.abs.gov.au/.

ABS 8153. (2001). *Catalogue No. 8153.0—Use of the Internet by Householders*. Australia. Retrieved May 2001 from the Australian Bureau of Statistics website: http://www.abs.gov.au/.

Alberta Education. (1997). *Learner Outcomes in Information and Communication Technology: ECS to Grade 12: A Framework.* Alberta, Canada.

ALLS. (1999). *ICT Literacy: Status Memorandum.* Retrieved May 2001 from: www.nces.ed.gov/surveys/all/documents/ict.pdf.

Arthur, W. & Hart, D. (1990). Empirical relationship between cognitive ability and computer familiarity. *Journal of Research on Computing in Education,* 21, 457.

Carroll, T.G. (2000). If we didn't have the schools we have today, would we create the schools we have today? *Contemporary Issues in Technology and Teacher Education,* 1(1).

Collis, B. & Anderson, R. (1994). Computer literacy for the 1990s: Theoretical issues for an international assessment. *Computers in the Schools,* 11(2), 55-68.

Davis, F. (1989). Perceived usefulness, perceived ease of use, and user acceptance of information technology. *MIS Quarterly,* 13(3), 319-340.

Eurydice. (2001). *Information and Communication Technology in European Education Systems.* Retrieved June 2002 from EEC Technology Education website: www.eurydice.org.as.

Evans, D. (2002). *A Nation Online: How Americans Are Expanding Their Use of the Internet.* Retrieved June 2002 from the U.S. Department of Education website: www.ntia.doc.gov/ntiahome/dn/nationonline_020502.htm.

Healy, J. (1999). *How Computers Affect Our Children's Minds—For Better or Worse.* New York: Simon & Schuster.

ILSSL. (1997). *Information Literacy Standards for Student Learning.* Retrieved May 2001 from: www.ala.org/aasl/stndsdrft.html.

ISR. (1999). *Measuring the Knowledge-Based Economy (ISR 1999-122).* Industry Analysis Branch, Department of Industry, Science and Resources, Canberra, Australia.

Karsten, R. & Roth, R. (1998). Computer self-efficacy: A practical indicator of student computer competency in introductory IS courses. *Informing Science,* 1(3), 34-36.

Kirsch, I., Jamieson, J. & Taylor, C. (1997). *Computer Familiarity Among TOEFL Examinees.* TOEFL Research Report #59, Princeton, New Jersey.

Lee, J. (1986). The effects of past computer experience on computerized aptitude test performance. *Educational and Psychological Measurement,* 26, 727.

Linden, R. & Adams, S. (1992). Technological change: Its effect on the training and performance of older employees. *Journal of Educational Research,* 5, 69.

Lowe, G. & Krahn, H. (1989). Computer skills and use among high school and university graduates. *Canadian Public Policy.*

Margolis, J., Fisher, A. & Miller, F. (2000). Caring about connections: Gender and computing. *IEEE Technology and Society Magazine,* volume.

Meredith, D. et al. (1999). *Real Time—Computers, Change and Schooling.* National sample study of the information technology skills of Australian school students, Australian Key Centre for Cultural and Media Policy.

Miller, F. & Varma, N. (1994). The effects of psychosocial factors in Indian children's attitude towards computers. *Journal of Educational Computing Research*, 10, 223.

NASBE. (1998). *Leader's Guide to Education Technology*. Alexandria, VA: NASBE.

NASBE. (2001). *Any Time, Any Place, Any Path, Any Pace: Taking the Lead on E-Learning Policy*. Alexandria, VA: NASBE.

NCES. (1999-011). *The Condition of Education 1998*. Retrieved June 2000 from the U.S. Department of Education website: http://nces.ed.gov/spider/webspider/1999011.shtml.

NCES. (1999-017). *Internet Access in Public Schools and Classrooms: 1994-1998*. Retrieved June 2000 from the U.S. Department of Education website: http://nces.ed.gov/spider/webspider/1999017.shtml.

NSF. (1998). *Webs, Wires & Waves*. Retrieved May 2001 from the National Science Foundation. Website: http://www.nsf.gov/od/lpa/nstw/teenov.htm.

Oderkirk, J. (1996). Computer literacy—A growing requirement. *Education Quarterly Review*. Statistics Canada, Catalogue No. 81-003-XPB.

OEdTech. (1996). *E-Learning: Putting a World-Class Education at the Fingertips of All Children*. Retrieved May 2001 from the U.S. Department of Education website: www.ed.gov/technology/elearning/e-learning.pdf.

Oliver, R. (1993). The perceptions of school leavers towards IT skills. *Australian Educational Computing*, (May), 45-56.

PISA. (2000). *OECD Project*. Retrieved May 2001 from the OECD website: http://www.pisa.oecd.org/Docs.Download/PISAsampleitemsEng.pdf.

Russell, G. & Holmes, D. (1996). Electronic nomads? Implications of trends in adolescents' use of communications and information technology. *Australian Journal of Educational Technology*, 12(2), 130-144.

Sacks, C., Bellissiomo, Y. & Mergendoller, J. (1993). Attitudes towards computers and computer use: The issue of gender. *Journal of Research on Computing in Education*, 26, 257.

Stein, A. & Craig, A. (1998). Preparatory IT practices & skills of transition business students. *Proceedings of the Third Pacific Rim Conference,* Auckland Institute of Technology, Auckland, July, 457-462.

Stein, A. & Craig, A. (1999). The Web chat & laptops: IT practices & skills of transition students. *Proceedings of ASCILITE99,* Queensland University of Technology, Brisbane, November, 125-135.

Stein, A. & Craig, A. (2000). IT haves & have nots: IT practices & skills of transition students. *Proceedings of ACE2001,* Monash University, Melbourne, December, 125-135.

The New Divide. (2001). *Technology Counts 2001: The New Divide*. Retrieved May 2001 from the Education Week on the Web website: http://www.edweek.org/.

USDoE. (2000). *The Power of the Internet for Learning: Moving from Promise to Practise, Web-Based Education Commission.* Retrieved June 2002 from the U.S. Department of Education website: http://interact.hpcnet.org/webcommission/index.html.

Wenglinsky, H. (2000). *Technology Counts.* Retrieved May 2001 from: www.edweek.org/sreports/tc98.

Chapter X

Strategies for Improving Instructor-Student Communication in Online Education

Stuart C. Freedman
University of Massachusetts Lowell, USA

Steven F. Tello
University of Massachusetts Lowell, USA

David Lewis
University of Massachusetts Lowell, USA

ABSTRACT

This chapter identifies potential communication barriers between instructor and students in an online educational environment, and suggests ways to reduce or eliminate them. There are at least five such barriers—social distance, conceptual confusion, fear and mistrust, isolation and disconnectedness, and lost efficacy—which, when present, are likely to diminish the effectiveness of an online course. Several approaches to structuring online lecture notes and composing individual student messages are proposed that are hypothesized to increase the likelihood that student satisfaction and learning goals will be achieved. It is assumed that the application of these communication tactics will enhance the attractiveness of online courses, particularly among students who would not otherwise have access to higher education. Suggestions for future research are proposed.

INTRODUCTION

Online education, also referred to as online instruction (Kearsley, 2000) or Web-based instruction (Khan, 1997), is becoming an increasingly popular approach to delivering academic courses (Saba, 2000). Online education is a form of technology-facilitated distance education. It occurs in a computer-mediated environment where the teacher and student are physically separated for some portion, if not all, of the instructional process (Turoff & Hiltz, 1995).

At one mid-size university in the northeast, for example, the number of students taking online courses has been increasing steadily over the past several years, as has the range of courses offered and the number of faculty participating. Between 1997 and 2002, the number of students rose from 410 to 5,430, and the number of courses offered increased from 25 to 265. Given the growth of online courses, and the likelihood that this growth will continue as Internet use increases, it is important to understand how best to design and deliver Internet-based instructional material in ways that facilitate both student learning and satisfaction with the overall educational experience.

CHARACTERISTICS OF ONLINE EDUCATION

Online courses may use a cohort model, where students move through the course material in a paced group (Motiwalla & Tello, 2000), or they may be self-paced, allowing individual students to start and complete courses at their own pace. Regardless of the pacing, students typically have access to course materials 24 hours per day from any Internet access point (Hiltz & Wellman, 1997). Students access the course website using Web browser software over an Internet connection (Kearsley, 2000; Motiwalla & Tello, 2000). Course lectures may be presented as text, as PowerPoint presentations or as streaming audio/video presentations. Course demonstrations or labs may be presented using streaming audio/video or graphic simulation software. Simulation software often allows students to manipulate variables in the simulation, affecting the outcome of the demonstration. Student assignments and projects may be returned to the instructor as e-mail attachments, through online Web forms or as student PowerPoint presentations. Communication, questions and discussion between students and faculty and among students are facilitated through the use of asynchronous (delayed) and synchronous (real-time, simultaneous) communication tools (Collison, Elbaum, Havind & Tinker, 2000; Kearsley, 2000; Motiwalla & Tello, 2000; Salmon, 2000).

COMMUNICATION BARRIERS

Online education is defined by the technology used to facilitate the delivery of course content, and mediate interaction between student and teacher and among students. Computer-mediated communication (CMC) is a central characteristic of online education (Hiltz & Wellman, 1997; Kearsley, 2000; Turoff & Hiltz, 1995). CMC, in its various technologies and forms, supports one-to-one communication, one-to-many communication and many-to-many communication in both a synchronous and asynchronous format (Ljosa as cited in Holmberg, 1995; Moore & Kearsley, 1995). These multiple approaches to communication support various methods of student access, pedagogical strategies and forms of interaction with course content, the instructor and fellow students.

As in traditional face-to-face (FTF) classroom settings, good practice in online education requires frequent instructor-student communication (Chickering & Ehrmann, 1996). Communication, or interaction, between student and instructor is considered essential to the learning process in both FTF (Chickering & Gamson, 1987; Kuh & Hu, 2001; Pascarella & Terenzini, 1976) and online education (Garrison, 1987; Holmberg, 1995; Moore, 1989; Smith & Dillon, 1999). However, unlike the FTF classroom, communication in online courses takes place primarily electronically and in writing. This poses some unique problems regarding communication quality that online instructors must overcome. For example, how can one communicate clearly and completely when there is no direct, face-to-face interaction? How does one know whether students received a message from the instructor as it was intended? How can students be involved in a course in which they rarely, if ever, meet anyone else in the class? What instructor communication style will increase the likelihood that students feel involved in the course, and believe that their educational needs are being met?

Research regarding the broader field of distance education, of which online education is one method, offers some direction regarding these questions. Moore suggests that the concept of distance "is not measured in miles or minutes" between the instructor and student, but is a function of the dialogue and individualization available within any educational program (Moore, 1991, p. 56). By dialogue, Moore is referring to essential two-way communication between student and instructor. He also introduces the term "structure," which refers to the extent to which the objectives, teaching methods and procedures within an educational program can be adapted to meet the needs of individual students. Moore suggests that the distance experienced between student and teacher is in part determined by the level of dialogue and structure within an education program. When dialogue is high and structure is low, the student and teacher experience less distance than when the converse occurs. Moore also suggests that an education program that supports high dialogue and low structure lends itself to a conversational approach between teacher and student, facilitating and encouraging communication between the two.

In his examination of print-based correspondence courses, Holmberg (1989) introduced the concept of guided, didactic conversation. Holmberg's theory proposes that student motivation and success in distance education courses can be facilitated through the development of course materials and instructor-student communication that is perceived as friendly and conversational in style (Mitchell, 1992). Holmberg suggests that distance education course materials should have the following characteristics: a) easy accessibility; b) explicit advice and suggestions to students; c) frequent invitations to students to communicate, question and exchange views; d) personal or professional relevance to students; f) an informal and conversational instructor communication style; and g) clear communications to students regarding changes in course themes and topics (Holmberg, 1983).

More recent research on the design and implementation of online courses has suggested a number of variables likely to influence course effectiveness. These include class size and prior experience with computer-mediated communication (Vrasidas & McIsaac, 1999); availability of technical and instructor support (Daughery, 1998); instructor attentiveness to student needs, and the extent to which there is synchronous, i.e., real-time, interaction (Lara, Howell, Dominquez & Navarro, 2001). Even with the greatest of care, however, courses do not always run smoothly. Hara and Kling (1999), for example, suggest that student frustration with Web-based courses can result from insufficient instructor feedback and ambiguous instructions regarding course procedures and requirements, often producing feelings of isolation. On a more behavioral level, Tello (2002) found that positive student attitudes regarding instructor feedback and use of asynchronous discussion tools were highly correlated with student course persistence rates. In general, this research suggests that online course effectiveness is determined in part by the type, quality and frequency of communication that takes place between students and instructor. To the extent these electronic interactions are poorly designed and managed, communication barriers are likely to arise that impede the achievement of course objectives (George & Jones, 2002, pp. 441-445).

The authors' experiences in the design, development and teaching of online courses suggest there are at least five types of barriers that can negatively affect student performance and satisfaction in an online course environment that must be overcome. These are: 1) the *barrier of social distance*, resulting from overly formalistic instructor communication that reinforces student-instructor status differences; 2) the *barrier of conceptual confusion*, resulting from poorly organized and presented course material; 3) the *barrier of fear and mistrust*, resulting from instructor communication that is perceived by students as non-supportive, indifferent to student needs or, in extreme cases, overtly hostile; 4) the *barrier of isolation and disconnectedness*, resulting from insufficient speed and frequency of instructor communication; and 5) *the barrier of lost efficacy*, due to instructor rigidity in applying course rules, procedures and policies. This chapter explores ways to reduce many of these barriers, and improve the student-instructor communication process.

Communication in online courses takes place, in part, through 1) the posting of online lecture notes that typically accompany textbook reading assignments, and 2) electronic responses to individual student messages communicated in the form of e-mails or discussion board postings. This chapter explores how instructors can approach these two general methods of communication in ways that reduce the communication barriers suggested above, and increase the likelihood that student learning and satisfaction goals are achieved. These approaches are grouped into three strategy categories, each addressing one or more of these barriers.

Online Lecture Notes—Context

How can an online instructor create lecture notes in a way that, apart from lecture content, reduces the *barrier of social distance*, and facilitates student learning and course satisfaction? Consistent with Holmberg's (1989) concept of guided, didactic conversation, it is suggested that an approach to electronic communication that simulates informal face-to-face interaction will more likely be experienced by students as *spoken* communication, and as more friendly and conversational **(Strategy 1)**. This is likely to improve the perceived "readability" and value of online lecture material and, as a result, enhance student learning and course satisfaction.

In practice, the authors have found several approaches that are hypothesized to facilitate this experience. These are:

- *Using contractions common in spoken language* (e.g., "*It's* likely that…" versus "*It is* likely that…"). Spoken language uses contractions much, if not most, of the time. Communication, particularly when it is spontaneous and informal, would appear awkward and robot-like if it did not. One exception is when emphasis, forcefulness or the communication of a high degree of certainty is intended by the speaker (e.g., "It *is* a good idea to be flexible with rules…" versus "It's a good idea…"). Using contractions is therefore likely to enhance the receiver's sense that an electronic message "sounds" more like direct face-to-face interaction.

- *Using spoken expressions at the beginning of written sentences, to create a tone and feeling of informality* (e.g., "Well, what this means to me is that…"). Spoken communication is often filled with words and expressions that have little or no informational content. They are often referred to as "time fillers" (e.g., "well"; "um"; "ya know"). When used too frequently, they can become distracting. When used occasionally, and in an intentional, targeted manner, they can facilitate the experience of talking rather than reading.

- *Writing in the first person, and in the active, rather than passive, voice.* For example, compare the following two sentences: 1) "What I'm saying is that if you reduce resistance, you'll more easily change an employee's behavior." 2) "In general, if resistance is reduced, employee behavior will more easily be changed." The first approach is no less precise or rigorous a statement than the second. It does, however, better reflect how people tend to speak, as compared to write.

- *Occasionally using what sound like incomplete sentences, as one often encounters in the dialogue of good novels* (e.g., "That's a fact. Hard to believe, isn't it?"). As the example suggests, this type of language does not necessarily contain ideas directly related to the content of the course. Rather, it can have the effect of reinforcing or emphasizing a previous statement in a way that is not appropriate when communicating in formal, written language.

- *Using "friendly" expressions that make it easier for students to perceive the instructor as approachable, and as someone with whom they can take intellectual risks* (e.g., "That's a fact, folks. Hard to believe, isn't it?") (compare this statement to the example in the previous paragraph). Formal written language does not refer to the message's audience as "folks." In fact, it generally does not refer to the recipient of the message at all. Spoken language, in contrast, permits an instructor this "linguistic license," and is therefore likely to enhance a student's sense of face-to-face communication, and connection to the "speaker."

- *Making consistent use of color, bold face and italics to communicate where emphasis of various kinds would be if a given statement were spoken, rather than written.* This may be thought of as a type of graphical, rather than text-based, tool that will be perceived and understood by students in the same way that a picture is perceived and understood differently than words. To apply this idea, one might, for example, use red and/or bold face to highlight important points in prose text, and italics to symbolize verbal emphasis (e.g., "*Now*, do you see the importance of **new information technology** as a key determinant of **organizational productivity**?").

Online Lecture Notes—Content

Regarding the content and structure of lecture notes, it is hypothesized that the *barrier of conceptual confusion* can be reduced, and the understanding and perceived value of online lecture material enhanced, by visually structuring course material **(Strategy 2)** in the following ways:

- *Creating lecture material that, to an appropriate degree, complements or supplements the course textbook (if a text is being used) rather than "rehashes" it.* This suggestion is self-explanatory, and often applies to traditional classroom settings as well as online courses. It may be more salient to students in an online environment, however, in that students in a traditional classroom are, in a sense, a "captive audience." Online students, in contrast, can "leave the classroom" if they become bored, or consider a lecture to be "useless," anytime they wish. If this happens too often, given that online courses tend to require more self-imposed discipline on the student's part over the course of the semester (i.e., walking out of a classroom is probably more difficult to do than walking away from a computer screen), the student is more likely to fall behind in an online course and encounter academic difficulty.

- *Drawing heavily on "real-world" examples of course concepts, particularly if the students are practically-minded working adults* (although the appropriateness of this depends considerably on the course subject). This suggestion may apply as readily to traditional courses as online classes. To the extent, however, that online students are more likely to be working adults who may be seeking a somewhat more direct correspondence between their academic courses and job applications, the regular use of practical examples can facilitate student understanding of, and satisfaction with, the content of an online course.

- *Developing a bulleted outline or PowerPoint graphic for each lecture topic within each weekly lesson that reflects or summarizes the flow of lecture material, and gives students a "bigger picture" of how the details of lecture content "hang together."* For example, in a course in organizational behavior, there is usually at least one lecture that analyzes the types of power tactics available to managers who seek to influence others at work. The inclusion of an outline or graphic that bullets the types of tactics discussed in the lecture, and lists them in the order in which they are discussed, will highlight the key concepts for students. This could facilitate their ability to understand and systematically integrate lecture details. That is, it will help them distinguish "the forest from the trees."

- *Systematically reducing font size as the outline moves from main title, to headings, to sub-headings, to bulleted points.* This is merely a graphical way to visually symbolize for students the development of lecture concepts as they flow from general to specific. It is another way to help them distinguish the "big picture" from the details.

- *Using one text color, background or font for lecture outlines and another for lecture notes.* Visually distinguishing outlines and lecture material in this way can potentially reduce the "monotony" of what might otherwise be perceived by students as a "boring" monochromatic presentation. Of course, the use of color should be judicious, keeping in mind that not all students perceive color contrasts or color. The use of color should be combined with another distinguishing marker such as size, font or underlining.

- *Dividing a large lecture into several smaller "pieces" that give students a sense of making progress when they reach closure on a "piece of the pie" (i.e., part of the online lecture), even though they may still have a lot further to go before the "pie" is fully "consumed."* Long online lectures can be experienced by students as tedious and difficult to read. Organizing a lecture into many smaller subtopics is similar to dividing a long novel into many smaller chapters. It provides the reader with natural break-points at which to "call it a day," and thus prevents arbitrary breaks in the continuity and flow of ideas. It also permits students to feel like they are making progress as they move toward completion of the lesson.

- *Using italics and boldface consistently to highlight key concepts and ideas.* This is another graphical technique to assist students in identifying what the instructor considers to be the most important points in a lesson. It is a way to communicate what is the "wheat" and what is the "chaff." Italics and boldface can be used separately for different purposes, or together to indicate the strongest possible emphasis.

Individual Student Messages

The *barriers of fear, mistrust, disconnectedness and lost efficacy* may be reduced through more personalized, supportive, complete and timely communication with students **(Strategy 3)**. It is important to recognize that online students are customers who are often "buying" more than just course content. They are often time-constrained, working adults who are also seeking flexibility and responsiveness from both the instructor and educational institution.

There are several ways in which instructors can convey to students that they are respected; that their unique concerns, uncertainties and pressures are understood; and that the instructor is willing to work with them as individuals to solve both anticipated and unexpected problems (e.g., an unforeseen business trip) that arise over the course of a semester. These more subtle, often indirect, messages from instructor to student may be conveyed through the exchange of e-mails, and possibly discussion board postings. They form the "between the lines," or "context," message embedded within instructor communications about such issues as course administration, student performance, Internet access problems, student requests for "special treatment" due to unavoidable job constraints and so on.

It is suggested that supportive context messages will be communicated to students when instructors directly or indirectly exhibit *flexibility and responsiveness* in their online communications. Instructors may send these messages in the following ways:

- *If a student asks that a particular e-mail be re-sent because the student "never received it," send the message out again "with a smile" (e.g., "sure, I'll send it right out").* It is easy for instructors to communicate to students "between the lines" that they are annoyed at having to do this. Instructor disapproval might even be sent inadvertently. If this type of negative message is communicated, the student will most likely "pick it up," and begin to perceive the student-instructor relationship as hostile and defensive, rather than friendly and supportive.

- *If a student cannot take an examination, or finish an assignment, at the scheduled time (e.g., due to temporary job overload or child care difficulties), permit the student to complete it at a different time,* if the explanation for the requested delay appears reasonable and honestly communicated. Always be aware that the goal of the instructor is to evaluate what students have learned, rather than how they respond to time pressure and other non-academic constraints.

- *If a student does poorly on an examination, and asks for help, give as much help as is reasonable and possible, without communicating annoyance "between the lines"* (e.g., "Sure, <<student's first name>>, what would you like some help with?" versus "O.K., but you're really expected to learn this material on your own."). This, of course, should not be done in a way that "spoon feeds" students, creates a "non-level playing field" for the rest of the class or reduces academic standards.

- *Begin each e-mail to a student with "Hi <<first name>>, or "Hello <<first name>>."* This will tend to personalize, and "de-formalize" an electronic message. If the message is an unpleasant one (e.g., to report a poor grade to a student), "hello" rather than "hi" might be an approach that is more congruent with message content. Also, the instructor should consider using his or her first as well as last name in all communications to reduce "social distance."

- *Anticipate what is going to confuse or create uncertainty for students, and address these issues as early in the semester as possible,* preferably at the beginning of the course (e.g., "I can't attend your chat hour because of a conflict with another class. Will this hurt my grade?"). One approach would be to create a series of e-mail messages clarifying these anticipated student difficulties, and stagger their distribution over the first week or two of the semester. Since students do not always read all of their e-mails, or might forget over time what they were told very early in the semester, it might even be appropriate to send some of these messages more than once.

- *Respond quickly to e-mails and other messages from students.* Until the instructor responds, online students with questions or problems, particularly ones that are not relevant to other students in the class, will have no idea what to assume or expect regarding the issue in question. If the instructor does not, or cannot, respond quickly, the instructor should apologize when he or she does respond (e.g., "Sorry for the late response…"), and tell the student why the response was later than it should have been, if appropriate. In addition to reducing the *barrier of self-efficacy*, this type of instructor response is also likely to reduce the *barrier of isolation and disconnectedness* by creating a "classroom climate" in which students will feel informed, secure and able to cope with the constraints in their lives that affect their ability to succeed academically .

CONCLUSIONS AND SUGGESTIONS FOR FUTURE RESEARCH

For any relationship to be productive and satisfying to participants, the parties must possess the interpersonal, or "people," skills needed to foster an environment that stimulates trust, spontaneity, risk-taking and creativity. When these conditions are present, the parties will more likely be motivated to continue their relationship and achieve desired goals. In general, these skills are reflected in the verbal and non-verbal behaviors each party directs toward the other. When instructor-student interaction takes place in an online environment, the challenge therefore is to identify how electronic communication tools can be used to approximate the positive experience students have when they are interacting face-to-face with an interpersonally competent instructor.

This chapter suggests three strategies for achieving this goal. The *first* is to reduce the barrier of social distance between student and instructor by writing in ways that approximate the characteristics of spoken language. Some approaches are to use contractions; include expressions used in spoken communication; and write in the first person, active voice. Instructors can also use "friendly" expressions; use color, boldface and italics to communicate verbal emphasis; and occasionally use incomplete sentences as is often done in everyday speech.

A *second* strategy for facilitating student trust, spontaneity, risk-taking and creativity is to reduce the barriers of fear, mistrust, disconnectedness and lost efficacy. This is likely to be achieved when an online instructor provides information and responds to student messages quickly; personalizes a message by beginning it with "Hi" or "Hello" and addresses students by their first names; communicates support for them "between the lines" rather than indifference; and is flexible with class rules and policies.

A *third* strategy is to reduce the barrier of conceptual confusion by visually structuring course-related information in ways that facilitate easier comprehension. Specific techniques include making extensive use of bulleted outlines and graphics; using color and font size to differentiate outlines from lecture text, and different levels of abstraction within outlines; using italics and boldface to highlight key ideas; and dividing long lectures into many self-contained shorter presentations.

Anecdotal experience suggests that the ideas presented in this chapter can attenuate the emergence of student-instructor communication barriers, and enhance student learning and satisfaction with the online course experience. Future research is required, however, to investigate the extent to which they have these positive effects.

One of the more general questions requiring empirical investigation is the extent to which the proposed taxonomy of communication barriers in online education is complete, and conceptually sound. It was proposed above that these potential barriers may be classified into five types—social distance, conceptual confusion, fear and mistrust, isolation and disconnectedness, and lost efficacy. Do online students in fact experience these barriers and, if so, under what conditions do they arise? Are there other barriers that are yet to be identified?

A related question is the extent to which these barriers are conceptually distinct, or overlap to some degree. If they are distinct, which specific behaviors lead to the emergence of which barrier? If they overlap, which ones tend to "hang together" and emerge as a result of the same instructor behaviors? It would be useful to determine whether the same instructor behavior can cause more than one barrier to arise. For example, if an instructor fails to address important course-related issues early in the semester that are likely to create uncertainty for students later on, might this create not only a feeling of lost efficacy, but also conceptual confusion and a sense of greater social distance? Likewise, an instructor who uses contractions and spoken expressions in written communications might not only reduce the barrier of social distance, but also the barriers of fear and mistrust.

Finally, do some communication barriers have a more salient effect on students than others, and might the importance of a particular barrier be mediated by student characteristics? For example, do older, more mature students who have had considerable work experience and go to school part time exhibit less concern about the barrier of social distance than younger, less mature students who are attending school full time and still live with their parents? Another question is whether students who have had considerable online course experience have fewer difficulties with an instructor who communicates poorly than students who are studying online for the first time.

An effective online instructor recognizes the unique problems that can arise in an online teaching, as compared to traditional classroom, environment, and finds ways to electronically simulate the positive aspects of direct face-to-face interaction with students. These issues are particularly relevant in settings where courses and programs are being provided to students who would not otherwise have access to higher education. It is our hypothesis that student learning and satisfaction with the overall online experience will be enhanced by creating a "virtual classroom" in which instructors are creative in the presentation of course content, flexible with the "rules" and responsive to student needs.

REFERENCES

Chickering, A. & Ehrmann, S. (1996). Implementing the seven principles: Technology as lever. *AAHE Bulletin,* (October), 3-6.

Chickering, A. & Gamson, Z. (1987). Seven principles for good practice in undergraduate education. *AAHE Bulletin,* 39(7), 3-7.

Collison, G., Elbaum, B., Havind, S. & Tinker, R. (2000). *Facilitating Online Learning: Effective Strategies for Moderators.* Madison, WI: Atwood.

Daughery, M. (1998). University faculty and student perceptions of Web-based instruction. *Journal of Distance Education,* 13(1), 21-39.

Garrison, D.R. (1987). Researching dropout in distance education. *Distance Education,* 8(1), 95-101.

George, J. & Jones, G. (2002). *Organizational Behavior.* Upper Saddle River, NJ: Prentice-Hall.

Hara, N. & Kling, R. (1999). Student's frustrations with a Web-based distance education course. *First Monday,* 4(12).

Hiltz, R.S. & Wellman, B.(1997). Asynchronous learning networks as a virtual classroom. *Communications of the ACM,* 40(9), 44-49.

Holmberg, B. (1983). Guided didactic conversation. In Sewart, D., Keegan, D. & Holmberg, B. (Eds.), *Distance Education: International Perspectives.* London: Croom-Helm, 114-122.

Holmberg, B. (1989). *Theory and Practice of Distance Education.* New York: Routledge.

Kearsley, G. (2000). *Online Education: Learning and Teaching in Cyberspace.* Belmont, CA: Wadsworth/Thomson Learning.

Khan, B.H. (1997). Web-Based Instruction (WBI): What is it and why is it? In Khan, B.H. (Ed.), *Web-Based Instruction.* Englewood Cliffs, NJ: Educational Technology Publishers, 5-18.

Kuh, G.D. & Hu, S. (2001). The effects of student-faculty interaction in the 1990s. *The Review of Higher Education,* 24(3), 309-332.

Lara, L., Howell, R., Heronimo, D. & Navarro, J. (2001). Synchronous and asynchronous interactions of bilingual Hispanic pre- and in-service teachers in distance learning. *American Journal of Distance Education,* 15(3), 50-67.

Mitchell, I. (1992). Guided didactic conversation: The use of Holmberg's concept in higher education. In Ortner, G.E., Graff, K. & Wilmersdoerfer, H. (Eds.), *Distance Education as Two-Way Communication.* Frankfurt: Peter Lang, 123-132.

Moore, M.G.(1989). Three types of interaction. *American Journal of Distance Education,* 3(2), 1-6.

Moore, M.G. (1991). Theory of distance education. *Distance Education Symposium: Selected Papers Part 3.* ACSDE Research Monograph 9, 53-67.

Moore, M.G. & Kearsley, G. (1995). *Distance Education: A Systems View.* Belmont, CA: Wadsworth.

Motiwalla, L. & Tello, S. (2000). Distance learning on the Internet: An exploratory study. *The Internet in Higher Education,* 2(4), 253-264.

Pascarella, E.T. & Terenzini, P.T. (1976). Informal interaction with faculty and freshman ratings of academic and non-academic experience of college. *Journal of Educational Research,* 70, 35-41.

Saba, F. (2000). Online education and learning. *Distance Education,* 4(1), 1.

Salmon, G. (2000). *E-Moderating: The Key to Teaching and Learning Online.* London: Kogan Page.

Smith, P. & Dillon, C. (1999). Comparing distance learning and classroom learning: conceptual considerations. *The American Journal of Distance Education,* 13(2), 6-23.

Tello, S. (2002). *An Analysis of the Relationship Between Instructional Interaction and Student Persistence in Online Education.* Doctoral Dissertation, Graduate School of Education, University of Massachusetts Lowell.

Turoff, M. & Hiltz, R.S. (1995). Designing and evaluating a virtual classroom. *Journal of Information Technology for Teacher Education,* 4(2), 197-215.

Vrasidas, C. & McIsaac, M. (1999). Factors influencing interaction in an online course. *American Journal of Distance Education,* 13(3), 22-36.

Chapter XI

Current Issues and Trends of Internet-Based Education in the Philippines

Bea V. Espejo
Ateneo De Manila University, The Philippines

Marlene P. Mana
Ateneo De Manila University, The Philippines

Sheila B. Bato
Ateneo De Manila University, The Philippines

ABSTRACT

The Philippines is one of many developing countries that has begun using the Internet to establish closer communication with entities abroad. Some educational institutions have begun engaging in Internet-based distance education to provide accessible, anytime, anywhere education. These ventures have focused on the tertiary level and post-graduate level of education. The quality of the Internet education that they provide has shown them to be at par with western institutions. However, in the primary and secondary levels of education, the situation is one of a large disparity between the levels of education provided by public and private schools of the nation. Many public educational facilities are located in remote areas where they do not even have electricity, telephone facilities, let alone Internet access. Due to lack of funding, the government has been forced to focus first on providing these schools with the most basic of amenities. Aside from these efforts, the government has also begun to provide ICT facilities to chosen schools that meet the basic requirements for ICT to function. The chapter discusses each of these major points in detail.

INTRODUCTION

This chapter focuses on the current issues and trends prevalent in the implementation of Internet-based education in the Philippines. Some Philippine educational organizations have responded to the need to have easily accessible, anytime, anywhere education. The authors aim to put forward the answers to the following points: (1) What is the current situation of Philippine public schools? (2) How prolific has Internet usage become in the Philippines? (3) What type of Internet-based education do Internet-based educational institutions provide? (4) What development stages did the institutions experience in setting up their Internet-based programs? (5) What support does the Philippine government provide for institutions that wish to engage in Internet-based education? (6) What actions should the Philippine government take to promote and provide Internet-based education nationwide?

BACKGROUND

The rapid growth of Internet-based distance education worldwide has prompted Philippine organizations to respond by developing their own Internet-based education programs. In comparison to their western counterparts, the Internet-based education program mentioned in this chapter is relatively young, being in effect from anywhere between two to eight years. Aside from the need to respond to this current trend in education, several factors that influenced the feasibility of these programs are listed in the following paragraphs.

Internet usage in the Philippines continues to grow each year. As of the fourth quarter of 2001, an estimated 1.5 million Filipinos had used the Internet out of the 78 million total population. About one-third of these users access the Internet using their home computers (Lugo, 2002), while others gain access to the facility at school or at work. Still others connect to the Internet by going to Internet cafes, whose proliferation has contributed greatly to the growth of Internet usage in the country (Toral , 2001).

The Internet cafes have become popular among the Filipino Internet users because they are able to gain access to the Internet at an affordable price of $.25 to $1.00 an hour (Toral, 2001). This can be used to show that Internet usage is influenced by the economic conditions in the country. If people can afford it, then they stay connected. Otherwise, they do not. In fact, a recent survey done by ACNielsen Philippines reveals that people from upper and middle classes use the Internet more than those in the lower class. Yet, the same survey shows that the number of Internet users who belong to Class D is slowly increasing (Lugo, 2002).

The Internet cafes are especially useful to those who do not own computers. Those who do, can conveniently connect to the Internet at home by subscribing to an Internet service provider (ISP). Actually, there are around 200 ISPs that exist in the Philippines today, and most of them offer 56K service at an average rate of $0.50 an hour. Some providers even offer DSL, wireless and fixed broadband, cable and satellite Internet facilities. However, people from the upper and middle classes, those who actually own a computer and can afford to subscribe, are the ones who can very well appreciate these services (Toral, 2002).

Internet usage in the Philippines, although very much influenced by the economic situation in the country, is affected by another factor, which is age. According to the survey done by ACNielsen, the majority of Internet users are aged 29 and below. The reason behind the large number is that this age group is the least resistant to technology and considers it, especially the Internet, a part of their lives (Lugo, 2002).

A growth in Internet access in the Philippine schools has been observed, particularly in the Visayas and Mindanao areas, and the occurrence is attributed to the age group mentioned above (Lugo, 2002). It is, however, imperative to note that most of these schools are private schools, those that use computer resources for teaching and learning. The public schools, on the other hand, use the computers mostly for administrative purposes and not for teaching (Rodrigo, 2001). This is why the bulk of Internet usage in Philippine education can be linked to the country's private schools.

Most of the schools in the Philippines today use the Internet as a supplement to traditional classroom methods. Some schools though are already offering full Internet-based education. Examples of schools with full Internet-based education are the University of Philippines Open University, De LaSalle University MBA Online, Ateneo de Manila's Center for Journalism and the Ateneo De Manila Loyola Schools.

SURVEY OF ONLINE DISTANCE EDUCATION INSTITUTIONS

University of the Philippines Open University

The University of the Philippines Open University was established by the UP board of Regents on February 23, 1995, when they recognized the "perennial challenge of providing high quality higher education to a growing population" in the

Philippines. Due to the limited resources available to the university, the different campuses cannot accept all of the students who apply for admission and qualify for entry. Through their Open University, the UP system was able to "respond to growing demands for quality graduate and undergraduate education even in areas which do not have a UP campus" (Open University, 2002).

The Open University is not the first distance learning program of UP. In 1967 the Los Baños campus started the first school-on-the-air program over the radio. In 1984 the Los Baños campus developed the Diploma in Science Teaching (DST) program, which aimed to upgrade science and mathematics teachers in the country. The DST program was launched in 1988; it was the first degree program offered through distance education. In 1992 the UP-Distance Education Program (UP-DEP) was approved by the Board of Regents, and in 1994 the UP-DEP committee began formulating the policies and programs with distance education as an alternative mode of instruction. In 1995 the UP Open University was established (Open University, 2002).

The Open University offers both undergraduate- and graduate-level courses, currently making use of their custom-made platform. The mode of instruction varies from course to course. Some courses are offered completely in an online environment, others are a mix, some sessions are held in the various learning centers of the open universities (Open University, 2002).

De LaSalle University MBA Online

The MBA Online program of De LaSalle University aims to give a convenient option for technologically literate and self-motivated learner. The program makes use of the WebCT platform to offer its courses (MBA Online, 2002).

MBA Online has two modes for their online courses—mixed mode and full online courses. In mixed mode the students meet their professor face-to-face around eight times during the run of the course, the rest of the course activities being conducted in an online environment. In full online mode students only physically meet their professor once, during the orientation session; all of the course activities are conducted online (MBA Online, 2002).

Ateneo de Manila University E-Learning Ventures

CFJ Online

The Konrad Adenauer Center for Journalism (CFJ) at the Ateneo de Manila University in conjunction with the Ateneo's Department of Information Systems and Computer Science (DISCS) began their e-learning venture in April 2001, offering online seminars on different journalism topics to reporters and editors from all over Asia. During the experimentation phase Blackboard.com was chosen as the initial platform to offer the seminars, due to the following reasons: Blackboard.com was evaluated as a very user-friendly interface for both students and instructors; it offers support for both asynchronous and online education; it is based on the World Wide Web and therefore could be ideally accessed through a minimum of technological requirements; and it may be used free of charge (Escaler, 2002).

In the latter part of 2001, Blackboard.com announced that it was discontinuing its free service and problems did emerge in this period, primarily due to the performance of the Blackboard.com software that made access to the online classroom difficult and frustrating for all parties involved. In December 2001, after another review of existing platforms, WebCT was purchased to launch the second year of seminars offered by CFJ (Escaler, 2002).

The online seminars offered by CFJ are conducted completely in an online environment. There is no actual face-to-face contact between the instructor and the students.

Loyola Schools Online

Several instructors in the Loyola Schools of the Ateneo de Manila University have been using websites, for the past few years, to complement and support their classroom lectures. The main purpose of the websites are to give the students basic information for the courses, such as course outlines, reference lists, downloading the PowerPoint Slides used in class, project specifications, links to related websites, related software and deadline details.

In June 2002, the Loyola Schools began using the WebCT platform. At present the platform is still being used as a supplement for the traditional face-to-face lectures with value added. The e-mail, discussion board and chat features of the platform allow for more communication between the students and the instructor. The testing feature is also being used to conduct quizzes and exams.

QUALITY ISSUES

This chapter makes use of the benchmarks developed by the National Education Association to measure the quality of Web-based distance learning programs of these key institutions in the Philippines. There are seven aspects to the benchmark (Institute for Higher Education Policy, 2000, pp. 2-3):

(1) *Institutional Support* covers the activities of the institution that helps to ensure the creation of an environment that is conducive to developing and maintaining quality in distance education.

(2) *Course Development* covers the benchmarks for developing the actual courseware, be it produced by an individual or a group of individuals such as faculty, subject experts or commercial enterprises.

(3) *Teaching and Learning Process* constitutes the activities that pertain to pedagogy, including issues such as: interactivity, collaboration and modular learning.

(4) *Course Structure* addresses policies and procedures that support the learning process.

(5) *Student Support* is the series of student services found in any campus such as admissions, financial aid and student expectations.

(6) *Faculty Support* covers the criteria that assist the faculty in teaching online, plus policies for faculty transition and continued assistance.

(7) *Evaluation and Assessment* are the policies and procedures that address how the institution evaluates Internet-based distance learning, including assessment and data collection.

All of the aforementioned institutions have performed well based on these benchmarks. In spite of their relatively 'young' age, these Internet-based education programs, based on the benchmarks, measure at more or less the same level as their western counterparts.

GOVERNMENT SUPPORT

The Philippine government supports the modernization of Philippine education, which includes Internet-based education. The Department of Education, Commission on Higher Education (CHED), and Technical Education and Skills Development Authority (TESDA) are the executive arms of the Philippine Government that work together with the private sector to provide Internet-based education in the Philippines. In addition, the Senate and the House of Representatives have been proposing bills to find funding and encourage the private sector in supporting government education modernization projects.

Unfortunately, the most involvement that the government agencies are able to provide is minimal. Private schools and other entities are still the ones initiating the development and implementation of Internet-based courses. The agencies are just there to authorize the private entities interested in providing Internet-based education. They are responsible for identifying standards and ensuring that those interested in offering Internet-based courses meet the standards. CHED is responsible for authorizing schools that offer long-term Internet-based courses that would lead to either an undergraduate or graduate degrees. On the other hand, TESDA is responsible for authorizing schools or other private entities that offer short-term Internet-based technical and specialized courses.

OBSTACLES IN IMPLEMENTING INTERNET-BASED EDUCATION

Due to economic factors, the Philippines as a developing country finds it difficult to implement this alternative teaching methodology. In comparison with most rich nations that spend as much as US$430 per child on non-salary education expenditures, other poor countries only spend approximately US$5 per child. That is why in most developing countries, school buildings do not have concrete flooring, furniture, electricity and water. This is clearly apparent in some provincial schools in the Philippines wherein classroom furniture such as chairs, tables, blackboards and laboratory equipments are lacking. Some of them do not even have electricity and water (Rodrigo, 2001, pp.130-132).

Not all areas where schools are located have electricity and Internet connection. Most of these schools are located in remote provincial provinces wherein local Internet service providers and telephone lines are not available. This poses a major obstacle in implementing Internet-based education.

DEPARTMENT OF EDUCATION ADOPT-A-SCHOOL PROGRAM

The obstacles mentioned in the previous section limited the Department of Education from venturing into developing Internet-based method of instruction. They are geared into providing information and communication technology (ICT) facilities first to schools that have the basic requirements needed to set-up an ICT facility, which is electricity and enough space to place the computer systems to be installed.

The obstacles have also led the Department of Education to establish the "Adopt-a-School Program" to augment the perennial problem of financial shortages. The program has its legal basis in Republic Act 8525 that encourages private sectors to support and provide assistance to various schools such as infrastructure, teachers, textbooks, equipment, health and nutrition, classroom learning kits and other instructional support. The program facilitates the strengthening of external partnerships with other education stakeholders. It is undertaken together with the interested private sector through a Memorandum of Agreement forged between DECS and the interested firms/companies (1999 DECS Annual Report).

The Adopt-a-School program has been in-charge of distributing computer hardware and software resources for the Department of Education modernization projects. Currently, one of their tasks is to allocate equipment to be used for ICT to improve teaching and learning the prescribed curriculum. Recipient schools, mostly from the provincial areas, are identified and notified prior to the delivery of the equipments.

DEPARTMENT OF EDUCATION BUREAU OF SECONDARY EDUCATION

The Bureau of Secondary Education (BSE) is one proponent under the Department of Education that promotes the application of ICT to teaching in Secondary Public Schools. One of their projects is the Distance Learning Program-Open High School (DLP). It aims to provide opportunity to all Filipinos to complete high school education regardless of physical condition, political affiliations, age, religious beliefs, geographical barriers and economic status. In this program, the students will spend most of their time independently. Flexible face-to-face sessions in headquarter schools between students and a regular secondary school teacher is also conducted for direct instruction, review of concepts learned and remediation. Aside from being a venue for face-to-face sessions, a headquarter school is also the center for enrollment and evaluation (Garcia, 2002).

Currently, the program uses hardcopy self-instructional modules to be given out to students availing of this program. The modernization effort of the Department of Education has prompted the BSE to consider another form of media to distribute the self-instructional modules. Since more and more headquarter schools are being equipped with ICT facilities, the BSE is planning to produce CD versions of the self-instructional modules. The CD version makes the production of instructional modules more cost-efficient and portable for the students. The headquarter schools can now also serve as a venue for viewing the instructional modules. But the true thrust of DLP is to make it available on the Internet, to be more accessible to a larger population and provide another venue for collaboration and interaction among the students and the teachers (Garcia, 2002).

As good as it is that a growing number of schools are being modernized and provided with ICT facilities, no monitoring or feedback mechanism has been implemented to ensure that the equipment delivered was indeed used for its intended purpose and whether it is still in good running condition (Garcia, 2002). It was also acknowledged by Department of Education Undersecretary Ramon C. Bacani that the Department of Education has no data regarding the use of ICT (Rodrigo, 2001, p.132).

FINAL ANALYSIS

The Philippine Government has realized the value of ICT and the benefits of Internet-based education. However, a lot of work still must be done to overcome the obstacles on its path. The government must first find a way to alleviate the perennial problem of financial shortages before any work can be done. It is not enough that a budget is being allocated for the modernization projects. It is also important that there be a proper amount of documentation that tells the government and other concerned entities about the status and results of the project to inform the government whether the funds are spent properly and that it is used for its intended purpose, and most importantly, help them determine how the scarce educational resources should be distributed.

REFERENCES

Department of Education Culture and Sport Annual Report. (1999).

Dynamic Business Education, Whenever, Wherever. (n.d.). Retrieved June 2, 2002, from: http://www.dlsu.edu.ph/mbaonline/main.htm.

Escaler, M. Personal Communication. April 9, 2002.

Establishing the UP Open University. (n.d.). Retrieved June 2, 2002, from: http://www.upou.org/upoupages/UPOU.HTM.

Garcia, E. Personal Communication. June 27, 2002.

Institute of Higher Education Policy. (2000). *Quality on the Line: Benchmarks for Success in Internet-Based Distance Education.* National Education Association.

Lugo, L.M.T. (2002, May 7). *Survey Shows Much Room to Grow for RP Net Access.* Retrieved from: http://itmatters.com.ph/indicators/indicator_05072002a.html. Last accessed: July 12, 2002.

Rodrigo, M.M. (2001). ICT use in Philippine public and private schools. In Cuyegkeng, M.A.C. (Ed.), *The Loyola Schools Review.* Office of Research and Publication, Ateneo de Manila University, 122-139.

Toral, J. (2001, September 30). *Philippines Responding to the Challenge of the Digitized Society.* Retrieved from: http://www.digitalfilipino.com/content.asp?FileName=%5Cecommerce%5Capecreport.ini. Last accessed: July 15, 2002.

Part IV

Effective
E-Learning

Chapter XII

Effective Online Learning – Both a Utilization of Technology and Methods

Jan Frick
Stavanger University College, Norway

Michael Sautter
Telenor Research, Norway

Svend Øvrebekk
Rogaland Training and Education Center, Norway

ABSTRACT

The authors have used modeling techniques to gain understanding of causes and relationships in online learning environments. The cases that the modeling relates to have their origin in the large Norwegian research project NettLæR, which runs online courses on various topics and levels. The modeling work seems to indicate that good learning models from earlier learning research may still be of relevance, but the conditions to make them work, and the context they operate in, are more limited and more critical than before.

BACKGROUND

It can be argued that industry today does not take full advantage of the possibilities within the traditional formal education system. This is mainly due to a lack of knowledge of the possibilities offered, and skepticism regarding the formal system not able to deliver according to industry's needs regarding content, time and place. At the same time new information and communication technologies (ICTs) provide new possibilities for flexible deliveries of courses and communication. In this new context there is even a greater need for a content deliverer like the formal educational system or a company buying courses to make sure that learning takes place as expected.

In Norwegian industry we have seen many examples of employees using much time attending courses with limited learning effects. Most of these courses are either standard education courses or tailor-made courses for a particular company. In many cases there seems to be an underestimated effect of learning in the context where you work—or tailor-making the learning context so that it is regarded to be of clear relevance to the challenges at work for the individual participant. At the same time, industry emphasizes the need for more effective learning, both regarding the need for the knowledge and a need to keep the training costs low (Frick, Hjulstad & Sun, 1996a, 1996b; Frick & Irgens, 1995, 1996; Frick & Riis, 1991; Riis & Frick, 1990; Sun, Hjulstad & Frick, 1999).

After doing some minor experiments with online distance courses over a few years, we set out in 1999 with a larger research project, NettLæR, to investigate relations between an effective learning process and various online learning methods. Acknowledging the vast complexity of the issues involved, we had no intention of researching every possible topic, but rather of identifying some guidelines that seemed to have a major impact on the participants' learning efforts. As "proof of the pudding," we decided to establish a set of pilot courses during the research process.

ABOUT NETTLÆR

NettLæR (an acronym in Norwegian for learning by use of Internet in Rogaland) is a research project in Norway supported by the Norwegian Research Council (NFR) that was established in 1998-99 (Frick, 2000b; Frick & Kaspersen, 2000). It will run for four years with a budget of 2,7M Euro not including the running of courses. It is based on five existing industrial collaboration networks with more than 80 companies as members, and with Rogaland Training and Education Center (in Norwegian Rogaland Kurs og Kompetansesenter, RKK) and Stavanger University College (in Norwegian Høgskolen i Stavanger, HiS) as the main educational vendors (Frick, 2001a).

The main focus for the project is to accumulate knowledge on how to provide and run vocational training as efficient as possible with the ICT tools available. All courses have a reference to the formal education system from 10th grade to PhD level.

The project is divided into four parts:

- Arena—studying the ICT and the course delivery infrastructure and specified/developed a new course administration tool, Coursekeeper™(patent pending). Coursekeeper™focuses on the participant in the course (Løkken, 2000; Quale, 2000).
- Pilot courses—seven courses developed for the project in order to provide a variation in pedagogical method, ICT tools, content level and type, and background of participants (Frick, 2000a).
- Empirical data collection and analysis—the collection of what happened both in the pilot courses and other related courses available for data gathering. (Brønnick & Pedersen, 2000; Tveterås & Vik, 2001).
- Optimal models—this is where we try to utilize different modeling techniques in order to test and eventually provide guidelines on how to deliver effective learning to industry (Frick, 2001c; Tveterås, 1997; Vennix, 1996).

The related courses delivered by various combinations of Internet include, as of June 2002, more than 5,000 post-education participants on different vocational topics such as full technical college for employees in mechanical industry, healthcare, offshore maintenance, economics for employees in a hotel chain, project management, fish farming, petroleum processing technology, congregation administration, etc. It is on levels from secondary school to PhD course. The PhD course runs with participants from all the five Nordic countries.

At the moment, we use two parallel administrative infrastructure systems, Coursekeeper™and WebOffice™ Its two vendors intend as a result of NettLæR experience to develop both tools further. We find the WebOffice™system useful in lower level classes where the teacher works in a traditional way and benefits from being able to control the participants and the progress, in other words a class management system. Coursekeeper™has another structure as it is made to be a learning management system where the individual participant chooses his/her own pace and uses the teacher as a coach and sparring partner. We have found this useful on the college level for vocational training for industry (Junge, 2002).

Rogaland Training and Education Center, RKK, has during the last decade established a profitable system for vocational education in the Rogaland area. It is now a virtual vendor of vocational training, with only four permanent employees in RKK itself, but based on a network of 32 local schools employing 1,000 teachers that generated an income of 4M Euro in 2000. Collaborating with Stavanger University College, HiS, RKK offers vocational training on levels from secondary school to master's degree (Frick, 2001a). NettLæR enhances the RKK system in several ways with the ICT. First, it increases the flexibility for industrial participants, as a portion of a course will be done wherever they are when they have the opportunity to study. Second, it increases the market for the institutions as they deliver their specialties to companies outside of their local area. Third, it improves the follow-up of participants, as the systematic use of chat and news groups together with e-mail improves the possibility for personal adjustment and dialogue. This reduces the number of dropouts from the courses (Brønnick et al., 2001; Frick, 2001a, 2001b).

Beginning Spring 2001, all RKK courses use Internet tools in various settings, and combine these with the administrative software that is WebOffice at the moment.

THE TRAINING AND EDUCATION CENTRE CASE, RKK AND E-LEARNING—A RETROSPECTIVE LOOK

RKK is a participant in "NettLæR," a joint project aimed at promoting the use of e-learning in Rogaland, and supported by NFR. The "NettLæR" project was launched in April 1998 and, as a result of its participation, RKK has gained valuable new experience and made useful contacts in the field of e-learning. This is a retrospective look to see what kind of trend we are in. It is not always easy to maintain perspective when a choice must be made of new methods and technologies almost every day. "NettLæR" has been a suitable arena for reflection and the exchange of views.

Winter 1998

At that time, RKK had for nine years focused primarily on running conventional courses and continuing education programs, with ever-growing success. Turnover was about 3.7M Euro a year, and more and more of the 32 upper secondary schools in Rogaland were contributing to its activities.

The system was (and is) that the profits were at the disposal of the schools themselves, which naturally attracted considerable goodwill. The result was good contact with industry and commerce, and competence development for both teachers and schools.

IT-based methods such as PowerPoint were being increasingly used and it became clear that RKK had reached a crossroads: Shall we concentrate on introducing more modern teaching methods, and if so what will this entail in the form of money and effort?

For RKK's part, it soon became clear that there was no way around it if we wanted to maintain our position as one of the market leaders for training and continuing education supplied by schools to the private and public sectors. The question was rather what form this should take and what specific tools and methods we should go in for.

A chance demonstration of the project management tool WebOffice proved significant. This represented just about the simplest system of communication one could envisage on the Internet, and at that time this seemed a highly significant factor. Some protests were heard, not least from players who wanted a greater degree of functionality immediately.

RKK's strategy was then formulated, and it stands if possible even firmer now than ever:

- Use simple systems that always work!
- Put the teacher in the center; the teaching environment will then also be the best possible one for the participants too!
- Critically try out new methods together with the teachers concerned!

WebOffice was chosen, and this tool has simple functions such as:

- Notice board (where the teacher can give brief messages to the participants)
- Discussions (teacher and participant can both contribute written comments on an equal basis)
- Chat channel (real-time chat online)
- Documents (file manager where the teacher can enter texts, presentations, pictures, videos, etc.; can also be processed information, depending on how ambitious the teacher is)
- Pointers (links to relevant websites)
- List of participants, with mail function

Given a clear interface, this is so simple that training has proved almost unnecessary to get started, both for teachers and participants. The choice of tool was vital if we were to get the system off the ground, with a large number of participants, without having to devote too many resources to course development and training in how to use it.

RKK's customers are mainly company employees, often without particularly extensive experience of working with PCs or the Internet. Much therefore depends on their getting used to this new tool quickly so that they can concentrate on the professional content and learning process.

Through "NettLæR," RKK chose a number of pilot projects, including courses leading to "technical college" qualifications for personnel working in the "Kverneland" concern, the world's largest manufacturer of agricultural machinery. Kverneland's main factory is about half-an-hour's drive away for the teachers, and teaching takes place one day a week using conventional methods. The rest of the week, contact between teacher and participants is maintained via WebOffice online. In a corresponding school-level scheme for workers in Sauda, extensive use is made of videoconferencing, as it would have meant a six-hour journey for teachers from Stavanger.

A main principle for RKK has always been to offer an optimal combination of methods:

- Conventional teaching; one-day, one-week or evening courses
- Online communication (Internet), at all times
- Videoconferencing, various types
- CD production and use of conventional texts

The Period from 1998 to 2001

Companies vary greatly in the way they follow up with employees on training schemes involving the use of new teaching methods. This is especially clear in regard to how far we can count on participants having their own PC, at home or at work. In 1998, several companies made it clear there was no guarantee that participants would have regular access to a PC, which made it difficult to implement many combined-method programs.

Today, RKK can almost take it for granted that everyone taking part in e-learning has his/her own PC, in one form or another. Internet access, preferably via ISDN line or better, will be a standard platform for RKK's programs from now on.

In 1998, RKK and corresponding course providers had to convince customers that a certain element of ICT in teaching could make courses more efficient and cost-effective. Companies have traditionally spent 80% of course budgets on non-teaching items such as travel, accommodation and daily allowances. In the last three to four years, RKK has tailor-made course programs with a considerable element of e-learning for a number of companies which have also calculated the cost savings this has brought them. The "Smedvig offshore" reckons it can save NOK 100,000 per participant on a half-year theoretical course for electro-personnel. It is also evident that results are just as good, and the drop-out rate less, with the right combination of the methods described.

In short, it is much easier today to argue in favor of e-learning, and there is now scarcely a company interested in anything other than a scheme that allows employees to combine work and education. It is essential, however, to take into account the participants' background and the framework conditions the company sets. The trend will continue, but no one knows for sure where we will end up in relation to ICT. The teaching itself is after all what really matters and methods must be chosen on that basis.

During these three years, the number of participants linked to WebOffice via the Internet has increased from virtually zero to over 3,000. RKK puts all courses which have even the smallest element of e-learning on the Internet, and all participants are given their own user ID and password. In some courses, active use is made of the Internet, in others to a lesser degree. This is a matter for the teacher responsible for the course to decide, in the same way as in the classroom. Sometimes a strong element of teaching and direct follow-up by the teacher will be chosen, while at other times virtually 100% online will be appropriate.

It is quite clear that some kind of new, online methodology is beginning to emerge, but no one today can say for certain what form this will take. It is important to distinguish between the different types of program and a rough classification may be:

- Participants following normal schooling, where a varying proportion of teaching will be ICT-based; a further distinction must be made between primary/lower secondary school and upper secondary level
- People working in companies and the public sector
- Participants at college and university level

There can be significant differences in how an e-learning program is organized for the various target groups. RKK has particularly extensive experience with setting up courses for employees working in companies who wish to combine work with further and continuing education, and where upper secondary schools are responsible for both the professional content and the choice of method. This is a customer group in which not many other course providers are engaged, but where the market is clearly expanding. The challenges are relatively great and not the same as arise in the case of, e.g., participants from colleges and universities. There the use of PCs is commonplace and independent study poses no problems. There are therefore no particular difficulties in organizing e-learning and following it up.

RKK's objective has always been to design simple, combined teaching programs adapted to the needs of the particular target group and company in each case. In the years from 1998 to 2001, many teachers got involved out of self-motivation and interest in using new methods in teaching. RKK has contributed software, hardware and training, so that it is not necessary for individual schools and teachers to use their resources on this aspect of the work.

RESEARCH METHODOLOGY

In the NettLæR project, we somehow try to sit on both sides of the table regarding research method. In the Arena and Pilot sub-projects, we generate the courses and their environment as we work. This work will typically be an action research type of work (Carr & Kemmis, 1986; Kember, 2000; McNiff & Whitehead, 2000; Schön, 1983; Winter, 1987). As with the Coursekeeper™ we have specified it, developed it, put it to real-life usage with online courses and participants from companies, and we test the results from the usage. But, in the data collection and analysis sub-project and in the modeling sub-project, we take on the observer's role, viewing the process and the results as they emerge.

By doing it this way, we hope to get the best of both the action research perspective, and more descriptive research methodologies. By combining the two, our experience so far is that we get a richer empirical base and the possibility to deploy different kinds of analytical perspectives. Likewise we acknowledge that is has become a slight problem: we to some degree mix people by using some of the people on both types of sub-projects. It can be argued that this to some degree might reduce the objectivity for some of the staff in the project.

In the same way as we have a duplicity in methods, we also have a duplicity in goals. NettLæR has as an overall goal to provide knowledge in models, guidelines, etc., that can enhance the efficiency when later making online courses. At the same time it is a clear-stated goal that the project shall significantly increase the amount of running online courses from the related providers, and if possible come up with new methods or tools regarding how to run such courses with an effective learning process for the participants.

MODELING

What is a Model in this Setting?

We have chosen to use a system thinking perspective, and hence a model is described as:

> An idealized, simplified description of real-life phenomena, often viewed as a picture or flowchart with some syntax guidelines.

We use modeling techniques widely known and recognized (Sterman, 2000; Vennix, 1996). Due to former experience we have used system dynamics with the iThink modeling tool as a primary method, but when relevant we have made use of other methods(HPS, 1992; Richmond et al., 1997; Richmond & Peterson, 1997a, 1997b; Soderquist, Peck, Johnston, Richmond & DeMello, 1997). Our models of the learning process are focused towards the learning outcome—both as measured as objectively as possible, but also as perceived and experienced by the individual. The models have been altered many times due to discussion on "what is learning" and "how do we measure learning in this kind of context." They include all the parameters that we, through our empirical studies, have found to have significance. They are extracted both from dialogue with teachers and participants in the pilot courses, and the more general empirical data collection such as questionnaire provided by the data collection subproject.

It is important to state that we consider the learning process and analyses we do as we work on the modeling process as the most important results from our work, not necessarily the models themselves. Thus, the models we have worked on are mainly regarded as "carriers" of our analyses and new understandings.

What Identifies Sound Models?

Sound models might be characterized by:

- *Recognizable relations or phenomena usually regarded as good practice*
- *Concrete common identifiable input and output situations*
- *A one problem-one solution type of situation that means that the model treats a well-defined limited situation, not the whole world*

We have tried to identify what goes on in our online course learning processes, and to limit the scope of the models and the number of parameters involved according to recognizable situations. This should not be considered a behavioristic approach, as our observations mostly are triangulated with the participants' own experiences. We have also made use of a kind of filter saying that a parameter, in order to be included, should have been "observed" in at least two or more situations. Besides the internal validation between observations, these parameters have also been validated through the use of questionnaires, qualitative interviews and more theoretic positions in literature.

As a model in our setting is expected to represent some important parameter use or relation for further interpretation, we have to be able to identify relations between the model and the real-life situation/observation.

Examples of Facts Stated in our Models for E-Learning or Online Learning Include:

- *Company need as a major motivation factor*
- *Frequent coaching by tutor towards the individual learner*
- *Groups as a social network, make everyone belong*

We have found many relations that give a meaning for the learning process. Some of these are obvious special cases coming from certain not-so-common conditions. Others have a more general usability. We thus try to extract understanding from our modeling work, and we would like to get this as general as possible. But, as quality of results is an issue here, we have to say that this understanding does not come from modeling a single course alone. Rather, it is an evolutionary process going back and forth between modeling work and dialogue with practitioners and data from their courses.

Many of our models state that old terms on how to achieve learning also apply to online learning. But it seems that in most cases, the requirements to the setup, the teacher/tutor, the structure of the content, the exercises, etc., are much more restricted than those for ordinary classroom or lecture hall teaching.

A major difference seems to be a shift in focus from the teacher being the center of the activities to placing the learner in the center. This has several implications both for the pedagogic and the technology to be used, and it sets clear demands for the infrastructure needed both in the ICT and regarding the content deliverer/coach. It also provides the learning process with possibilities to increased use of the learner's context, which again may benefit both the company/learner organization involved and the learning process.

Motivation plays a major role in online courses, even more than in ordinary courses, and for company employees attending, the relation to the need of their company is important. Other factors that have a major role are the frequency of coaching towards the learner and the creation of an infrastructure to include the learner in some kind of society.

Other Examples that May Not be Similar General, but Seem to Have Impact in Many Cases are:

- *When someone the learner regards as an authority shows interest for his/ hers individual progress such as the company manager or professor/ teacher*
- *Content and progress schedule adjusted for the learner's capabilities and background*
- *Groups when the learner needs a social network as discussion partners for learning tasks*

Motivation is a frequently returning issue, but with many variations regarding both learner background and course level and characteristics (Atkinson, 1974). One easy way to promote motivation is to make the learner feel that it matters what he/ she does. This can be achieved by attention from the learners superior in the company setting, but is also possible with frequent personal coaching from superior people in the course setting.

A similar effect can be derived from the possibilities of having content and schedule adjusted for personal background and capabilities. Using group members as discussion partners is another way of extending the learners' capabilities. Both these are closely related to motivation. But, as mentioned earlier, many of these guidelines gathered from a course and treated in models do something to our technical need and usage. We are used to having technological people providing us with possibilities about future use in online learning and related administration and communication. It has become a way of technological push.

Our work with models does not only suggest how to arrange courses to achieve effective learning, but it also suggests demands to the technology. These demands are both easy and hard to implement. Technical solutions talk often about flexibility but seem to prefer many kinds of standardization on technology's terms. Such standardization may and may not be an advantage when we talk of a need for flexibility on the learner's terms.

If we want freely functioning discussion in learner groups, individual adjusted content or frequent personal coaching, etc., with learners spread out in different towns and courses run in a wide span of time, then we need to implement a technological infrastructure and tools that support these kind of guidelines (Brønnick et al., 2001).

We have so far described what we have "found" during the modeling process. With all such work we have a need to validate both the process and the results. In our case this has been done over some time. It is not finished. We started out in the mid-90s with test cases in online teaching that we tried to model. Then this was taken into the NettLæR project, previous ideas and guidelines were discussed with practitioners from different companies, and the emerging ideas were taken into new courses and then again information was gathered for both models and discussion. This has been done in several cycles.

PARAMETERS THAT PROMOTE LEARNING

As indicated above, we have found many parameters that promote learning. Some of these are method oriented, some are mainly technology based, but most seem to be a combination where the technology facilitates the learning method (Gertsen, 1993; Riis, 1978, 1997; Riis & International Federation for Information Processing, 1995). Such parameters are (Frick, 2001a; Frick, Hansen, Gertsen, Sun & Sautter, 2002; Frick & Jonsson, 2002; Frick & Sautter, 2002; Sautter & Frick, 2002):

- Group work (Brønnick et al., 2001)
- Activating of learners (Hansen, Gertsen, Larsen & Frick, 2002)
- Set up according to learners' background/situation (situational approach) (Marsick & Watkins, 1990, 1999)
- Flexibility in delivery regarding time and place
- Blended learning (which is various combinations of gatherings, Internet-based guidance and group work) (Rosenberg, 2001)
- Exploitation of the Internet as an information source and reference

This may imply a move where educators change from focus on daily deliveries to focus on course development and implementation?

RETHINKING E-LEARNING

Some of the methodological and technological implications of organizing e-learning emphasizing the parameters outlined above may be:

- Moving of responsibility of progress from educator towards learner.
- Infrastructure of learner gains a more active role; a paradigm shift that has importance for the functionality requested from technology that implies higher requirement on the functionality of the technology, i.e., being able to interact with the company's Enterprise Resource Program (ERP) system.
- Various set-ups with high-frequency follow-up from lecturer or some tutor towards the individual learner seems to have a high learning efficiency impact.

But there are several issues that may be stated from comparing the various e-learning cases (Frick & Sautter, 2002):
- E-learning is not for every student in every set-up.
    - Many students are not prepared for working that much on their own.
    - The more mature students, the better possibility for success.
    - Lack of technical knowledge may often block otherwise good possibilities.
- E-learning may not be an advantage for everyone, even when well prepared.
- E-learning frees up fixed time for the educator, but it is much more work if quality is to be maintained.
- E-learning should not emulate classroom, but focus on learning and flexibility possibilities.
- Faculty cost is normally substantially higher in e-learning compared with face-to-face education. This is due both to more extensive preparation needed and more time used, as most learners tend to operate as individuals, not a coordinated class.
- E-learning is available anywhere for learners all day, all week, thus providing flexibility in place and schedule for learner, as compared with once or twice a week in one location in ordinary courses.
- Blended learning, mixing e-learning with physical gatherings or/and videoconferencing, seems in all our cases to provide confidence to learners and thus better results.
- Strict requirements for deliveries from learners seem to promote learning, both with high and low frequency on deliveries.
- Highly interactive e-learning seems to indicate no more than 20 learners in a class.
    - The exception is when learners are using learners' communities in various types of group work; then, inter-community communication may allow higher number of learners. The main reason is that the community then may react as a single learner unit.
    - Very structured classes with low interaction may have more learners, but will often demand extreme detailed preparations in advance.

- Efficient e-learning seems to relate to coordinated activation of learners.
- Learning and thus creation of knowledge in an "e-" context seems to emphasize relation to:
  - Coordination
  - Integration
  - Cooperation
- E-learning may be regarded as a generating process by a social and working context in virtual interactions.

FUTURE SCENARIO

Although many questions and open issues remain, we see some trends in technology-based vocational training. As mentioned we believe the main focus in vocational training will move from the training now being the "baby" of teachers and tutors to a situation where the outset is the learner's situation and his/her learning goals. This may move some of the responsibility from the teacher to the learner for actually keeping progress on the course.

Similarly, we believe the technology will enable us to return from a homogeneous standard teaching mode, teaching large uniform classes to individually customized teaching and close follow-up of learners.

The company role will increase in vocational training due to the last point, as a consequence of individual adjustment also enables the companies to have their employees learn through tutored projects within their own companies.

CONCLUSION

We have found that the use of modeling is a profitable way to accumulate knowledge when working in a complex research project setting. As for the online learning, we have seen little new in how people learn. But, new tools and new context sets constraints on old methods and provides new possibilities when we combine old methods and new tools. These possibilities relate to many parameters in a complex learning environment, but much is closely connected to a shift in focus from teacher/teaching to the learner and his/her learning process and objectives.

REFERENCES

Atkinson, J.W. (Ed.). (1974). *The Mainsprings of Achievement-Oriented Activity*. Toronto: New Looks.

Brønnick, K.S. & Pedersen, C. (2000). *NettLæR—Evaluering av Faget "Prosjektledelse i Industrien," Nettbasert Versjon, Høsten 1999.* (RF-2000/258, ISBN 82-490-0068-4). Stavanger: Rogalandsforskning.

Brønnick, K.S., Frick, J., Junge, A., Løkken, A., Sautter, M. & Øvrebekk, S. (2001). *Læreprosesser og Virtuelle Grupper.* Paper presented at the NettLæR workshop, Stavanger, December.

Carr, W. & Kemmis, S. (1986). *Becoming Critical. Knowledge and Action Research.* City: The Falmer Press.

Frick, J. (2000a). *NettLæR—Teori og Metodegrunnlag for Pilot Prosjekter.* Stavanger: Høgskolen i Stavanger.

Frick, J. (2000b). *The NettLæR project.* Unpublished manuscript, Stavanger.

Frick, J. (2001a). Emerging of a model for vocational training. *Industry and Higher Education, 15*(December), 403-408.

Frick, J. (2001b). *RedMeis Evaluation Report.* Stavanger: Høgskolen i Stavanger.

Frick, J. (2001c). *Working Paper Regarding Standards for E-Learning* (version 1). Stavanger: Høgskolen i Stavanger.

Frick, J., Hansen, P.H.K., Gertsen, F., Sun, H. & Sautter, M. (2002). Experiences from research and use of technology in e-learning. *Engineering Education and Lifelong Learning,* (in press), 19.

Frick, J., Hjulstad, R. & Sun, H. (1996a). *Achieving Competitiveness from Technological Developments.* Paper presented at the FAIM96, Flexible Automation & Intelligent Manufacturing 1996, Atlanta, Georgia, USA.

Frick, J., Hjulstad, R. & Sun, H. (1996b). *A Study of Technological-Organizational Development and Market Dynamics in Denmark and Norway.* Paper presented at the Fifth International Conference on Management of Technology, Miami, Florida, USA.

Frick, J. & Irgens, C. (1995). *The "Learning Organisation" as an Approach to Increasing Manufacturing Competitiveness.* Paper presented at the Nordic Conference on Business Studies, København.

Frick, J. & Irgens, C. (1996). *Increasing Technology Benefits (Achieving Benefits from Technology) Through Organizational Learning.* Paper presented at the MoTV, The Fifth International Conference on Management of Technology, Miami, Florida, USA.

Frick, J. & Jonsson, M. (2002). *Technology Enhanced Learning Environment Used in Real Case.* Paper presented at Euroma 2002, København, June 4.

Frick, J. & Kaspersen, B. (Eds.). (2000). *NettLæR—Informasjonshefte NettLæR; Samling fra Ulike Notater for å Informere om Prosjektet.* Stavanger: Høgskolen i Stavanger.

Frick, J. & Riis, J.O. (1991). *Organizational Learning as a Means for Achieving Both Integrated and Decentralized Production Systems.* Paper presented at the Computer Application in Production Engineering, Bordeaux, France.

Frick, J. & Sautter, M. (2002). *Effective Online Learning–A Matter of Making Sound Models Work.* Paper presented at IRMA 2002, Information Resources

Management Association 2002, Issues and Trends of Information Technology Management in Contemporary Organizations, Seattle, Washington, USA.

Gertsen, F. (1993). *Perspektiver for Indførelse af ny Teknologi.* Paper presented at the Fornyelse i Industriell Produktion: Udviklingsperspektiver fra et Forskningsprogram om Integrert Produktion.

Hansen, P.K., Gertsen, F., Larsen, J.H. & Frick, J. (2002). *Does Efficiency and Project Based Learning Comply?* Paper presented at the Nordesign Education, Trondheim Norge, August.

HPS. (1992). *iThink User Manual* (Version 2.01). Hanover, NH: High Performance Systems, Inc.

Junge, A. (2002). *Vurdering av Nettbaserte Learning Management Systemer* (RF–2001/260). Stavanger: Rogalandsforskning.

Kember, D. (2000). *Action Learning and Action Research: Improving the Quality of Teaching and Learning.* London, Sterling, VA: Kogan Page, Stylus Pub.

Løkken, A. (2000). *Coursekeeper, A Learning Portal for your Company (pp. 4): Boxer Technologies as.* ***info missing???***

Marsick, V.J. & Watkins, K.E. (1990). *Informal and Incidental Learning in the Workplace.* London: Routledge.

Marsick, V.J. & Watkins, K.E. (1999). *Facilitating Learning Organizations: Making Learning Count.* Aldershot: Gower.

McNiff, J. & Whitehead, J. (2000). *Action Research in Organisations.* London, New York: Routledge.

Quale, C. (2000). *NettLæR—ARENA, Forretningsgrunnlag, Funksjonelle Krav og Planer* (RF-2000/248, ISBN 82-490-0064-1). Stavanger: Rogalandsforskning.

Richmond, B., DeMello, S., Peterson, S., Stevenson, R., Wolstenholme, E. & Soderquist, C. (1997). *Business Applications, iThink Software.* Hanover, NH: High Performance Systems, Inc.

Richmond, B. & Peterson, S. (1997a). *An Introduction to System Thinking, iThink Software.* Hanover, NH: High Performance Systems, Inc.

Richmond, B. & Peterson, S. (1997b). *A Technical User Guide, iThink Analyst Software.* Hanover, NH: High Performance Systems, Inc.

Riis, J.O. (1978). *Design of Management Systems: An Analytical Framework.* Copenhagen: Akademisk Forlag.

Riis, J.O. (1997). *Fornyelse i Virksomheder: Baseret på Danske Erfaringer* (1st edition). København: Børsen.

Riis, J.O. & Frick, J. (1990). *Organizational Learning: A Neglected Dimension of Production Management Systems Design.* Paper presented at the Advances In Production Management Systems, Helsinki.

Riis, J.O. & International Federation for Information Processing. (1995). *Simulation Games and Learning in Production Management.* London: Published by

Chapman & Hall on behalf of the International Federation for Information Processing.

Rosenberg, M.J. (2001). *E-Learning: Strategies for Delivering Knowledge in the Digital Age.* New York: McGraw-Hill.

Sautter, M. & Frick, J. (2002). *Contextualised Online Learning; How a Strong Focus on Context Affects Online Learners, Teachers and Developmental Models for Producing and Managing Content.* Paper presented at IRMA 2002, Information Resources Management Association 2002, Seattle, Washington, USA.

Schön, D. (1983). *The Reflective Practitioner.* New York: Basic Books.

Soderquist, C., Peck, C., Johnston, D., Richmond, B. & DeMello, S. (1997). *Getting Started with the iThink Software, A Hands-On Experience, iThink Software.* Hanover, NH: High Performance Systems, Inc.

Sterman, J. (2000). *Business Dynamics: Systems Thinking and Modeling for a Complex World.* Boston: Irwin/McGraw-Hill.

Sun, H., Hjulstad, R. & Frick, J. (1999). Critical success factors in implementing AMT by Norwegian companies. *International Journal of Management,* (12).

Tveterås, R. (1997). *Econometric Modelling of Production Technology Under Risk: The Case of the Norwegian Salmon Aqualculture Industry.* Bergen: Norges Handelshøyskole.

Tveterås, R. & Vik, I. (2001). *Computer Mediated Distance Education at Public Contact Universities: Barriers to Entry and Modes of Entry* (Arbeidsnotat). Stavanger: Høgskolen i Stavanger.

Vennix, J.A.M. (1996). *Group Model Building: Facilitating Team Learning Using System Dynamics.* Chichester, New York: John Wiley & Sons.

Winter, R. (1987). Fictional-critical writing: An approach to case study research by practitioners. *Cambridge Journal of Education,* (16), 175-182.

Chapter XIII

A 3-Dimensional Framework for Evaluating Multimedia Educational Software

Eshaa M. Alkhalifa
University of Bahrain, Bahrain

Fawzi Albalooshi
University of Bahrain, Bahrain

ABSTRACT

This chapter introduces a three-dimensional framework aimed at evaluating multimedia educational software. It argues that the current means of evaluations is highly dispersed and ailed with "no significant result" findings mainly due to the evaluation techniques used and not the systems themselves. The framework proposed combines the two approaches currently followed in three dimensions of evaluations which are: system architecture, educational impact and affective measures. System architecture studies the design of the system itself and the technologies it takes advantage of. Educational impact concerns the differences between student levels prior and following exposure to the system. Affective measures concern student motivation issues when using the system. The goal is to provide a solid framework that is general enough to evaluate all types of multimedia educational systems.

INTRODUCTION

Multimedia systems invaded the educational world without allowing educators enough time to formulate proper evaluative techniques to assess their usefulness. The attractive nature of these systems, that allowed them to waltz into our lives, may eventually wear off and raise the necessary question: Are they capable of delivering what they promise? This chapter analyzes several approaches to evaluate multimedia and utilizes them as a basis of a new framework. The evaluation procedure proposed here emphasizes the participation of all parties involved in the evaluation process, such as educators, technical experts and the target learners. Background information is first collected about the system content and its technical performance, in addition to finding a method through which the effect of the CBI on students' learning outcome is measured. The collected evaluation information then is analyzed in rigorous detail to determine the suitability of the CBI under analysis as a teaching medium. A three-dimensional framework is proposed such that its dimensions are: system architecture, educational impact and affective measures. System architecture analyzes the system components, how they work together and their design. Issues such as speed of display of information and logical bugs are evaluated along this measure. Educational impact measures the effectiveness of the system when compared to a benchmark classroom lecture. Issues such as types of knowledge gained are measured through pre- and post-testing of students. Affective measures are evaluated through a written survey along with system architecture questions. Issues such as how students regard the system and whether they are willing to learn on such a system are addressed. A case study of a multimedia data structures tutoring package (DAST) is evaluated within this three-dimensional framework to show its applicability as an effective evaluation method of multimedia tutoring systems.

TRADITIONAL EVALUATION PROCEDURES

Computer-based instruction provides educators with a powerful technological tool to aid them in reaching their teaching objectives. Recent advancements in multimedia made it possible to incorporate sound and animation into the same presentation, clearly providing more means for information transfer than classroom whiteboards and textbooks. This tool may even aid in reinforcing student learning as well as overcoming traditional problems that commonly exist with the traditional approaches. However, many researchers— including Beatte (1994), Reiser and Kegelmann (1994)—believe that educational software must be evaluated to ensure its teaching benefits on the learners before being approved for use. Questions such as "Do the students like the software?" and "Who's using it?" are inadequate as a measure of effectiveness. What is being emphasized is the most fundamental evaluative question: "What's being learned by the students?" A good evaluation must establish whether this type of representation is able to overcome a particular learning problem, and then follows that by a deeper search to investigate the nature of the learning experience and its benefits to students.

A review carried out by Reiser et al. (1994) showed that in most cases the people who took part in evaluations were teachers that had to go through the software similar to a student, and then fill out a rating form by comparing the system to what would occur in a classical classroom session. Usually a wide variety of the CBI features are reviewed, including content, technical characteristics, documentation, instructional design, learning considerations, software objectives and the handling of social issues. Only a small number of evaluators gathered evidence to demonstrate the effectiveness of the CBI in teaching. The authors concluded that organizations should incorporate students as active participants in the evaluation process, in addition to assessing how much students learn as a result of using the software.

McKenna (1995) highlighted major flaws in some of the approaches that followed, indicating that the "no significant difference" problem has persistently appeared partly because of failing to describe the unique dimensions of the innovation under study. She also added that there was no enforcement of strict control measures in the lessons presented through different mediums for comparison. Beattie (1994) suggested a number of evaluation techniques, some of which are pilot testing, before/ after testing, expert criticism and student questionnaires.

Some evaluators used these types of techniques to study the effectiveness of the use of particular media as opposed to another. Pane, Corbett and John (1996), for example, examined the impact of computer-based animations and simulations on students' understanding in time-varying biological processes. They setup two student groups based on prior test performance in the course to compare computer-based and paper-based instruction, using as main measure for comparison the pre- and post-test results. They used strictly similar materials as per the results found above. Further tests of the animation presentations was attempted by Byrne, Catrambone and Stasko (1999), who examined whether animations would help students learn computer algorithms more effectively. Their approach was mainly based on pre- and post-testing the student groups participating in the experiments. While the last experiment highlighted the importance of overall effectiveness, the one for Lawrence, Badre and Stasko (1994) concentrated on finding the difference in student performance in carefully selected pre- and post-test questions to show the difference between the learning of declarative and procedural questions.

Although the importance of evaluation as a vital player in any instructional software is evident to all researchers, there do not exist any guidelines through which such evaluations could take place. An example of a problem that may exist is the series of experiments that were aimed at testing the differences in instructional effectiveness of the animation versus textual media. These tests depended on providing a clear sequence of photographs to show the procedure while in the animated versions, the animation was shown on a screen. Freyd (1987) showed through a large number of experiments the basis of what she called "representational momentum." This theory explains a natural tendency to treat any series of images, as equivalent to an animation and vice versa. Therefore, comparing the two media through tests of effectiveness may not result in any desirable results because what is estimated does not indicate the difference in "cognitive load" during the learning process. Students learning from these textbooks may learn as effectively as the ones that learn through animation, but end up with a smaller overall efficiency when their learning rate is measured by time. The "no significant difference" results seemed to persist throughout these experiments.

Tam, Wedd and Mckerchar (1997) went one step further, when they proposed a three-part evaluation procedure including peer review, student evaluation, and pre- and post-testing. In a way, this approach attempts to include a user and expert survey in the evaluation process to combine the two approaches described above, surveys versus pre- and post-testing. Scriven (1967) describes two main aspects of evaluation of instructional material that was further described by Bloom, Hastings and Madaus (1971). Evaluations are of two types: formative evaluations that occur during the early design, and development of the system to estimate whether or not it achieves expectations and summative evaluations. The latter is concerned with the evaluation of the completed systems, with respect to how effective they are in teaching.

Although this classification is crucial to understanding the types of possible evaluations, it fails to fully describe all that is of importance in the evaluations process. An example of this is a full categorization of the types of objectives of an educational system (Bloom, 1956; Bloom et al., 1971): knowledge, comprehension, application, analysis, synthesis and evaluation. At the knowledge level a student is capable of recalling a fact or a term, but not to understand or apply it. The comprehension level implies that the student can use the material to some degree where he can give definitions or draw direct conclusions. The application level allows a student to apply the knowledge into concrete situations, and the analysis level implies that the student can identify the underlying concepts as well as compare them and examine their relationships to each other. The synthesis level implies that the student can also organize presented materials to generate new ideas, while evaluation involves the ability to judge the value of the knowledge.

Mark and Greer (1993) identified seven principles that could be used for Intelligent Tutoring System evaluations. These are:

1. *Proof of correctness:* Here a designer attempts to mathematically test the validity of the algorithm used to answer the question: Does it do what it is supposed to do? This technique is unsuitable for Artificial Intelligence programs that deal with intractable problems, but may be used for conventional program-ming. It is usually undesired due to the complexity and time-consuming nature of the mathematical analysis involved.

2. *Criterion-based evaluation:* In another approach to evaluation, a system is considered successful if it displays no major inadequacies within its intended

application environment. The care with which this criteria is developed is of utmost importance as it determines the value of the knowledge gained from it. Mark and Greer (1993) believe that this technique is best suited during development when criteria can be specified and measured precisely.

3. *Expert knowledge and behavior:* This technique required that an expert, and in this case an educator, be brought in to evaluate the educational system. The expert can judge the material used as well as the behavior of the system. Yet again this seems best suited for formative evaluations rather than summative.

4. *Certification:* An independent body of teachers could set some basic requirements for certification and review all submitted details of educational systems to assess whether or not they meet these requirements. This technique requires standard requirements to be set by a certification board, and so far no such standards seem to exist.

5. *Sensitivity analysis:* This technique is only applicable to adaptable tutoring systems that alter their material or method of teaching according to student preferences or level. The analysis would check how sensitive the system is to differences in the student model and can therefore not be generalized to all multimedia systems.

6. *Pilot testing:* Testing can be done on prospective users of the system, and this branches out into three types of testing. One-to-one testing is usually done early on in system development, followed by small-group testing, and that in turn is followed by field testing.

7. *Experimental research:* Experimental techniques that are commonly used in psychology are also suitable to evaluate educational systems. Although these tests are useful to identify the effects of a single factor, more complex designs are required to example multiple factors and their interactions.

3-DIMENSIONAL FRAMEWORK FOR EVALUATING MMTS

The framework proposed here is composed of three dimensions, one for each of the major forces that may affect the final product that is obtained. They are as follows:

1st Dimension: System Architecture

This dimension is concerned with the system's main modules, their programming complexity as well as their interactions. Evaluation within this dimension should be performed in any or all of the following methods:

- Each system module must be described in detail, as well as the interactions performed between them, and checked to ensure that the system as a whole works in that way.
- Expert survey of the system should be capable of assessing the viability of the architecture as a teaching medium. This usually implies that experts or educators would test run the system and fill out a questionnaire.
- Student evaluations could allow students to test run the system and fill out a questionnaire from the perspective of potential users of the systems. This would give their opinion of the suitability of the architecture from their own standpoint.
- Any architectural design must be based on cognitive findings that test the effects of different modules or types of representation. The literature is already there and is extensive, so there is no harm is using it to advance the effects of the system. This should decrease the amount of "no significance" in test results that fall under the educational impact dimension.

2nd Dimension: Educational Impact

This dimension is concerned with assessing the benefits that could be gained by students when they use the system. Classically, these are done in pre- and post-tests, and this is carried on in this framework with more attention given to detail.

- Student groups must be selected according to a common mean grade to ensure that further testing can be compared in reference to changes to the means.
- Pre/post-tests done before and after students use the system, contrasted with a regular class session, as well as given following a class session.
- Questions in the pre/post-tests must be mapped to each other, such as the same types of knowledge are measured, and not overall ability. Types of questions should cover several types of knowledge, at least including declarative versus procedural knowledge. Depending on the application the types of knowledge or depth of answers required may vary.
- The tests should best be attempted with students who were never exposed to this material previously to assess their learning rate. In a sense, this is combining the power of a controlled experiment and a field study, as student numbers are limited even though they are the potential users of this system.

3rd Dimension: Affective Measures

This dimension is mainly concerned with student opinions on the user friendliness of the system and allows them to express any shortcomings in the system. This could best be done through a survey where students are allowed to add any comments they wish freely and without restraints.

CASE STUDY: EVALUATING DAST

The Data Structure Tutorial (DAST) system is a multimedia tutoring system that was developed at the Department of Computer Science in the University of Bahrain. The system aims at teaching and/or reinforcing the basic concepts of the Data Structures course by presenting its content in combined animated and textual mediums simultaneously.

1st Dimension: System Architecture

The evaluation procedure must go in stages, starting with the development of the system itself and ending with the tests of how effective it is in transferring the information to students. This system started out with a thorough analysis of the educational content, which was done by expert review of educators experienced in the same course materials. They first tested the system for programming errors and then filled out a specially designed questionnaire. Caffarella (1987) proposed some guidelines for such an evaluation form and these have been adopted in the form presented here. Most questions require subjective judgment to the effectiveness of the CBI program and how capable it is in meeting its education goals, including questions about program goals, content, audience, instructional strategies, design, appropriateness, etc. Experts gave the system an average rating of 5.33 on the same scale of 0 to 6.

In addition to these tests, an evaluation questionnaire was given to students to highlight any weak or strong areas they found while interacting with it. In a sense, this would allow students to take an active role in the evaluation process and describe their point of view. Students of groups two and three who were exposed to the system were asked to fill in a similar evaluation form. With respect to the DAST system, students in general gave ratings of around 4 to 5 on a scale that went 0 to 6, with the highest for "The use of graphics, sound and color contributes to the student's achievement of the objectives" and "The user can control the sequence of topics within the CBI program." The lowest score was 3.559 for "The level of difficulty is appropriate for you." Therefore, it seems that the students in general enjoyed learning from the system, although they found the level of difficulty of the concepts presented as challenging.

Both questionnaires were broken up into several main sections with two to three questions in each. These include:

1. *Program goals:* This includes questions to see if students understood the aim of the CBI.
2. *Program content:* This includes one question requesting students to judge if the CBI is in line with the university taught materials.
3. *Audience for the CBI Program:* This section includes four questions about the suitability of the CBI to this particular group.

4. *Instructional strategies:* This section includes two questions about the suitability of the CBI's approach to teaching and if it can be stopped at any time.
5. *Program design:* This section has six questions about feedback, speed of presentation, user control, the use of graphics, sound, etc. and readability issues.
6. *Appropriate use of computers:* Two questions here ask students if this application is appropriate to be presented on a computer and if it takes advantage of the interactivity offered by computers.
7. *Program techniques:* This section has four questions that ask about issues related to software execution, including the clarity of directions and programming errors if any.
8. *Cost/benefit analysis:* Two questions ask about the required time a student needs to use this system and if it is worth the investment.
9. *Overall evaluation:* Questions concerning listing the software's strengths, weaknesses, the user's overall evaluation on a scale and whether they believe the university should adopt it.

2nd **Dimension: Educational Impact**

Students were pre-tested to assess their levels in comparison to each other with respect to their learning abilities and then separated into three groups of 15 students by keeping the means of their test grades equal. The aim of this step is to allow an even distribution of students in the groups based on their learning abilities. Without this test, it is quite possible that by accident, a group exposed to a particular condition may have students who are sharper and more capable of learning than another group. Therefore, this step was essential to isolate the variable of student ability from the comparison table.

Two tests were then prepared composed of seven and eight questions to be exact, where one of the questions in the first test was broken up into two in the second. The questions were carefully written to ensure that each question on the first test mapped exactly onto one or more on the second test to allow for comparisons on a question-by-question basis to check for differences in student levels within particular domains. Byrne et al. (1999), for example, found that the use of interactional animation improved student responses to procedural questions, while Lawrence et al. (1994) made similar findings simply through interactive laboratory sessions.

An example of the mapping implemented in this particular case can be seen in these two questions: "List and explain the data variables that are associated with the stack and needed to operate on it?" and "List the data variables and operations associated with the stack?" The first would appear as Question Number 4 on the first day, and the second would appear as Question Number 3 on the second day. A sample diagram of the mapping is as shown in Figure 1.

Figure 1: A Sample Mapping of the Questions Between the Post-Test and the Pre-Test

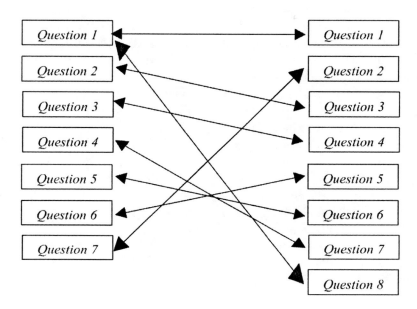

Figure 2: The Evaluation Procedure

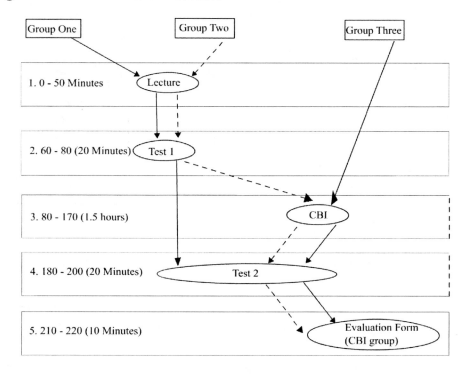

The evaluation procedure concentrated on testing all possible conditions, which implied that students had to be tested if they used the system only, attended the classroom session only or attended the classroom followed by the system. The first two conditions would test for the differences in the effectiveness of teaching in a classroom versus through a multimedia system. The third condition would then be compared to the two above by showing if the system provides any reinforcement to the learning level attained after a regular classroom and if so how much reinforcement resulted. In general the technique followed is shown in Figure 2.

The three groups followed the paths shown. Note that the variation between the two tests allows them to be directly mapped onto each other without any serious problems. They were, however, reworded to reduce the chances of students remembering the answers of the first test. Therefore, the only factor of difference was the time duration between the two types of presentation of material and the use of the system versus the classroom lecture. Students were allowed to take their time during a lab session that usually takes approximately two hours, of which they took at most the period shown of 1.5 hours. Additionally, Steps 1 and 2 of the evaluation procedure took place on Day One and steps 3, 4 and 5 took place on the following day. This allowed students to rest following the classroom lecture and also to forget the questions they were asked in the first test. Students were not informed that they

Table 1: Total Student Scores in Pre- and Post-Tests

Group One		**Group Two**		**Group Three**	
Test One	Test Two	Test One	Test Two	Test One	Test Two
6	4.5	9	16.5		12.5
8	12.5	9	11		8.5
8.5	8	11.5	14		10.5
7	8	8	10.5		6.5
12	13	7.5	7.5		13
22	24	6	14		13.5
10	19	12	13		9.5
9	8.5	8.5	14		12.5
8.5	6	5	10		8.5
17	18.5	11.5	18		6
6	8	7	7.5		12.5
8.5	9.5	5	9.5		13.5
11.5	13.5	8	12		11.5
8.5	6.5	16.5	15		10.5
7.5	7.5	10	12.5		16.5
SD= **2.923**	SD: **2.880**	SD= **4.167**	SD= **5.305**		SD= 2.759
X>10.5= **4**	X >10.5=**6**	X>10.5= 4	X>10.5=**11**		X>10.5=**10**
X<10.5=**11**	X <10.5=**9**	X<10.5=**11**	X <10.5=**4**		X <10.5=**5**

would be retested on the following day, so they were unaware of the events of the following day and had no reason to wish to retain any information concerning the first test. Evaluation questions were asked to experts who have previously taught the course, as well as to students who were subject to this experiment.

Analysis of the results

To avoid falling into the pitfalls of previous systems, a thorough analysis of the results was carried out with respect to all the data that was collected. The student marks in the two tests that were given were analyzed using the Analysis of Variance (ANOVA) test. This test allows one to test the difference between the means by placing all the data into one number, which is F, and returning as a result one p for the null hypothesis. It will also compare the variability that is observed between conditions, to the variability observed within each condition. The static F is obtained as a ratio of two estimates of the students' variances. If the ratio is sufficiently larger than 1, the observed differences among the obtained means are described as being statistically significant. The term of null hypothesis represents an investigation done between samples of the groups and with the aim that learning was not a product of the treatment. In order to conduct a significance test, it is necessary to know the sampling distribution of F given that the significance level needed to investigate the null hypothesis. It must also be mentioned that the range of variation of averages is given by the standard deviation of the estimated means. Student scores and the standard deviation (SD) according to their groups were as shown in Table 1.

The aim of this data is to arrive at some measure of the effectiveness of this system without falling into the temptation of comparing the effects of the different media with each other. Therefore, the benchmark used here and proposed in general is to compare this type of CBI with a regular classroom lecture. The ANOVA tests did indeed show that there is a significant improvement in Group Two between the first test that was taken after the lecture and the second test that was taken after using the system. However, this was not sufficient to be able to pinpoint the strengths of the system.

Therefore, a more detailed analysis was done of the student performance in the individual questions of Test One and Test Two. Since the questions were mapped onto each other by design as is shown in Figure 1, it was easy to identify significant changes in student grades in particular question types in the students of Group Two who responded to similar questions before and after the use of the system. An example is a highly significant improvement, with $F=58$ and $p<.000$ observed in the question "Using an example, explain the stack concept and its possible use," which is an indication that the use of the system did strongly impact the student understanding of the concept of a "stack" in a functional manner. Another advantage for mapping the questions as was done is the ability to compare between subjects in Groups One and Three who either attended the lecture only or used the system only. Oddly enough, the same question comes up again, only this time favoring the classroom-only case and with F=5.02 and p <.03. This raises a serious question that would not be identified if not for the evaluation design assumed here. The question is: If the system did worse than the classroom lecture in that particular question, then how can they so strongly reinforce the understanding of the concept following the classroom lecture?

Another point of view is to examine the scores by using the total average, which is 10.639, therefore approximating to the borderline becomes 10.5 and the rest of the scores will be divided around this line. It is worth noticing that the scores of the third group were not so high, but most of them were over the average and, comparing with the second group, the results are close even if the third group took only the CBI package, while Group Two had both lecture and CBI package learning. It also underlines how much the second group improved their test results after taking the CBI and at the same time showing that the first group had not improved much only with the lecture learning. Alkhalifa (2001) showed through two experiments that the difference in error levels between students who are exposed to a logical task may significantly differ whether the task is a "moving" system or a stationary one. Without the use of this particular statistic, the advantages of having animation in this multimedia system would not fully be assessed.

These results seem to indicate that the use of the system may introduce a "limiting" effect that follows the initial introduction to the concepts of Albalooshi and Alkhalifa (2001). Classroom lectures introduce students to the concepts allowing them all the freedom to select all types of applications, which is in some ways overwhelming. The use of the system, on the other hand, produces a safe haven to test their ideas and strongly pursue the examples they can imagine. It goes without saying that such a conclusion would have been impossible to reach if the questions were not purposely set in the shown mapped fashion.

3rd Dimension: Affective Measures

Part of the questionnaire above concentrates on student opinion and their views towards the educational system. In general, they seemed highly enthusiastic to incorporate the use of this educational system into the course curriculum as is shown by achieving a rate of 5.085 on a scale of 6. They also voiced some comments requesting more examples that go more in depth into the theory to solve more complex questions that they face during the course. Other affective measures were included in the Audience for CBI program sections where questions included asking students what they feel about the course materials, level of difficulty and necessary prerequisites, and how much they learned from it. These questions allow students to tailor their assessment of the system to their own individual needs.

FUTURE TRENDS

With the dawn of the age of information, it does not seem that any "not significant" measures will result in multimedia educational systems' disappearance from the world. Their attractive colors and animations were enough for them to be welcomed with open arms into our lives and educational systems. The hope then for the future is to identify their points of strength and weaknesses through the use of effective educational techniques. The DAST system shows that the system tested was more efficient in transferring one type of information than another. So perhaps evaluations can guide future work into a forever continuing self-improvement path into the future.

CONCLUSION

It goes without saying that software evaluation is critical to any educator, and when the concerns about the effectiveness of the evaluation procedures grow as cognitive researchers pinpoints inadequacies in presumptions, one has to turn to an "overall view" of the system. Although the DAST system presented has both an animation module as well as a textual module within the same framework, the individual testing of each seemed fruitless. Past studies (Lawrence et al., 1994; Byrne et al., 1999) found the two to be equivalent because their methods of evaluation concentrated on comparing the two media with respect to performance. Freyd (1987) showed through several experiments that a comparison of this type is fruitless because the human mind seemed to cognitively interpret one form into another. However, this does not inform us of anything concerning the cognitive load on memory and whether it enhances learning to use one or the other. This implies that separating the media in testing is not informative at all when evaluating a CBI as a whole because results can be misleading. On the other hand, we have shown here that when all the types of different media are presumed to be one united system, and when evaluating it from an instructor's, a student's, as well as a performance perspective, results are much clearer. The framework used for this evaluation was clearly presented, showing why the mapping of pre- and post-test questions is essential to the success of this procedure. Another point worth mentioning is the equal distribution of questions between procedural and declarative with the addition of a conceptual question that combines both. These tools allowed a deeper analysis of the system that gave interesting insights into the points of the strength of the CBI. It is these little surprises that everyone seeks when evaluating the abilities of CBI programs to help guide future designs.

REFERENCES

Albalooshi, F. & Alkhalifa, E.M. (2001). Multimedia as a cognitive tool: Towards a multimedia ITS. *Proceedings of IEEE International Conference on Advanced Learning Technologies: Issues, Achievements and Challenges,* Madison, Wisconsin. August, pp. 231-234.

Alkhalifa, E.M. (2001). Directional thought effect in the selection task. *Proceedings of the Third International Conference on Cognitive Science,* Beijing, China, August, pp. 171-176.

Beatte, K. (1994). How to avoid inadequate evaluation of software for learning. *IFIP Transaction A [Computer Science and Technology],* A-59, 245-258.

Bloom, B.S. (1956). *Taxonomy of Educational Objectives: Cognitive Domain.* New York: David Mackay.

Bloom, B.S., Hastings, J.T. & Madaus, G.F. (1971). *Handbook on Formative and Summative Evaluation of Learning.* New York: McGraw-Hill.

Byrne, M.D., Catrambone, R. & Stasko, J.T. (1999). Evaluating animation as student aids in learning computer algorithms. *Computers and Education,* 33(4), 253-278.

Caffarella, E.P. (1987). Evaluating the new generation of computer-based instructional software. *Educational Technology,* 27(4), 19-24.

Department of Computer Science, McMaster University, Hamilton, Ontario, Canada (1999). *Abstract Data Type Demonstration Web Site* [online]. Available: http://www.cas.mcmaster.ca/cs3ea3/1997/ (October 12, 1999).

Freyd, J. (1987). Dynamic mental representations. *Psychological Review,* 94(4), 427-438.

Lawrence, W., Badre, A.N. & Stasko, J.T. (1994). *Empirically Evaluating the Use of Animation to Teach Algorithms* (Technical Report GIT-GVU-94-07), Georgia Institute of Technology, Atlanta.

Mark, M.A. & Greer, J.E. (1993). Evaluation methods for intelligent tutoring systems. *Journal of Artificial Intelligence and Education,* 4, 129-153.

McKenna, S. (1995). Evaluating IMM: Issues for researchers. *Occasional Papers in Open and Distance Learning,* No 17. Open Learning Institute, Charles Sturt University.

Pane, J.F., Corbett, A.T. & John, B.E. (1996). Assessing dynamics in computer-based instruction. *Proceedings of the 1996 ACM SIGCHI Conference on Human Factors in Computing Systems,* Vancouver, B.C., Canada, April, pp. 197-204.

Reiser, R.A. & Kegelmann, H.W. (1994). Evaluating instructional software: A review and critique of current methods. *Educational Technology, Research and Development.* 42(3), 63-69.

Scriven, M. (1967). The methodology of evaluation. In Stake, R.E. (Ed.), *Curriculum Evaluation.* Chicago: Rand-McNally.

Shaffer, C. (1997). *Swan* [online]. Available: http://geosim.cs.vt.edu/Swan/Swan.html (October 12, 1999).

Shaffer, C.A., Heath, L.S. & Yang, J. (1996). Using the Swan data structure visualization system for computer science education. *SIGCSE Bulletin,* 28(1), 140-144.

Tam, M., Wedd, S. & McKerchar, M. (1997). Development and evaluation of a computer-based learning pilot project for teaching of holistic accounting concepts. *Australian Journal of Educational Technology.* 13(1), 54-67.

Chapter XIV

Performance Assessment: A Case for Rubrics in the Virtual Classroom

Apiwan D. Born
University of Illinois at Springfield, USA

Carol M. Jessup
University of Illinois at Springfield, USA

ABSTRACT

This chapter examines a performance assessment tool (i.e., rubric) that is increasingly being utilized in online courses. The concept of performance assessment in the virtual classroom environment is discussed, including the proposition that using traditional assessment tools alone is not sufficient. Issues related to rubrics are identified, and guidelines are presented for online instructors and course developers. Emerging trends and future research opportunities are also provided.

INTRODUCTION

"What did I do to deserve a C on my paper?"

This question probably sounds familiar to faculty members, who have heard it countless times from students. Online instructors may receive many e-mails asking variant forms of this question. The problem stems from assigning activities without absolute answers (e.g., true or false; multiple choice formats), in which students oftentimes do not know what is fully expected from them. An instructor needs to communicate clearly in advance the required assessment criteria, in the form of a rubric, which is commonly organized into a grid or scale.

The concept of a rubric is not new. Rubrics have been widely used in educational settings for decades. As information technology, especially the Internet, has created a new means of course delivery and a new educational environment, the issue of student assessment needs to be revisited since tools used in a traditional classroom may no longer be applicable for this new setting. This chapter will, therefore, explore the use of assessment rubrics in teaching technologies in the virtual classroom in higher education.

The objectives of this chapter include a description of performance assessment and a recommendation on how it can be used successfully in the virtual classroom. Arguments are provided herein as to why traditional assessment tools alone are not sufficient. The chapter addresses one of the performance assessment tools known as 'a rubric' that has been utilized successfully in the virtual classroom. Issues related to rubrics are identified, and guidelines are provided for online instructors and course developers. Emerging trends and future research opportunities are presented at the end of this chapter.

BACKGROUND

Student performance assessment is a continuous process examining what a student is able to do. Performance assessment consists of two major components: tasks and criteria (Rudner & Boston, 1994). Assessment tasks include identifying learning objectives and audiences, matching assessment techniques to learning objectives, and specifying illustrative tasks where students demonstrate sets of skills and mastery of the desired outcomes (Herman et al., 1992). Assessment criteria, or "the standards of achievement," need to be communicated to students before the tasks are assigned (Wangsatorntanakhun, 1999). One of the most popular tools used to organize and present these criteria is known as a rubric.

The word rubric dates to the Middle Ages, derived from the Latin word "ruber," meaning "red." According to *Webster's Unabridged Dictionary* (1998), the earliest references to rubrics include when scribes would write performance instructions in red for the priest in church missals to distinguish prescribed actions or rules from the actual text that the priest would deliver. Modern use of rubrics within education has increased in the last decade; the use of this tool is congruent with the recent movement towards alternative and authentic assessment.

A rubric serves as both an assessment and communication instrument between students and an instructor. To measure how much students learn, a rubric provides a clear list of assessment criteria that the instructor intends to measure and a numerical score associated with each criterion. A student's performance is compared directly to these predefined criteria and only indirectly to other students (Elliott, 1995). A well-written rubric can also serve as a means to convey an instructor's expectations to students. Both instructor and students will have a common tool to assist an evaluation process and to monitor student progress. In addition, to promote student collaboration and motivation, a faculty invitation for student input in the rubric process is an option (Kordalewski, 2000). This technique of self-assessment would further empower students as independent learners and is illustrative of the formative nature of assessment. The next section will discuss issues related to performance assessment as well as rubrics and their use in the virtual classroom.

ISSUES RELATED TO PERFORMANCE ASSESSMENT AND RUBRICS

The performance assessment tool of a scoring rubric is widely acknowledged as appropriate to measure student knowledge and skills, especially with high order and critical thinking skills. Rubrics serve as self-assessment tools, which are suitable for a student-centered environment such as the virtual classroom where students need to discipline themselves and manage their time properly. Despite the benefits of rubrics, the use of rubrics has not been discussed widely in the virtual education literature. To raise the awareness of rubric use among online instructors and course developers, this section discusses issues related to performance assessment and concerns in rubric use, rubric design, validity and reliability, and lessons from the field.

Reasons for Using Performance Assessment and Rubrics

Student assessment is defined as "the systematic collection, review and use of information about educational programs undertaken for the purpose of improving student learning and development" (Palombra & Banta, 1999). Assessment is an on-going process (Angelo, 1995) and is a means, not an end in itself (Angelo, 1999). There are two major types of assessment: formative and summative. Formative assessment is conducted during a course or program with the intent of providing feedback to be used for improvement. On the other hand, summative assessment is given after a course or program has been completed to evaluate its quality or value compared to a predefined set of standards.

Traditional assessment such as standardized testing tends to be summative in nature and does not provide feedback to students until they complete a course or a program. This type of assessment has been criticized for being superficial and measuring only what students are able to recall. Formative assessment overcomes this weakness, as feedback on an interim basis is a critical element in synthesizing and integrating complex knowledge. Beginning in the early 1990s, an increasing number of calls began to appear for authentic assessment (Madaus & Raczek, 1996).

Performance assessment, which is a formative tool, is proposed as an alternative and authentic means of measuring student learning (Wangsatorntanakhun, 1999). Unlike traditional tests and quizzes (e.g., selecting from a list of possible responses), performance assessment tools allow students and teachers to engage jointly in knowledge construction, where teachers progressively turn over the metacognitve processes to students who are learning to think about thinking (Gipps, 1996). These tools are authentic since students are required to perform tasks under defined conditions similar to what happens in the real world.

As introduced earlier in this chapter, one of the performance assessment tools is a rubric. In order to consider the comprehensive nature and multiple facets within learning, rubric use provides more meaningful and stable appraisals than traditional scoring methods. The use of the rubric involves acts of scoring, interpreting, and judging (Simon & Forgette-Giroux, 2001). Scoring entails alignment of a rubric description that most closely matches observed performance; interpreting is the assessment of the level of skill mastery observed; judging compares the actual performance level with predetermined standards.

Rubric Design

Rubric design needs to focus on assessment criteria that are observable and measurable in the virtual classroom. A rubric is usually presented in a matrix or checklist format. Rubrics can be designed for the evaluation of specified tasks or for general categories (Moskal, 2000); either category is appropriate in an online educational setting. For example, when a stated purpose is to develop typing skills, the general scoring rubric must contain criteria such as typing speed and accuracy, which would allow students to use any feedback obtained to improve their next typing exercise or on the job in functions involving typing.

Assessment criteria can be grouped in two different ways: analytical and holistic (Betts, 1997). An analytical rubric contains several dimensions, each of which is then divided into multiple levels of competency. Figure 1 shows an analytical rubric for a short paper assignment. The rubric contains four dimensions: application of background knowledge, presentation of new ideas, demonstration of analytical skills and overall writing quality. Each of these dimensions is divided into three to four levels of competency. The expectation of each level is explained clearly; therefore, students know what to expect. The total score of this rubric is based on a summative scale of all criteria.

A holistic rubric, on the other hand, provides a summary of all assessment criteria on one scale. Holistic scaling views the entire activity as a set of interrelated tasks. One score or one level of achievement is used to capture simultaneously different aspects of the learning outcomes. In other words, a holistic scale is divided

Figure 1: Analytical Rubric

Instruction: Write a short paper (1-2 pages) and incorporate answers to the following questions.

1. Give an example of a Web site that you are familiar with and explain what it does.
2. Critique the usability of the site based on factors such as layout, color, text, hyperlinks, and accessibility.
3. Suggest what can be done to improve the usability of the site you selected.

Points in a possible range from 0 - 10 will be awarded based on a summation of scores received from each the following four criteria.

Student Uses Background Knowledge
☐ 2 Integrates background knowledge to explain the questions
☐ 1 Incomplete background knowledge; Mostly copied from other sources
☐ 0 Did not submit the paper

Student Presents New Ideas
☐ 3 Presents new and well-thought out ideas with a reasonable justification
☐ 2 Presents developing ideas that are not fully thought through; Ideas have some major flaws
☐ 1 Presents old ideas that do not add value to the paper; Ideas are copied from other sources without applying them within the context of the paper
☐ 0 Did not submit the paper

Student Demonstrates Analytical Skills
☐ 3 Makes a clear and sound argument with supporting evidence; Clear evidence of analytical skills (e.g., applying lessons from the textbook or lectures to solve the problems and provide a reasonable explanation); provides constructive recommendations
☐ 2 Makes a clear argument without supporting evidence; Beginning analytical skills (e.g., attempting to apply lessons learned to solve the problems but does not provide rationale); Provides constructive recommendations
☐ 1 Does not make an argument, or makes vague arguments; Does not apply lessons learned to solve the problems; Does not provide a recommendation
☐ 0 Did not submit the paper

Writing
☐ 2 Grammatical and spelling errors are few to none
☐ 1 Grammatical and spelling errors are many
☐ 0 Did not submit the paper

Figure 2: Holistic Rubric

Instruction: Write a short paper (1-2 pages) and incorporate answers to the following questions.

1. Give an example of a Web site that you are familiar with and explain what it does.
2. Critique the usability of the site based on factors such as layout, color, text, hyperlinks, and accessibility.
3. Suggest what can be done to improve the usability of the site you selected.

Short Paper Rubric: A possible grade of A - F will be awarded based on the following levels of performance.

A - A submission integrates background knowledge to explain the questions, presents new and well thought out ideas with a reasonable justification, and makes a clear and sound argument with supporting evidence. The submission shows clear evidence of analytical skills (e.g., applying lessons from the textbook or lectures to solve the problems and providing reasonable explanation) and provides constructive recommendations. Writing is free of grammatical and spelling error.

B - A submission integrates background knowledge to explain the questions mostly copied from other sources, presents new and well thought out ideas with a reasonable justification, and makes a clear argument without supporting evidence. The paper shows beginning analytical skills (e.g., attempting to apply lessons learned to solve the problems but does not provide a rationale) and provides constructive recommendations. Writing is free of grammatical and spelling errors.

C- A submission contains incomplete background knowledge, is mostly copied from other sources, presents developing ideas not fully thought through (some ideas have major flaws), and makes a clear argument without supporting evidence. The paper shows beginning analytical skills (e.g., attempting to apply lessons learned to solve the problems but does not provide a rationale) and provides constructive recommendations. A few grammatical and spelling errors.

D - A submission contains incomplete background knowledge, is mostly copied from other sources, and presents old ideas that do not add value. Absence of analytical skills exhibited. The ideas are copied from other sources without applying them within the context of the paper. Lack of argument or making vague arguments. Fails to apply lessons learned to solve the problems; fails to provide recommendations. Many grammatical and spelling errors.

F- Did not submit the paper.

into different levels of competency, and either a letter grade or a point base is assigned to each level. An example of a holistic rubric for the same short paper assignment can be created as shown in Figure 2.

While holistic scoring provides a quick and easy way to evaluate student work, it does not provide detailed feedback about student performance in specific content areas. Analytical scoring, on the other hand, divides learning objectives into many categories, each of which is assigned one score. This grid or scale provides more detail of what criteria will be evaluated than a holistic scale, although it is time consuming for an instructor to evaluate student work or a product based on one category at a time.

At the present time there are many tools that exist to help educators develop rubrics; an abundance of electronic tools are accessible through the Internet. Also rubrics related to nearly every imaginable discipline can be found on the Internet. For example, the Teach-nology.com website (retrieved January 7, 2003 from http://www.teach-nology.com/web_tools/rubrics/) contains a wide variety of rubric generators used to create rubrics in numerous disciplines.

Validity and Reliability

The issues of validity and reliability are important in the design and use of rubrics. Although information technology makes it more convenient to evaluate student performance at anytime and anywhere, bias (invalidity) and unfairness (unreliability) of an assessment instrument are not completely eliminated (Linn et al., 1991). Evidence of validity of the assessment rubric is generally categorized into content, construct and criterion; reliability issues most applicable in rubric use are inter-rater reliability and intra-rater reliability (Moskal & Leydens, 2000).

Content validity addresses "sample-population representativeness" (Cronbach, 1971) where knowledge and skills measured by an assessment instrument should reflect knowledge and skills of the subject area of study. For example, in a Web design class, a student is assigned to create a Web page using HTML codes. A rubric for evaluating a student's code should contain criteria relevant to HTML coding skills. An expert in the area such as a Web developer can be brought in to validate content of the rubric.

Construct validity in the context of assessment refers to the degree to which a tool measures what it is purported to measure. Constructs refer to "processes that are internal to an individual" such as a student's reasoning ability, problem solving, creativity, writing process, self-esteem, and attitudes (Moskal & Leydens, 2000). To measure a construct, a scoring rubric needs to emphasize not only the product but also the process. Take the previous example of the HTML activity. To measure a student's HTML coding skills, both the product (i.e., the Web page) and the process (i.e., the reasoning) need to be examined. In this case, the rubric's criteria need to address that the Web page functions properly, and that student explanations are reasonable (e.g., comments[1] and logic underlying the code).

Criterion validity is concerned with generalizability of student performance (Rafilson, 1991). It refers to "the extent to which the results of an assessment correlated with a current or future event" (Moskal & Leydens, 2000). In performance assessment, activities focus heavily on applying knowledge and skills to a real-world situation. Using the previous example of the Web design course, an instructor typically requires a group of students (similar to a Web development team in the real world) to create a real website that is accessible via the Internet. A rubric is designed to assess how well these students are prepared to be professional Web developers. Criteria in the rubric must emphasize relevant knowledge and skills required in the field of Web development. A high score derived from a valid rubric suggests high performance in the future career as a Web developer.

To ensure reliability of a rubric scale, more than one rater can be used in pilot testing, with individual results subsequently compared. This is called "inter-rater reliability." If there are discrepancies among scores, further discussion among raters would uncover potential reliability issues such as inconsistencies in performance observed or misinterpretation of the predetermined standard. It is possible that discrepancies are caused by ambiguous wording in the scale or by inappropriate dimensions or criteria. The scale needs to be revisited periodically to make sure that it measures what it is supposed to measure.

Another form of reliability is intra-rater reliability, which refers to the consistency of an individual rater's response to the same scale at different times. Many external factors such as fatigue, weather and stress may impact a rater's judgment or attitudes when evaluating student work. To minimize an inconsistency, criteria in a rubric must be written clearly with detailed descriptions and each rater needs to revisit those descriptions frequently during the grading process (Moskal & Leydens, 2000).

This subsection pertains to how validity and reliability can be established in a rubric scale. More detail about when and where a rubric should be tested for validity and reliability in an assessment process will be discussed in the Recommendations section. One caveat for those who adopt an existing rubric is that one size does not fit all. Although the rubric may appear to be valid and reliable for a certain task in one course, it is not necessarily valid and reliable for the same task in another course. It is recommended that validity and reliability of a rubric is examined prior to its implementation no matter whether that rubric is borrowed or created from scratch.

Lessons from the Field

We began using rubrics in our online courses during the summer of 2001. Several rubrics were designed for different types of assignments including short papers, group discussion and case analysis. For example, these rubrics were used with graduate students in an introduction to Management Information Systems

(MIS) course offered fully online via the Internet (i.e., without a face-to-face meeting). The class interacted using Blackboard and electronic mail; rubrics were introduced when the semester began. Two or three class activities were assigned every week; the instructor emphasized clearly which rubric would be used for assessing each activity. Over 75% of the class members (n=20) were satisfied with the use of rubrics and the clarity of the language in explaining each rubric criterion. In subsequent semesters, use of rubrics was also extended to another online course in the accounting discipline, including rubrics used for financial statement analysis tasks and team presentations that integrated analysis within PowerPoint presentations. Feedback received from online students is mostly positive. Examples of feedback include the following comments.

"Rubrics gave me a better understanding of what the instructor's expectation is."

"Before I began to work on my assignment, I referred to the rubric to see what criteria I needed to meet. It made it a lot easier to complete the assignment."

"I didn't know what a rubric was so I was confused at first because the instructor had many different rubrics for different assignments. But after she showed how she used it to grade my assignment, I thought I understood what it was for. I think it is a useful tool."

"Rubrics were constructive in getting me to think."

"Criteria for grading stress the importance of insight and analysis into course materials."

"Rubrics are fair and reasonable."

Each rubric emphasizes criteria considered as standards of excellence. When criteria are stated clearly, the rubric is useful in helping the entire class to identify and apply the preferred practices. Students are not compelled to compete against each other but with themselves to meet those criteria. In the meantime, students are not left guessing what is required in each activity. A majority of our online students have not previously been exposed to a rubric device in prior coursework, but they readily grasp the benefits to be derived from the tool. While several students appreciate the use of rubrics in an online course, some have reservations.

"This was the first class that used assessment rubrics. It took a couple of weeks to find out what was wanted and how to satisfy the requirement."

"The rubric that is used to evaluate group members had too many criteria in each area making it difficult to give a proper evaluation of the member."

"Break the rubric items up more. Some items were combined so much that the assessment wasn't accurate. Allow for open comments."

The above comments from students imply that open communication between the instructor and students is critical. Students who are not familiar with rubrics need to be guided and shown how the rubrics are used. Examples of student products (e.g., papers, projects and essays) can be used to demonstrate each performance level (excellent, fair or poor) and how each example meets certain criteria specified in the rubric. Rubrics should be made simple enough for students to use as a self-evaluation tool as well as for them to engage in rubric development.

Rubrics have made the task of evaluating student work easier and more organized because of a checklist and rating scale associated with each criterion; one benefit exists in forcing faculty to revisit their expectations with specificity. The introspection involved in the development and use of rubrics engages faculty members in honest self-assessment of their teaching style. It is important to keep track of the shortcomings and strengths for a given rubric as faculty move through the on-going development process of testing and revision of the rubric.

RECOMMENDATIONS

To utilize rubrics successfully in the virtual classroom requires not only a sound plan but also patience and persistence from participants, including course developers, instructors and students. A three-phase student assessment project life cycle consisting of planning, implementing and responding has been proposed by Angelo and Cross (1993) and is presented in Figure 3. Although this life cycle is proposed for use with traditional classroom assessment, the following recommendations will suggest how rubrics can be deployed in the virtual classroom.

Phase I: Planning

The first phase, planning, begins with choosing a course to implement a scoring rubric. When a target course is selected, an instructor must identify a "teaching goal" and formulate an "assessable" question. An assessable question is one that is well focused and limited in scope and can be easily answered mostly through the use of one student assessment technique (Angelo & Cross, 1993). Wording in both the goal and the question must be clear because it will subsequently guide development of assessment activities. Once the question is formed, the tasks of determining the

Figure 3: Adapted from Angelo and Cross' Assessment Project Cycle (1993)

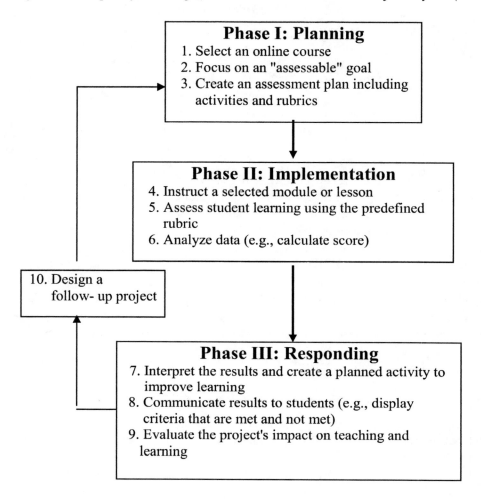

required student responses and the appropriate techniques to collect responses remain (Angelo & Cross, 1993). Thus, an assessment activity as well as its corresponding rubric must be created. Regarding validity and reliability of a rubric scale, an instructor or rubric designer should use the goal and the assessable question to guide the rubric development (Moskal & Leydens, 2000). An expert in the subject area can be invited to provide input and ensure content validity of the rubric.

Phase II: Implementation

In the implementation phase, the selected lesson or module is instructed and student learning is assessed. Using the selected assessment technique in the planning phase, the instructor can collect and analyze student responses with the predefined rubric. The important issue that needs to be addressed in this phase is when assessment should be delivered. It can be delivered before, during or after instruction as described next.

Assessment given before instruction is used for identifying student background knowledge, directing student attention to important issues and establishing "baseline" performance (Student Assessment in Online Courses, 2001). During instruction, students' work is evaluated to identify areas that need to be improved and to remind students of the desired outcomes they are expected to meet. After instruction, assessment is used for measuring student learning, preparing students to apply their knowledge and determining whether the learning outcomes are met. Different rubrics can be used to evaluate a student's responses at any stage of the instruction. Concerns should be made that criteria in those rubrics are relevant to the content area (content validity), measure the intended construct (construct validity), and address knowledge and skills related to practices in the field (criterion validity).

Phase III: Responding

Lastly, the responding phase transforms student responses collected from the implementation phase into a meaningful output ready to be presented to students. The instructor informs the students whether their overall responses indicate that the goal is achieved. This can be easily done by displaying to students which criteria in the predefined rubric they meet or do not meet. If the goal is not reached, the instructor must discuss with the student what needs to be done. Conveying comments to students in the virtual classroom can be time consuming since the comments need to be typed. A rubric can ease this task because the instructor can create a rubric template (in a word processing or spreadsheet format) and fill it out while grading student responses. Once the grading is finished, the instructor can send the complete rubric to the student electronically. In addition, instructors should keep an inventory of assessment activities and rubric templates, with an attached comment as to how they were conducted and whether they were well accepted by students. The inventory makes it easy to retrieve for future use and to ensure consistency in a grading process.

FUTURE TRENDS

Traditional assessment tools are criticized as they measure what students are able to recall or reproduce, rather than what they integrate and produce (Huerta-

Macias, 1995). Today, assessment of student progress is changing mainly because current real-world situations require workers who possess not only knowledge but also abilities to think critically and to solve problems they encounter quickly (Bond, 1995). As an increasing number of activities tend to require application of knowledge and critical thinking rather than memorization and recollection alone, traditional tools are no longer adequate. An alternative tool such as a rubric is required to evaluate skills that do not generally lend themselves to objective assessment.

Success of an assessment rubric depends on its implementation. Instructors teaching in a virtual classroom the first time should begin with a simple rubric and slowly roll into a more complex one. Starting simple provides an indication whether the rubric technique works and is worth pursuing. Rubric implementation is an on-going process that requires patience and persistence from participants, including course developers, instructors and students. To succeed, everyone involved must understand what work needs to be evaluated and why they are doing it.

Many scholars (Rudner & Boston, 1994; Herman et al., 1992) suggest that successful implementation of performance assessment requires a coherent plan and a clear understanding of what students need to master. While there are thousands of websites that provide instructors ready-made rubrics on a wide variety of subject areas, the best rubric that satisfies course needs is the one oriented to the specific course learning objectives. Since each course has its unique set of objectives, it would be difficult to adopt a generic rubric without modification.

The more work one does with rubrics generates an increased awareness of how rubric devices can be adapted to varied courses and assignments. Once rubrics are in place, further investigation of the use of rubrics is beneficial, with some questions meriting further research. Does using a rubric in online courses improve student performance compared to other sections of the course that do not use this tool? Does inclusion of a rubric within each assignment achieve improved student awareness of assessment criteria compared to merely posting the rubric on the course management system with reference to that posted document in the assignment? For what types of assignments do students prefer the use of an analytical rubric or a holistic rubric? Do graduate students prefer the use of a holistic rubric to an analytical rubric? In the virtual classroom, is there an optimal number of assignments or tasks for which a rubric can be used before it loses its effectiveness? Once exposed to rubrics, will students vocalize their preferences in subsequent courses with the same instructor where the tool is not used? Is a one-shot use of rubrics in the virtual classroom detrimental to the assessment process? Will students voluntarily partake of involvement in rubric design in the virtual classroom when asked to do so? How does the use of a rubric in the virtual classroom impact the instructor's time? How do rubrics impact the quality of assessment from the instructor's perspective? These and other questions pertaining to reliability and validity issues merit further investigation in the use of the rubric as an assessment device.

CONCLUSION

Compared with traditional assessment, performance assessment if used properly may be a more valid indicator of students' knowledge and abilities since it requires active demonstration of what they know (Sweet, 1993). This chapter focused on how using rubrics, an instructor can identify strengths and weaknesses of students and of his/her own teaching styles. When designed and implemented properly, rubrics are found to be viable tools in assessing teaching and learning. Rubrics provide valuable information regarding the degree to which a student has achieved a desired learning outcome based on a predefined set of criteria.

REFERENCES

Angelo, T.A. (1995). Improving classroom assessment to improve learning: Guidelines from research to practice. *Assessment Update*, 7(6), 1-2, 13-14.

Angelo, T.A. (1999, May). Doing assessment as if learning matters most. *AAHEBulletin*. Retrieved December 5, 2001, from http://www.aahe.org/Bulletin/angelomay99.htm.

Angelo, T.A. & Cross, K.P. (1993). *Classroom Assessment Techniques: A Handbook for College Teachers* (2nd Ed.). San Francisco: CA: Jossey-Bass.

Betts, B. (1997, August). *Assessing Student Learning.* Paper presented at Ruamrudee International School, Bangkok, Thailand.

Bond, L.A. (1995). Critical issue: Rethinking assessment and its role in supporting educational reform. *North Central Regional Educational Laboratory.* Retrieved February 12, 2002, from http://www.ncrel.org/sdrs/areas/issues/methods/assment/as700.htm.

Cronbach, L.J. (1971). Test validation. In Thorndike, R.L. (Ed.), *Educational Measurement* (2nd Ed.). Washington, DC: American Council on Education.

Elliott, S.N. (1995). *Creating Meaningful Performance Assessments.* Reston, VA: ERIC Clearinghouse on Disabilities and Gifted Education. (Eric Document Reproduction Service No. ED 381 985).

Gipps, C. (1996). Assessment for learning. In Little, A. & Wolf, A. (Eds.), *Assessment in Transition: Learning, Monitoring and Selection in International Perspective.* Oxford: Pergamon.

Gottleber, T.T. & Trainor, T.N. (2000). *More Excellent HTML.* Boston, MA: Irwin-McGraw-Hill.

Herman, J.L., Aschbacher, P.R. & Winters, L. (1992). *A Practical Guide to Alternative Assessment.* Alexandria, VA: Association for Supervision and Curriculum Development. (Eric Document Reproduction Service No. ED 352 389).

Huerta-Macias, A. (1995). Alternative assessment: Responses to commonly asked questions. *TESOL Journal*, 5, 8-10.

Kordalewski, J. (2000). *Standards in the Classroom: How Teachers and Students Negotiate Learning.* New York: Teachers College Press.

Linn, R.E., Baker, E.L. & Dunbar, S.B. (1991). Complex, performance-based assessment: Expectation and validation criteria. *Educational Researcher,* 20(8), 15-21.

Madaus, G.F. & Raczek, A.E.A. (1996). Turning point for assessment: Reform movements in the United States. In Little, A. & Wolf, A. (Eds.), *Assessment in Transition: Learning, Monitoring and Selection in International Perspective.* Oxford: Pergamon.

Moskal, B.M. (2000). Scoring rubrics: What, when and how? *Practical Assessment, Research and Evaluation,* 7(3). Retrieved January 25, 2002, from http://ericae.net/pare/getvn.asp?v=7&n=3.

Moskal, B.M. & Leydens, J.A. (2000). Scoring rubric development: Validity and reliability. *Practical Assessment, Research and Evaluation,* 7(10). Retrieved February 12, 2002, from http://ericae.net/pare/getvn.asp?v=7&n=10.

Palombra, C. & Banta, T. (1999). *Assessment Essentials: Planning, Implementing, and Improving Assessment in Higher Education.* San Francisco: Jossey Bass.

Rafilson, F. (1991). The case of validity generalization: Practical assessment. *Research & Evaluation,* 2(13).

Rudner, L. & Boston, C. (1994). Performance assessment. *ERIC Review,* 2(1), 2-12.

Simon, M. & Forgette-Giroux, R. (2001). A rubric for scoring post-secondary academic skills. *Practical Assessment, Research and Evaluation,* 7(18). Retrieved from http://ericae.net/pare/getvn.asp?v=7&n=18.

Student Assessment in Online Courses. (2001). Illinois Online Network Resource. Retrieved from http://www.mvcr.org/sa/index.html.

Sweet, D. (1993). Performance assessment. *Education Research Consumer Guide,* 2(September). Retrieved January 15, 2002, from http://www.ed.gov/pubs/OR/ConsumerGuides/perfasse.html.

Wangsatorntanakhun, J.A. (1999). *Designing Performance Assessments: Challenges for the Three-Story Intellect.* Retrieved April 3, 2002, from http://www.geocities.com/Athens/Parthenon/8658.

Webster's Revised Unabridged Dictionary. (1998). Plainfield, NJ: MICRA, Inc.

ENDNOTE

[1] Comments in programming refer to "documentation of choices made while writing a program or HTML page, including explanations of why those choices were made" (Gottleber & Trainor, 2000, p. 514).

Chapter XV

Cognitive Styles, Metacognition and the Design of E-Learning Environments

Ray Webster
Edith Cowan University, Australia

ABSTRACT

This chapter considers the use of cognitive styles and metacognitive skills in the design and development of e-learning environments. Participants involved in a unit in Human Computer Interaction used the results of a Riding's Cognitive Styles Analysis to assist in the design and development of Web-based Individual Learning Environments (ILEs). Student reflections and cognitive styles results are considered in terms of their impact on the design process. They are also used to consider participants' metacognitive awareness of their own cognitive and learning styles. It is suggested that the use of cognitive styles in this manner will produce interfaces and environments more suited to the learning requirements of each individual. In addition, the process of reflecting on and using the style results will help develop more metacognitively aware learners. The individual environment and metacognitive awareness are both desirable elements for a student-centered learning system for successfully participating in virtual education.

INTRODUCTION

This chapter considers the use of cognitive styles and metacognitive skills in the design and development of e-learning environments. The cognitive styles of individual students were used to help construct individual learning environments for Web-based learning. To facilitate this, a computer-based cognitive styles test was administered to a group of 64 Human Computer Interaction students. As an assessed part of the unit, students were then asked to document the process of designing and developing a Web-based Individual Learning Environment (ILE) with specific reference to their own cognitive style. Coyne has suggested that when using technology for design, *"we discover new ways of acting and thinking"* and that we *"reveal aspects of our practice"* (Coyne, 1995), and it was considered that the ILE design exercise would be particularly suitable for students considering their own cognitive styles.

For the purposes of this study, the cognitive style measure used was Riding's Cognitive Styles Analysis (Riding, 1991, 1998). Riding's cognitive style construct has two major dimensions which affect how each individual holds and processes information and thus impact on learning style and personality. The dimensions of the cognitive style construct were used by the participants for reflection and to inform the design of Web-based learning environments for interfacing with learning resources. An additional consideration was that student awareness of the learning process has become increasingly relevant with the shift of emphasis towards active learning and the increased use of learning technologies. This implies a need for students to become more actively involved in the management of their own learning and an associated need for each student to be more metacognitively aware of his or her personal resources. It is suggested that each student can use knowledge of his or her cognitive styles in ways that could help the individual develop his or her learning skills and strategies in the light of useful self-knowledge.

BACKGROUND

A gap has emerged between the model of student learning in higher education being proposed (active, resource-based, student-driven learning) and the experience of many students and lecturers. A continuing problem with the current scenario in higher education is that while there may have been a much expanded student intake and a move to a mass system, many of the processes and practices in use are those developed for an instruction-based elite system. While many of the processes and practices developed are and will remain useful and relevant, we have to ensure that those in use are suitable for functioning effectively within the resources and constraints of a mass system. Some central processes and practices (forms of assessment, tutorials which functioned effectively with eight participants but struggle with 16 to 20, personal tutoring) are increasingly under-resourced and under strain. In addition, a perception has developed, especially among higher education managers, that the provision of information and communication technologies will, *by themselves*, provide useful and cost-saving solutions. This approach often misses the point that the learning systems we are concerned with are social systems of which technology is only one aspect, often acting simply as an information carrier or interaction enabler.

Metacognition and the Autonomous Learner

Several writers (Tait & Knight, 1996; Goodyear, 2000) have discussed the concept of independent learning and the emergence of the *autonomous* learner. Goodyear in particular concerns himself with the question of "*How we should approach the design of learning environments that are consistent with the needs of autonomous lifelong learners*" (Goodyear, 2000). It can also be argued that the autonomous learner needs to be metacognitively aware, while Phelps et al. (2001) make the connection between metacognition and the concept of the expert learner. Metacognition can be described as thinking about thinking. A more comprehensive definition was provided by Flavell (1976) who suggested that:

> "*Metacognition refers to one's knowledge concerning one's own cognitive processes or anything related to them, e.g., the learner-related properties of information or data. For example, I am engaging in metacognition if I notice that I am having more trouble learning A than B; if it strikes me that I should double check C before accepting it as fact.*"

In a study concerning the potential role of reflective learning and metacognitive processes in the development of capable and competent computer users, the authors came to the conclusion that "*Reflection and metacognition is central to the development of 'expert learners' and thus can be seen to provide a sound framework for the development of 'capable' computer users*" (Phelps et al., 2001). One aim of this study was to increase student awareness of their own learning resources via metacognitive processes and investigate the effects of this awareness on the design and completion of a personal learning environment.

Cognitive Styles

Cognitive style can be defined as "an individual's preferred and habitual approach to organizing and representing information" (Riding & Rayner, 1998). Many different measures have been developed over the past few decades (Jonassen & Grabowski, 1993, Morgan, 1997; Riding & Rayner, 2000), but this main assertion of the relationship between cognitive style and individual information processing has remained central to all definitions. Ford studied the implications of the distinction between holists and serialists in learning for supporting individual users through user interface design (Ford, 2000). Another study looked at the possible impact of cognitive styles on the user-model-based design of adaptive human-computer interfaces (Averbukh et al., 1997). With the advent of Web-based learning, the amount, range and quality of information available to students and other academic users has increased enormously in recent times. This information can be regarded as a resource of great educational significance. However, it can be suggested that it is not a true resource until users possess the required skills, knowledge and suitable interface to maximize its utility. There has been an increased interest in, for example, the relationship between cognitive style, online database search experience and effectiveness in Web search performance (Palmquist & Kim, 2000).

Additional studies have attempted to look at the relationship between cognitive style and the format of learning materials for computer-assisted instruction or Web-based learning (Pillay, 1998; Boles & Pillay, 1999; McKay, 1999). Although much work has been done on the nature of cognitive and learning styles, the application of styles to interface design and learning has proved more problematic. These studies often reflect a continuing problem with the quasi-experimental approach to this type of study in that the results often find no significant relationship between the material presentation/interface style and learning. The use of single quantitative measures to capture a representation of students' cognitive style and measures of learning has often produced inconclusive results. Several authors have commented on the need for qualitative research concerning the ways in which individuals with different cognitive styles interact with Web-based learning environments (Summerville, 1999; Chen, 2000). In the general area, Ellis (2000) provided an example of the richer data that could be uncovered by using qualitative approaches to studying technology-supported learning. Another study (Felix, 2001) considered student comments as sources of information for Web-based learning design.

In an attempt to provide an alternative approach to exploring this area, a different and more process and qualitatively based methodology was developed. In this approach, one of the main aims was to involve the students in the design and development of the interface while at the same time getting each student to reflect and comment on both his or her cognitive style elements and the interface design and development process. A review of literature plus discussions with a range of colleagues, including those in the field of educational psychology, led to the choice of the Cognitive Styles Analysis (Riding, 1991) as the measure to be used. This was on the basis of the large number of empirical studies available establishing the reliability and validity of the measure (Riding & Cheema, 1991; Riding & Rayner, 1998). In both studies, the main alternative measures of cognitive and learning style were considered and the related empirical evidence reviewed. For example, Witkin's Group Embedded Figures Test (GEFT) is often put forward as the most reliable measure of cognitive style (Witkin et al., 1977). When Riding considered the GEFT as a measure of cognitive style, he did not question the validity of the field-dependence-independence construct. However, he did conclude that the way it is used to measure cognitive style is more likely to come up with results which correlate with ability (Riding & Rayner, 1998, p. 111).

COGNITIVE STYLES ANALYSIS

The Cognitive Styles Analysis (Riding, 1991) is a 15-minute, computer-based test which measures personal preferences for representing and processing information.

Two principle cognitive style dimensions are identified by the CSA and have the following characteristics:

- **Verbal-Imagery**—an individual's position on this dimension determines whether that person tends to use images or verbal representation to represent information when thinking.
- **Wholist-Analytic**—an individual's position on this dimension determines whether that person processes information in parts or as a whole (Riding and Cheema, 1991).

Measurements on the two dimensions produce four basic classifications—analytic-imager (AI), analytic-verbaliser (AV), wholist-imager (WI) and wholist-verbaliser (WV). In terms of the presentation of material and interface design, Riding and Rayner (1998) suggest that the following guidelines are applicable:

- **Analytic-Verbaliser**—the individual will prefer information presented in a textual form (VI), and as analytics tend to break down and structure material, assistance with the overview of material (WA) may be helpful.
- **Analytic-Imager**—the individual will prefer information presented in an image or pictorial form (VI), and as analytics tend to break down and structure material, assistance with the overview of material (WA) may be helpful.
- **Wholist-Imager**—the individual will prefer information presented in an image or pictorial form (VI), and as wholists tend to take a general overview of material, assistance with the structure of material (WA) may be helpful.

- **Wholist-Verbaliser**—this individual will prefer information presented in a textual form (VI), and as wholists tend to take a general overview of material, assistance with the structure of material (WA) may be helpful.

METHOD

Sixty-four students took part in the study to the extent that they completed the Cognitive Styles Analysis (CSA) and also completed the unit. The CSA and data collection procedures were an agreed part of the course content of a human computer interaction unit which had a reasonable amount of material on the cognitive aspects of HCI. The assessment procedures of the unit were designed to allow further data collection via reflective journals and the development and documentation of the Individual Learning Environment. The cognitive style measure was considered to be part of the process of user modeling for HCI and interface design.

The elements of the cognitive style outlined above can be viewed as the independent variables in the study (WA and VI dimensions). A series of measures, which can be viewed as dependent variables, was designed to measure the impact of the elements of the cognitive style on the learning process and learning outcomes. These included reflective journals; ILE (website) assessment—interface characteristics; ILE (website) assessment—documentation on development process; feedback survey; interviews with a subset of students.

The Individual Learning Environment

The process of designing and implementing an Individual Learning Environment had two purposes:

- It gave the student experience of the cognitive aspects of Human Computer Interaction via the cognitive profiles.
- It allowed the students to work on a system and develop a set of interfaces in a particularly well-known area for the group (education)—a functional context application.

The following definition was provided:

An Individual Learning Environment (ILE) is a system which is designed to support the information retrieval, information handling and learning support needs of the individual student. In its entirety, the ILE is a hardware and software system which is set up to replicate as many of the Learning Resource Center functions as possible. These functions can include: Learning Support; Study Skills; Media Services; IT Support

(Administrative); IT Support (Academic); Learning Resources and Career Services. The ILE should allow the student to store, retrieve and manipulate information from internal sources (storage, scanner, etc.) and external sources (Internet, WWW, etc.).

The functions of the ILE were to be organized around a series of Web pages which would contain URLs and processes relevant to that function. The majority of the processes (file/open/save/delete, etc.) would be provided by the operating system and browser.

The assessment criteria requested that the system should be structured around the student's current and future units and any learning resources he or she wished to include. For example, resources for a particular unit could include URLs to articles, newsgroups or even the websites of similar units at other institutions. Learning resources could include, for example, links to information on graduate courses the student might be considering or URLs to information considered useful to studies and learning in general.

Elements to be considered in the design of ILE included:

- Conceptual structure (the needs for an organizer or an overview)
- Type of content (verbal or visual)
- Layout of information (e.g., tables, tree diagrams, etc.)
- Choice of mode of presentation (words or pictures) (Riding & Rayner, 1998)

RESULTS

The first figures for the CSA are a simple frequency count for each of the four main classifications. The cognitive styles were distributed in the manner shown in Table 1.

The distribution of the cognitive styles as measured by the CSA show that the largest category is the analytic-imager, comprising nearly one-third of the population (32.8%). Also, while the verbaliser and imager categories are almost evenly split between the group (51.6% and 48.4%), there are more analytics than wholists (57.8% and 42.2%).

Survey Comments on the CSA

The survey asked a range of questions about students' views on the use and relevance of the cognitive style measures to both the unit and the design of the ILE. Of the 60 students completing all the relevant assessments, 39 (65%) also completed the feedback survey. Both quantitative and qualitative responses were recorded. The quantitative responses were measured using five-point Likert scales with 5

Table 1: Distribution of Cognitive Styles

Style	Frequency	Percentage
Analytic-Imager	21	32.8%
Analytic-Verbaliser	16	25.0%
Wholist-Imager	10	15.6%
Wholist-Verbaliser	17	26.6%
Total	64	100.0%

indicating 'strongly agree' and 1 indicating 'strongly disagree.' Due to restrictions of space, only selected results will be summarized here.

When asked to consider the accuracy of the CSA as a measure of their cognitive style, 98% of the respondents either strongly agreed (44%) or agreed (54%). This was rather more than those who held these views for CSA as a measure of personality where 72% agreed with 26% strongly agreeing **(sa)** and 46% agreeing **(a)**. In terms of the format and content of the ILE, 87% of the respondents considered the CSA "important in terms of helping to determine the format of the ILE design" (sa—36%, a—51%), while 66% considered the CSA important in helping determine the content of the same (sa—15%, a—41%).

Cognitive Style and Impact on a Range of Assessments

In Table 2, cognitive style as measured by the CSA is considered with reference to a range of assessment tasks. Of the 64 students who completed the unit, 60 completed all of the above and other assessments. Table 2 demonstrates that, in this study, students with either an analytic-imager or analytic- verbaliser cognitive style consistently scored higher marks across the range of assessments than those with the wholist-imager or wholist-verbaliser cognitive style.

Table 2: CSA and Assessment Marks (%)—Means & Rankings

Ass.	AI	AV	WI	WV
RJ1	70.9	68.9	67.6	63.7
	1	2	3	4
ILE doc	72.1	72.9	66.2	64.4
	2	1	3	4
ILE Int	79.4	78.5	74.9	75.3
	1	2	4	3
Exam	64.0	64.7	56.4	59.8
	2	1	4	3
Final	69.3	68.9	64.2	64.4
	1	2	4	3

KEY:
Assessments: *RJ1—First reflective journal, ILE Int—ILE interface, ILE doc—ILE design documentation, Exam—Final examination, Final—Total unit mark*
Cognitive Styles: *AI—analytic-imager, AV—analytic-verbaliser, WI—wholist-imager, WV—wholist-verbaliser*

STUDENT COMMENTS

A large number of student comments and qualitative data were sought and received via various methods. Reflective journals were used to reflect on each individual's cognitive style. Interface documentation described the design and development process of the ILE and again related it to elements of the cognitive style. Interviews were conducted and survey comments elicited. The range of student comments and reflections included those on how aspects of their cognitive style might impact on interface design and the development of the ILE. For the CSA and cognitive style, an important factor was a preference for text or graphics. While all students recognized the need for the added dimension of textual information, they often differed considerably on their own stated preferences for informational form and content. The material below presents example comments by different students. Some journal reflections are first presented, followed by descriptions of how different cognitive styles might have impacted on the design process for the ILE.

Cognitive Style (CSA)—Reflection

The students found the CSA to be an accurate measure of their cognitive style as described and discussed in class and the readings. The reflective journal comments below are but a small selection of those which often showed students to be at least partially aware of their different cognitive styles, but lacking a framework in which to place and discuss related issues.

The two statements below, the first a wholist-verbaliser, the second an analytic imager, contrast some of the possible cognitive style preferences very well:

"In learning, I agree that I prefer to have the facts set out in a clear structured order and that diagrams and pictures help a great deal." **(analytic-imager)**

"I have always been puzzled as to why teachers would always recommend to us to draw diagrams to help us understand better as I have always found diagrams to be more of a bane than a boon." **(wholist-verbaliser)**

An analytic-verbaliser was surprised by the accuracy of the results:

"(I found the results to be) true as I tend to hold and process textual information in place of graphical information...The test itself did not give any hint as to what the results would be like. In fact I was astounded by the results. My result—analytic-verbaliser, was like reading a book about myself when referring to the description of an Analytic-Verbaliser."

One multimedia student had been confronted with usability problems stemming from different interface designs and had already reflected on them:

"I have also wondered why some people seem to pick up a new piece of software really easily, while I sometimes can seem to struggle for hours. For example (with this software)...the interface seemed com-

pletely foreign to me relative to other programs, and I had no idea where to start...Thus any subject that focuses on how we can improve the problem of difficulty with software is of great interest to me as a multimedia software developer."

Whereas not all respondents were similarly impressed:

"Riding's report claims that I am 'reasonable spatially and have a sense of geographical direction.' I beg to differ on this one. From previous experience, my sense of direction has not been all that wonderful and I have a reputation for getting lost, whether it be in the physical sense or on the Net."

Cognitive Style (CSA)—ILE Development

Participants were especially able to use the cognitive style measure to influence the design of the ILE. This was because, as it gave measures of their supposed preferences for the format and content of information, there was a direct link to the design process that required little further reflection. There was a drawback to this in that some students took the classifications to be absolute rules rather than preferences or guidelines with which they were able to agree or disagree.

This was not always the case though, and several students reflected well and extended that reflection to the design of the ILE. The analytic-imager above commented:

*"When I study, one of the most important things is that all the information is in one place and not scattered about. This structured approach to learning is characteristic of my cognitive style, an **analytic-imager**, and is the foundational element in the design of my ILE. The structure of the ILE was set out in way that allowed me to see the different available categories at all times, i.e., by means of the top frame. This frame acted as an overview that could be referred to at all times."*

One design problem was the issue of strengthening preferences (the verbaliser-imager dimension) or balancing them (the wholist-analytic dimension). As wholists tend to get a good overview of information quite easily, it might have been better for the following participant to impose structure via frames:

"To facilitate the viewing of the Web pages as a whole, I have included a page summary at the top of each Web page. Additionally, the first page (index.html) includes a description of what the ILE

contains. This was to allow me to complement the Wholist section of my cognitive style according to the CSA tests. The Verbaliser section of my cognitive style indicates that I prefer a textual layout to a graphical one and learn best from verbal presentations. I felt that this was a very accurate reflection of my cognitive style and took definitive steps to incorporate this into my ILE." **(wholist-verbaliser)**

Similarly, this participant is strengthening the analytical structure of his ILE when providing features similar to those in the previous example would have been preferable.

"I received an Analytic score of 2.24 and a Verbal score of 0.89. More so an analytic than a verbaliser which also illustrates that I may be more of a "bimodal" person...(that is—either imager or verbaliser)...Viewing information in an analytic form as described in a CSA format, I tend to separate it into parts. This is evident in the ILE as the use of LHS and RHS frames segregate the choice and display of relevant of information." **(analytic-verbaliser)**

It is hoped that these issues can be considered and acted upon in future design and development exercises.

DISCUSSION

When considering an approach where the participants are more fully involved in the research process, and that process involves aspects of an assessed unit, one must be aware of several potential pitfalls. Because the work was assessed, it is possible that students might over emphasize the positive aspects of the process in documents such as the reflective journal, ILE documentation and the feedback survey. To counter this, some cross-checking of comments and opinions is available because of the multiple measures. In addition, the fact that the CSA test was a computer-generated test rather than a self-administered questionnaire gave some assurance as to the objectivity of the results.

It would appear that the cognitive style of each individual has an important impact on how each person internally represents and processes information. Cognitive style, then, could be an important factor in the design of more effective individual interfaces. The integration of style elements with new technologies such as agent-based interfaces could also be a further development (Webster, 2001). The development of agent-supported and cognitive style-related interfaces and learning environments would further help support the student in the demanding activities of online and e-learning. Problems continue to exist with the overall development cycle (Hook, 2000), but continued work in this area will help overcome them.

The current political, organizational and social changes occurring in higher education provide serious challenges for allocating resources to reorganizing student learning. Many institutions are combining the need for change driven by decreasing resources with the potential offered by information technology developments to support student learning. This produces additional problems in the form of easy access to enormous amounts of relatively unstructured data and information. It is suggested that modeling and combining knowledge of an individual's cognitive style and integrating that with adaptive interface design and the use of Internet agents provides a possible solution to some of these problems. This could be a significant factor in the production of environments which would help students to learn more effectively by locating and processing information from the Web and other networks in a more effective and efficient manner.

CONCLUSIONS

The survey results indicated a high level of agreement with the relevance of the overall process and the accuracy of the CSA. Further work is needed to cross-check the range of measures in more detail and to attempt to verify that the survey responses match the comments in the reflective journals, documentation and interviews. From this study, the data suggests that those students who had an analytic-imager or analytic-verbaliser cognitive style consistently outperformed those with a wholist-imager or wholist-verbaliser style across a range of assessment types on the human computer interaction unit. This effect was least on the actual ILE/website development and greatest on the ILE documentation. These differences, while not large, were consistent.

The qualitative data and student comments suggested that knowledge of and reflection on the characteristics of individual cognitive styles could affect the design of the individual learning environment. The study and results also indicate that the ability of each individual to develop a personal learning resource and reflect on the role of their metacognitive characteristics could be a useful instrument in their development as an autonomous lifelong learner. The student comments and qualitative data suggest that knowledge of and reflection on the characteristics of the different individual cognitive styles dimensions could also affect the design and content of individual learning environments in different ways. The design of the Individual Learning Environment was affected in terms of both structure and content. Many found that the different dimensions of the CSA gave them directly useful information. The wholist-analytic information helped develop the format of the ILE while the verbaliser-imager dimension informed the design of the content.

Several respondents questioned why they had not had access to this type of metacognitive information earlier in their school or university careers. They also suggested that they would have found the knowledge particularly useful for the transition to university life and the greater demands of independent learning. Responses and comments often showed that participants were aware of their cognitive and learning styles in a relatively uninformed way. The information provided by the cognitive style measure allowed them to reflect on their learning-related characteristics and preferences in a much more structured and informed manner. The outcome of applying the results of this reflection was enhanced metacognitive skills and knowledge. As autonomous learning in virtual environments becomes more the norm, the awareness of cognitive styles and the application of metacognitive skills will become increasingly valuable resources for the individual learner.

REFERENCES

Averbukh, E., Gavrilova, T., Johannsen, G. & Voinov, A. (1997). User-model based design of adaptive human-computer interfaces. *Proceedings of the 1997 IEEE International Conference on Systems, Man, and Cybernetics, 2,* 1693-1697. Piscataway: IEEE.

Boles, W. & Pillay, H. (1999). A study on the impact of designing computer-based instruction considering preferred cognitive styles. *Proceedings of the 11th Annual Conference and Convention Australasian Association for Engineering Education,* pp. 66-71. AAEE.

Chen, C. (2000). Individual differences in a spatial-semantic virtual environment. *Journal of the American Society for Information Science, 51,* 529-542.

Coyne, R. (1995). *Designing Information Technology in the Postmodern Age: From Method to Metaphor.* Cambridge: MIT Press.

Ellis, R.A. (2000). Writing to learn: Designing interactive learning environments to promote engagement in learning through writing. In Sims, R., O'Reilly, M. & Sawkins, S. (Eds.), *Learning to Choose, Choosing to Learn. Proceedings of the 17th Annual Australian Society for Computers in Learning in Tertiary Education. Southern Cross University.*

Felix, U. (2001). Students as informants for Web-based learning design. In Kennedy, G., Keppell, M., McNaught, C. & Petrovic, T. (Eds.), *Meeting at the Crossroads. Short Paper Proceedings of the 18th Annual Conference of the Australian Society for Computers in Learning in Tertiary Education,* pp. 53-56. Melbourne: Biomedical Multimedia Unit, The University of Melbourne.

Flavel, J.H. (1976). Metacognitive aspects of problem solving. In Resnick, L.B. (Ed.), *The Nature of Intelligence,* 231-235. Hillsdale, NJ: Lawrence Erlbaum.

Ford, N. (2000). Cognitive styles and virtual environments. *Journal of the American Society for Information Science,* 51, 543-557.

Goodyear, P. (2000). Environments for lifelong learning: Ergonomics, architecture and educational design. In Spector, J.M. (Ed.), *Integrated Perspectives on Learning, Instruction and Technology.* Dordrecht: Kluwer Academic Publishers.

Hook, K. (2000). Steps to take before intelligent user interfaces become real. *Interacting with Computers,* 12, 409-436.

Jonassen, D.H. & Grabowski, B.L. (1993). *Handbook of Individual Differences, Learning, and Instruction.* Hillsdale, NJ: Lawrence Erlbaum.

McKay, E. (1999). An investigation of text-based instructional materials enhanced with graphics. *Educational Psychology,* 19, 323-335.

Morgan, H. (1997). *Cognitive Style and Classroom Learning.* Westport: Praeger.

Palmquist, R.A. & Kim K.-S. (2000). Cognitive style and on-line database search experience as predictors of Web search performance. *Journal of the American Society for Information Science,* 51(6), 558-566.

Phelps, R., Ellis, A. & Hase, S. (2001). The role of metacognitive and reflective learning processes in developing capable computer users. In Kennedy, G., Keppell, M., McNaught, C. & Petrovic, T. (Eds.), *Meeting at the Crossroads. Proceedings of the 18th Annual Conference of the Australian Society for Computers in Learning in Tertiary Education,* 481-490. University of Melbourne.

Pillay, H. (1998). An investigation of the effect of individual cognitive preferences on learning through computer-based instruction. *Educational Psychology,* 18, 171-182.

Riding, R. & Cheema, I. (1991). Cognitive styles: An overview and integration. *Educational Psychology,* 11, 193-213.

Riding, R. & Rayner, S. (1998). *Cognitive Styles and Learning Strategies: Understanding Style Differences in Learning and Behaviour.* London: David Fulton Publishers.

Riding, R.J. (1991). *Cognitive Styles Analysis.* Birmingham: Learning and Training Technology.

Riding, R.J. & Rayner, S.G. (2000). *International Perspectives on Individual Differences - Volume 1: Cognitive Styles.* Stamford: Ablex Publishing Corporation.

Summerville, J. (1999). Role of awareness of cognitive style in hypermedia. *International Journal of Educational Technology,* 1.

Tait, H. & Knight, P. (Eds.), (1996). *The Management of Independent Learning.* London: Kogan Page.

Tait, H., Entwistle, N.J. & McCune, V. (1998). ASSIST: A reconceptualisation of the approaches to studying inventory. In Rust, C. (Ed.), *Improving Student Learning,* 262-271. Oxford. Oxford Centre for Staff and Learning Development.

Witkin, H.A., Moore, C.A., Goodenough, D.R. & Cox, P.W. (1977). Field-dependent and field independent cognitive styles and their educational implications. *Review of Educational Research,* 47(1), 1-64.

Webster, W.R. (2001). Interfaces for e-learning: Cognitive styles and software agents for Web-based learning support. In Kennedy, G., Keppell, M., McNaught, C. & Petrovic, T. (Eds.), *Meeting at the Crossroads. Proceedings of the 18th Annual Conference of the Australian Society for Computers in Learning in Tertiary Education,* 559-566. Melbourne: Biomedical Multimedia Unit, University of Melbourne.

Part V

IT Teaching
Cases

Chapter XVI

Designing and Implementing an E-Government Application

Derek Asoh
State University of New York at Albany, USA

Salvatore Belardo
State University of New York at Albany, USA

Jakov Crnkovic
State University of New York at Albany, USA

ABSTRACT

Today, citizens have grown accustomed to highly customized products and services from private sector firms. As a result, they have begun to demand that government agencies become similarly responsive as well. In order to address the ever-increasing expectations of its citizens, governments will need to become more customer-centric. Some government agencies have begun to do this through such IT-enabled initiatives as e-commerce and e-government. This chapter presents a case study of a successful IT project, MACROS, designed to help implement a new vision of business for state agencies within New York State. This new vision requires greater organizational and system transparency, and a culture of collaboration and sharing that is essential to learning how to better serve citizens. The discussion of the methodology employed in the implementation of this e-government application and the lessons learned lends itself to both traditional and virtual educational processes.

INTRODUCTION

The statistics concerning IT project implementation are discouraging. Forty-five percent of all systems that are begun are never completed and of those that are, over 55% take twice as long to complete and cost twice as much as originally planned. While it is good to learn what not to do, it is perhaps more important to learn what should be done in order to ensure success. In this chapter we will report on a successful effort to implement systems in a governmental organization. This case is important because it discusses many ideas that are currently being taught in systems courses at universities.

This case examines the successful initiation, adoption and diffusion of IT within the Office of the State Comptroller (OSC, 2001b) of New York State that is intended to support a new vision of business for government. In particular, we focus on the Multi-purpose Access for Customer Relations and Operational Support (MAC-ROS) project within OSC's Division of Municipal Affairs (OSC-MA). The MAC-ROS project reflects a unique vision of what, why and how one government agency has been able to prepare for business success in the turbulent new economy where constituents demand more responsive customization of service[1] at ever-decreasing costs.

The OSC provides services to the population of New York State through a program of regulation designed to control government agencies (OSC, 2001d). Because of this role, there has been an adversarial relationship between OSC and other state agencies. In mid-1993, a new vision was established at OSC that emphasized the need for new concepts of partnership and quality management. At the heart of this new vision is the use of information technology (IT) to help facilitate the changes needed to better serve the citizens of New York State.

The MACROS project was the first effort designed to improve the quality of OSC-MA services. What used to be, up until the late '90s, a mammoth semi-automated operating environment is now fully automated. Thanks to MACROS, municipalities can now receive, complete and file annual financial reports (AFRs) and/or annual update documents (AUDs) electronically. Today, MACROS has evolved to serve as the cornerstone of an operational enterprise network in OSC-MA that links all employees, helps OSC-MA respond to most requests for information and facilitates communication among OSC-MA's far-flung offices and personnel. It is a highly customized adaptation of the InterTrac software suite from the vendor, ComputerWorks (2001), that is based on the Lotus Notes/Domino architecture. It employs 13 integrated databases designed to fit OSC-MA's needs.

BACKGROUND

OSC-MA was one of the first departments in OSC to embrace the new concept of partnership with customers as a way to achieve managerial goals. Such a shift in the way business is conducted in public organizations would not be possible if accompanying measures (strategic planning, continuous process improvements, etc.) were not taken into account in order to create the proper environment.

Creating and maintaining a supporting environment is neither straightforward nor easy. In fact, it was the top priority of the OSC Administration for close to four years (1994-1998) prior to the start of the MACROS project. As in any change effort, it was essential to gain the support of staff members who will be affected by the new program. The approach to executing OSC-MA's traditional auditing functions also had to be reviewed, taking into consideration the need to build relations among stakeholders. In 1998, the idea of a Municipal Affairs Contact Repository Operating System (MACROS)[2] project was proposed. OSC-MA's personnel are distributed within its two functional branches (Services and Support) operating in several remote locations through the State. The customer base served includes local government officials, and external contacts such as federal agencies, legislatures, taxpayers, professional organizations, financial institutions, vendors and citizens at large.

For a better understanding, let us examine two scenarios that illustrate the daily problems that MACROS helped to solve:

Scenario One: A newly elected official calls OSC-MA with questions concerning AUD, needing immediate feedback.

Scenario Two: A town board member calls OSC-MA asking for an expert who could help explain how their town budgeting works before a vote on the budget scheduled to take place in just three hours.

Traditionally, the role of OSC-MA is to routinely gather, organize and distribute information to its customers. Prior to MACROS, the information was found in many places and in a variety of forms: written correspondences, news articles, media reports, formal reports, professional publications, staff notes, legislature records, etc. Personal contact was the preferred means of communicating with the municipalities. Since the field staff quite often operated independently, the absence of an appropriate network and comprehensive IS support created the emergence of "islands of information." This situation required considerable prior preparation before OSC-MA could respond to customers' requests. In order to keep everything working, OSC-MA had to rely heavily on directives, audits and corrective actions from the central office. This worked as long as the goals of OSC-MA were clear and its activities covered usual and frequent needs, or what is known in IS terminology as well-structured information requests.

SETTING THE STAGE

The OSC is an independent government agency that manages State funds, and has custody over the assets of State and Local Government Retirement Systems. Headed by a comptroller, OSC is charged with specific pre- and post-audit functions. To effectively execute its functions, the OSC has a number of supporting divisions, where the primary responsibility is to oversee the operation of local governments and their political subdivisions, of which there are over 10,000 in New York State (OSC, 2001b).

As noted above, a new vision of customer service started at OSC-MA in 1994. With the new vision, improving the quality of relationships between OSC and local government became a primary goal. New services were provided including: training, consulting, analysis of information products manufactured by local governments and risks assessment. Unfortunately, because each region was doing the same things but in its own way, "Islands of information"[3] were scattered all over OSC-MA. Consequently, there was no way to ensure uniformity and accuracy of information. The information required by staff to do their jobs was likely to be unreliable and redundant or not accessible. With no enterprise/statewide network in place, the manual approach to information processing and exchange often resulted in slow business transactions and poor decisions. The strategy devised by OSC-MA offered people the opportunity to improve performance by providing them with appropriate IT.

In 1998, OSC-MA established a partnership with the Center for Technology in Government[4] (CTG) at the State University of New York at Albany (CTG, 2001), to study the potential for sharing information across the divisions. The mission of the Center is to work with state government agencies to help develop information strategies that foster innovation and enhance the quality and coordination of symbiotic relationships.

Organizational Changes and Technology Issues

Historically, IT at OSC-MA depended on the Bureau of Information Technology Services (BITS)—the IT shop within OSC that provides infrastructure, application and database support to all divisions of OSC. Being internal to OSC-MA, MACROS was not seen as a BITS responsibility. This led to a major decision within OSC-MA to create a unit called Info Tech (see Figure 1), which took on the full responsibility for MACROS.

This change had significant implications for OSC, especially pertaining to the relation between Info Tech and BITS. BITS remained fully involved in a number of activities dealing with MACROS, like writing technical specifications, reviewing the request for proposals and reviewing bids. They were not, however, involved in system implementation of OSC-MA's MACROS project. The Center for Technology in Government (CTG) assisted OSC-MA in developing a policy, management

Figure 1: Operation of BITS and Info Tech Reflecting IT Area of OSC-MA (Note: Info Tech is not a part of BITS, but BITS kept their role in OSC-MA like in other OSC divisions)

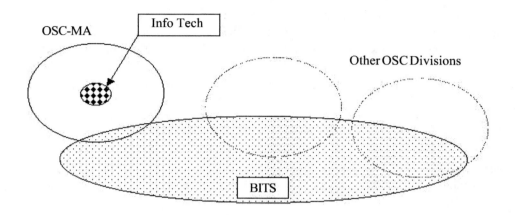

and technological framework for using its rich, but unstructured information to support new service goals. The starting point was the creation of a working team, comprised of staff from OSC-MA and BITS on the one hand, and their counterparts from CTG on the other hand.

CASE DESCRIPTION

Following a stakeholder analysis, a strategic framework for OSC-MA was established. This was followed by business problem analysis where business problems were defined and various options as part of an overall solution were recommended. This "business like" approach in governmental agencies will continue in other applications, particularly in e-government applications. Implementing MAC-ROS is and has been the sole responsibility of OSC-MA.

The business problem analysis showed that the existing strategies[5] caused numerous problems, including:

1. *Inability of staff to:* track or be informed of previous contacts and communication exchanges with current customers; coordinate the distribution of information to customers even within OSC-MA; design responsive and tailored services for a specific customer or group of customers.
2. *Absence of information support mechanisms to:* facilitate critical tasks; properly integrate newly elected officials or appointees.

3.   *Lack of a repository of information resources* that would enable staff to share experiences, collaborate and learn.

The business process analysis quite naturally opened the door for re-engineering. In addition to developing a better understanding of its needs, the approach employed by CTG enabled OSC-MA to understand its current organizational environment and the problem and limitation that it presented.

In making plans for the necessary changes identified as a result of CTG's analysis, a pilot conversion process was selected in order to avoid possible large-scale costly system failures. Thus, it was necessary to limit the scope of the MACROS as much as possible, while trying to obtain concrete results that would provide the rationale for moving forward. Consequently, a single process—the Technical Assistance (TA)—was selected to serve as the test case. The TA transaction created a central information repository within OSC-MA.

The TA transaction exhibited most of the service characteristics and frequently encountered business problems at OSC-MA. It provided an information service that municipalities could access before making any decisions. Based on the business case, one of three alternatives was chosen in the design of MACROS: one that focused on the staff, one that focused on the customer and one that focused on both. The alternative selected would not only influence benefits, but also determine the process models to be implemented, which documents would be captured in the repository and finally the information required for the TA.

To minimize chances of failure, a staff design approach[6] was agreed upon as the major focus.

The service objectives were subsequently formulated in 1998 as follows:
1.   conduct targeted dissemination of information to local governments,
2.   assess the need for service delivery to local governments, and
3.   document contacts between MA staff and specific local government,

   so that:
1.   local governments receive useful information provided by or through OSC,
2.   staff can determine municipalities at risk,
3.   staff can maintain a contact history between OSC and local governments,
4.   staff have timely and accurate information designed to guide regional staff in delivering consistent services to municipalities, and
5.   staff can produce a reliable, accessible, uniform centralized list of local officials.

After setting the service objectives, the next step was to identify and describe the appropriate business activities. The rationale was to make the TA service process as transparent as possible, so that the overall business value of MACROS could be easily evaluated. Following the Joint Application Development[7] approach, a workshop was organized, in which the CTG "Model for Action Tool Kit" (CTG, 2001) was employed to identify, review and describe all the steps of the TA processes, as well as the associated records and system requirements. In this phase, many more OSC-MA staff, especially those from the regional offices, were involved. Participants agreed that TA was the most cost-effective way to start MACROS.

Given the importance of gaining and maintaining broad and top management support, the OSC-MA team adopted a knowledge management (KM) strategy that involved the practice of sharing the story of the MACROS projects and its prospects with all involved. This led to the establishment of a solid foundation of agency support, paved the way for more efficient and effective stakeholder analysis, and also served as a stimulant for the desired inter-division collaboration.

A formal evaluation of the stakeholders' involvement was categorized according to several broad areas of service objectives including internal and external objectives. The OSC-MA staff was once again selected as the primary stakeholder. The relative needs of the stakeholderers and the value of the proposed services that MACROS would provide to each stakeholder were assessed. This was done in order to gain an appreciation of stakeholder expectations and the level of commitment necessary for success.

Both internal and external factors needed to achieve specific service objectives were analyzed using CTG's *Making Smart IT Choices: A Handbook* (CTG, 2001). This analysis helped establish the framework for OSC-MA. It is a way to enable organizations to "think out of the box," so that they can better understand the operational environment—resources, innovative opportunities, customers and new partners (see Table 1).

Following the stakeholder analysis and the establishment of the strategic framework, the business problem analysis was conducted using three modeling tools—cost performance, surveys and best practices. The cost performance modeling addressed issues concerning the system functionality, level of system implementation (modest, moderate, elaborate), associated cost/gain and required timeframe. Stakeholders were surveyed to ascertain the business practices within OSC associated with collecting and documenting contact information, the nature and availability of such information, who is responsible and what stakeholders expected of MACROS.

Based on the business problem analysis, three options were considered as possible solution components. These components turned out to be complementary and included a Document Management System, a Workflow System and a Records Management System. These systems were expected to positively impact the efficiency, effectiveness and quality of OSC-MA services.

The assessment showed that MACROS would be able to offer the following benefits (OSC, 1998):

Table 1: OSC-MA Operational Environment

Resources	Primary	Secondary
	Existing systems, media reports, local government reports, operational policies, legal opinions and OSC-MA staff knowledge	BITS, OSC divisions, network resources, personnel, vendors, Internet, local government associations
Innovative Opportunities	Products	Services
	Central repository, communication tracking and document management	CTG project, communication center, search capabilities, online access and decision support
Customers	Internal	External
	OSC-MA staff and managers, legal services, press office	Local officials, other state agencies, federal agencies, taxpayers, legislature, media, professional associations, vendors and financial institutions
New Partners	Legal Division, Press Office, Justice Court, Mail Room, BITS, Management Services	State agencies, local governments, CTG, Office for Technology

1. reduce redundant records;
2. provide historical information, better background information for services, more consistent policy and action, and better context for planning;
3. deliver services on the spot;
4. improve day-to-day communication and performance;
5. ensure more timely delivery of services; and
6. increase local awareness of available state-sponsored services.

Additional recommendations included the creation and implementation of a system vision with appropriate technological solutions, and maintenance of effective communication to educate stakeholders on the importance and necessity of MAC-ROS.

MACROS: Design and Implementation Approach

A call for bids was made in 2000. The bid articulated all the objectives of OSC-MA and the system vision of MACROS. Proactively, the bid went a step further to emphasize an OSC-wide integration perspective (scalability) and in making it clear that MACROS would be adding processes over time.

A local company, ComputerWorks (2001), a Lotus Premier Business Partner[8], emerged as another collaborator in the MACROS project. MACROS was designed to include a system of integrated databases to serve the purposes of auxiliary forms (audit and reports), business processes, calendar, calls, contacts, correspondences, filing services, form letter library, help desk and knowledge base, reports and time management. The Lotus Notes/Domino architecture on which MACROS is based offered an environment with powerful facilities for free-form managing of documents, and the ability to replicate information for off-line use. Although MACROS has the ability to integrate products from several platforms, the focus is on the Microsoft Office Suite. From an operational perspective, MACROS is transparent to its users. All components seamlessly operate together and are accessible through various graphical user interfaces. Functionally, MACROS offers important features and services such as: information access, dissemination and business process support.

Project realization resulted in providing staff with the opportunity to collaborate and learn from each other, while better serving customers. Described as an organization in transition towards a service-oriented way of working (CTG, 2001), OSC-MA's new strategies are in the hands of Info Tech—now the IT "flag bearer" of OSC-MA.

CURRENT CHALLENGES AND MACROS PERSPECTIVES

MACROS, while a success, nevertheless created a number of challenges that we have categorized according to the following three areas: Philosophical and Organizational, Information Resource Management and Knowledge Management.

Philosophical and Organizational Challenges

1.   Eliminate difficulties in describing what MACROS is and what it is trying to accomplish.

2.   Build and sustain credibility and support.
3.   Ensure that Info Tech works with all division managers, staff and customers to better understand their respective objectives, and craft the best IT solutions.
4.   Overcome geographical barriers that exist as a result of the dispersed location of the regional offices.
5.   Start working to eliminate the resistance to change, which is one of the greatest obstacles to the successful introduction of new concepts and systems.
6.   Promote interdependence among various departments.

Information Resource Management Challenges

1.   Continue working on establishing an appropriate relationship between BITS and Info Tech.
2.   Establish a more stable IT network in order to implement MACROS for remote users. (The current Internet service provider is not reliable.)
3.   Solve time constraints and provide for the transfer of the current legacy system to MACROS.

Knowledge Management Challenges

1.   Get people to share knowledge.
2.   Create an organization where everyone is willing to contribute and share information with others, even if they do not understand how helpful it might be to the others.
3.   Introduce the best analytical tools to enable communication and ensure knowledge exchange among the different stakeholders.
4.   Educate the staff and help them to understand that MACROS will not cause them to lose their jobs, but will help them to do their job better.

In order to manage the above challenges, a number of significant improvements were made, including:
1.   A MACROS Advisory Committee with members from OSC and CTG was created.
2.   A monthly newsletter called "State of Affairs" (OSC, 2001c), through which staff is informed and educated, was initialized.
3.   Leaders capable of handling the high expectations the administration placed on the success of MACROS was designated.
4.   A flexible MACROS philosophy was promoted in order to support the evolutionary and changing nature of the acronym MACROS[9].

The next phase in the MACROS project is being geared towards establishing an OSC-wide collaborative environment. The MACROS Advisory Committee in May 2001 completed another study (OSC, 2001a). From the study, it was determined that the best strategy for OSC-MA requires a focus on Info Tech, rather than just on MACROS. A strategic plan for the realization of the mission of Info Tech (2001) has been summarized as: "Users will be able to access information they need when they need it, regardless of their location, in the format that is most appropriate for their needs." It is in fact the "Anyone-Anything-Anywhere-Anytime" paradigm, that clearly requires enormous resources for full execution- resources well beyond those possessed by Info Tech.

Greater demands on the public sector for better services seems logical given that citizens have become accustomed to a greater variety of customized products and services provided by private sector firms (Asoh, Belardo & Neilson, 2002). In response to these ever-increasing expectations, governments are currently engaged in such initiatives as e-commerce and e-government. Success in these endeavors, however, depends to a large extent on how well public agencies are prepared for change. Evidently, with MACROS, OSC-MA is poised to deliver services—very elegantly, timely, with a high degree of accuracy, to the satisfaction of all parties concerned and at minimum cost.

We complete our discussion by summarizing the solutions of the two scenarios introduced earlier. In the first scenario, the actions undertaken reflect *How MACROS Serves Customers*. As a result of MACROS, OSC-MA staff can instantly: 1) consult a complete contact list of specialists, 2) track and consult relevant past communications of the outgoing officials, 3) re-assign jobs, 4) collaborate with each other in real-time to assemble a solution or generate the answers to questions that have not been previously asked or problems that have previously been solved, and 5) provide a solution to the official in whatever form requested. In the second scenario, the actions undertaken reflect the *Use of MACROS as the Municipal Electronic Library*. Here, OSC-MA staff can: 1) identify and gather training material on budgeting on the spot, through appropriate keyword searches, 2) mobilize competent personnel or re-assign roles to respond to the board member, and 3) participate in the board meeting accordingly.

LESSONS LEARNED

We believe that this case is interesting to experienced system designers and managers, as well as novices in the areas of IS design, IT and management. We will conclude our discussion by presenting several important lessons learned.

Lesson 1: The Importance of Applying a Business View

Business Problem Analysis opens new opportunities for using sound business practices in governmental and other non-profit organizations. As in any situation these ideas should be applied very carefully, but even more so in the public sector where it is important to keep in mind the needs and interest of an extremely wide variety of stakeholders, including the public, staff, elected officials, volunteers, etc. Similarly, it is important to understand the "customer" in order to deliver the products or services appropriate to the customer's unique needs.

The IS/IT needs of agencies, such as election boards or the State Agency for Mental Health, are significantly different than those of, say, the Department of Motor Vehicles or State Parks and Recreation. Serious managerial and IS/IT problems surface when governmental and non-profit entities begin to employ a business view. For example, the introduction of e-government—started to promote business-like relations between governmental agencies themselves, and between governmental and for profit organizations—had become necessary, yet requires a new and very different mindset for governments.

Lesson 2: Key to Successful IS/IT Application: Reengineering, KM and Collaboration

Critical to the success of the MACROS project was the use of various models and such tools and techniques as reengineering and knowledge management. Reengineering is essential if we are to overcome the inherited problems that entrenched islands of information pose. Attention to the need for reorganization in the IS/IT area needed, helped identify the need to establish the Info Tech group and limit the influence of the established BITS. Knowledge management was also instrumental in ensuring the success of the effort, not only because it emphasized the need to share information/knowledge, but also because it helped identify the need for a strategic partnership. The collaboration that resulted from the partnership between OSC-MA, CTG and ComputerWorks has helped make MACROS a success story.

Lesson 3: Employing a Proven System Development Methodology

Fundamental to the success of any IT project is the underlying development methodology and the development team. Various components of the CTG SmartIT Methodology (CTG, 2001) were employed in the MACROS project. Using this methodology, OSC-MA was able to: 1) choose a "good" problem, 2) identify and test the practicality and feasibility of solutions to the problem, and 3) evaluate alternate solutions and make a smart solution choice based on a realistic business case. In the case of MACROS, the smart IT Choice was for OSC-MA to outsource rather than build the application.

Key to the success of any outsourced effort is the preparation of a bid that explicitly includes detailed future needs, especially scalability considerations. A good bid description and a well-orchestrated bidding process enabled OSC to obtain an excellent software company partner (ComputerWorks). The IT shop of OSC, BITS, was aware that its role in the system implementation was very limited; however, BITS used its expertise when it was needed (e.g., in the bidding process) and to facilitate cooperation with the newly established Info Tech group. The MACROS design team ensured that roles were properly defined for all actors. Applying the Joint Application Design (JAD) methodology and prototyping insured that stakeholders, especially key personnel, would assume the role of "champion" and be fully involved in the whole system analysis, design and implementation process.

REFERENCES

Asoh, D., Belardo, S. & Neilson, R. (2002, January). *Knowledge Management: Issues, Challenges and Opportunities for Governments in the New Economy.* Paper presented at the 35th Hawaii International Conference on System Sciences (HICSS35), USA.

ComputerWorks. (2001). *ComputerWorks Website.* Available: http://www.computerworks.com [2001, October 11].

CTG. (2001). *Center for Technology in Government Website.* Available: http://www.ctg.albany.edu.

Info Tech. (2001). *Info Tech Strategic Plan.* Albany: OSC-MA.

OSC. (1998). *MACROS: Municipal Affairs Contact Repository Operating System. Business Case.* Albany: OSC-MA.

OSC. (2001a). *Conducting the Investigation and Feasibility of Expanding MACROS as an Agency-Wide Tool: Identifying Needs and Commonalities.* Albany: OSC-MA.

OSC. (2001b). *Office of the State Comptroller, New York State.* Available: http://www.osc.state.ny.us [2001, October 11].

OSC. (2001c). *State of Affairs.* Albany: OSC-MA.

OSC. (2001d). *What's the Comptroller's Responsibilities?* OSC. Available: http://www.osc.state.ny.us/about/response.htm [2001, October 11].

ENDNOTES

[1] An earlier version of this paper, entitled "Preparing a Government Agency for Business Success in the New Economy: A Success Story," was presented at the IRMA International Conference in Seattle, May 2002, and printed in the

Conference Proceedings: *Issues and Trends of Information Technology in Contemporary Organizations*, edited by Mehdi Khosrow-Pour, Idea Group Publishing, Hershey, PA, 2002. This case encapsulates discussions and suggestions made by conference participants after the presentation.

[2] The project title MACROS remains the same, but the original acronym developed over time into: Multi-purpose Access for Customer Relations and Operational Support, showing the special flavor for dynamic needs and approach.

[3] Islands of information **between** governmental agencies are not in the focus of this paper

[4] The CTG has received the prestigious "Innovations in American Government" award from the Ford Foundation in recognition of its creative partnerships and problem solving in the public sector.

[5] Briefly presented in the section "Background" of this paper.

[6] When building a completely new informational system for governmental (or any other) organization, other approaches are more likely to be chosen (Crnkovic, 2001).

[7] For example, see Hoffer, J.A., George, J. & Valacich, J. (1999). *Modern Systems Analysis and Design*, 2nd ed. Reading, MA: Addison Wesley.

[8] ComputerWorks has clients all over the world, including several state agencies (CWK, 2001). In 2000, ComputerWorks won the "Best Industry Solution Public Sector" award from IBM Lotus Development Corporation in recognition of its works in the government and health care segments.

[9] See footnote numbered [1].

Chapter XVII

Learning to Analyze Unstructured Systems Using Forster's
A Passage to India

Athar Murtuza
Seton Hall University, USA

Muhammad Ali
Tuskegee University, USA

ABSTRACT

The chapter seeks to promote use of literary works as a teaching resource for management information systems (MIS) courses. It does so by using a novel written by E.M. Forster to illustrate what may be done. The use of such a resource to supplement MIS teaching can help students' communication skills and raise their awareness of cultural diversity in the global village. The main focus in this chapter, however, is to provide a way for instructors to impress upon students the need to be aware of the great number of managerial decisions that cannot be made using boiler-plate recipes. Managers who make decisions often must deal with unstructured situations involving non-recurring and non-routine issues. Such situations do not fit established models and conceptual frameworks; consequently, managers have to rely on their expertise in dealing with them. The education of MIS analysts and managers needs to include such awareness so they will be better prepared to deal with a world where the only constant is change.

The chapter starts by discussing the various benefits that can result from using literary works in systems analysis courses. Works such as A Passage to India *combine elements associated with both case studies and experiential learning. This makes literary works potentially a very useful resource for MIS curricula even though such an idea may seem unconventional. Even though MIS educators do not use literary works, other curricula aimed at various professions, such as medicine and law, are using them as a teaching resource. After discussing the potential benefits of this untapped resource, the chapter provides a synopsis of the novel. It then discusses the specific relevance of Forster's novel for MIS and suggests ways of using it in systems analysis context.*

INTRODUCTION

Managers who make decisions often must deal with unstructured situations involving non-recurring and non-routine issues. Such situations do not fit established models and conceptual frameworks; consequently, managers have to rely on their expertise in dealing with them. The education of the managers needs to include such expertise. They must know how to deal with an ever-changing world. The education of management information system (MIS) students and professionals must include the appreciation of the considerable extent to which unstructured decisions take up the resources available to system managers and analysts. One way to improve their ability to deal with unstructured situations is by making sure they can practice, while still in classrooms, repeated applications of their skills as systems analysts to unfamiliar contexts and unstructured situations.

LITERATURE AS A TEACHING RESOURCE

It is imperative for MIS instructors to impress upon MIS students that communication of information and its use for organizational decision-making involves more than bits and bytes. It is important to give MIS students the opportunity to practice the application of skills they are taught, such as system analysis and mapping to unstructured situations. This chapter shows how such objectives may be realized by the use of literary works, such as E.M. Forster's novel, *A Passage to India,* as a teaching resource in MIS courses dealing with systems analysis and process mapping. While this chapter uses the novel about South Asia to make its case, other literary works can also be used. The world represented in the Forster novel can be seen as an organization where cultural and behavioral factors impede effective communication of information leading to harmful and ineffective decisions. British India as dramatized in the novel will be an unstructured situation for MIS students, and getting them to map how crucial decisions were made and how communication of information took place in this literary classic would be a good way to engage their critical thinking skills.

BENEFITS OF USING LITERARY WORKS IN MIS COURSES

There are collateral benefits to using literary works to supplement other more familiar teaching resources, such as cases, games, experiential exercises and simulations. It can help improve students' abilities to communicate. Communication skills can be learned through such practice. Even though reading a novel is time consuming, such reading is precisely the kind of practice needed to learn communication skills—all too often such investment of time serves as intellectual stimulation rather than busy work. In addition, a novel such as *A Passage to India* can raise students' global awareness by showing them how the global village is made up of diverse cultures. Yet another benefit to MIS students is to emphasize the importance of knowledge and skills learned in liberal studies courses.

Traditionally, the required liberal studies courses are the primary tools designated to teach undergraduate MIS general studies. But the skills and knowledge acquired through liberal studies are rendered less effective because the liberal studies courses are seen as stones to step over rather than as stepping-stones to the acquisition of knowledge and its management (Coe & Merino, 1987, pp. 1-6). Among such skills acquired through liberal studies are those that permit enhanced and effective communication as well as a greater understanding of cultural and behavioral issues. Time after time, the importance of such skills in the blueprints for MIS curricula have been emphasized; one need not browse further than the suggested MIS curriculum on the IRMA website.

One way to make MIS students value and retain the skills and knowledge taught in liberal studies courses is by calling on them to use what is taught in their MIS courses. This would be an apt way to make the MIS students see the knowledge gained and skills taught in liberal arts courses as stepping-stones that help reinforce what they are learning in MIS, accounting and business courses. Such a recollection of what should have been learned in liberal studies courses would, in turn, mean that MIS teachers are not outsourcing entirely to the arts and science faculty the concern with the teaching of human aspects of information communication and knowledge management. In fact, communication and human behavior should not be left entirely to liberal studies; MIS courses ought to reinforce what is taught in liberal studies courses. Using resources conventionally associated with liberal studies, such as literary works, in MIS courses is one way to keep students from seeing liberal studies as stones to step over.

LITERATURE AS A SURROGATE FOR EXPERIENTIAL LEARNING

There is a considerable body of research that has dealt with the value of experiential learning for some time (Coleman, 1976; Kolb, 1974; Umapathy, 1985; Walter & Marks, 1981). It is generally agreed that the experiential approach to teaching behavior can facilitate a greater student involvement, promote class discussion and facilitate the understanding of complex behavioral concepts. Experiential learning stays with students much longer than other approaches do. Students tend to remember an experience much longer than they do parts of lectures or pages from a textbook. Games, business simulations, behavioral exercises in the classroom and case studies seek to bridge the gap between abstract lectures and experiential learning. These approaches contrast with courses relying strictly on lectures, where human behavior is talked about rather than observed, felt or experienced.

Culture, art and literature can also help improve students' perceptions about human behavior. For thousands of years and in virtually every civilization, cultural artifacts such as music, paintings, novels, poems and plays have dramatized human behavior. The hold literature has on the human imagination can be attributed largely to its ability to evoke empathy in its readers. While reading a novel, reciting a poem or watching a play, readers and audiences are able to empathize with the characters and actions being portrayed and are able vicariously to experience it themselves. Literature may be seen both as a mirror that reflects human behavior and a lamp that helps illuminate it. Because literature evokes empathy and permits readers to experience life vicariously, it can serve as a resource for vicariously experiencing life and through it human behavior. Some will argue that not only do literary works capture life more effectively than do the narratives in case studies, they happen to be more readable as well. One ought to be able to use literature as a surrogate for vicarious experiential learning pertaining to human perception, motivation, anxiety, conflict, attitude and attitude change, interpersonal communication and the complex diversity of human behavior.

Such a use of literary works in the context of accounting and systems courses seemingly fits the various definitions of creativity quoted by Cougar (1995). Among the definitions quoted by Cougar is the one by Bruner that sees "effective surprise" to be the essence of a creative approach. Ciardi sees creativity to be imaginatively recombining known elements into something new, while the French mathematician Poincare equated the creative process with a fruitful combination that reveals an unsuspected relationship between facts long known but wrongly believed to be antithetical to each other. In order to merit classification as creative, an activity must be new or unique, and it must have utility and/or value, according to Cougar (1995, p. 14), which is what use of literary works in MIS courses would do.

Even though MIS pedagogy has yet to make use of literature in its courses, other professions have been using alternative resources such as literature to enhance their

Exhibit 1

Tool	Profession	Citations
Films	Communication	Adler, 1995; Griffin, 1995; Proctor; 1993, Proctor & Adler, 1991; Serey, 1992; Zorn, 1991
Films	Medicine	Green et al., 1995
Films	Business	Berger & Pratt, 1998
Literature	Medicine	Downie, 1991; Green et al., 1995; Carson, 1994; Weisberg & Duffin, 1995; Coles, 1989
Literature	Law	Webb, 1996; Coles, 1989
Literature	Business	Shepard et al., 1997; Coles, 1989; Kennedy & Lawton, 1992; McAdams, 1993; McAdams & Koppensteiner, 1992

teaching. In Exhibit 1, the chapter cites studies that talk about use of alternative resources used to educate professionals. The list is representative and even the sample citations show the extent to which professions other than MIS have made use of literature and similar resources to enhance the diversity of educational resources available to them.

SUMMARIZING THE NOVEL'S PLOT

Before talking about how to use Forster's novel in an MIS course, it would be helpful to provide the readers with a synopsis of the novel. Such a summary would be of special benefits to readers who have not read the novel or even seen the movie. Incidentally, the movie left out most of material belonging to the third part of the book.

The plot of *A Passage to India* can be well summarized if it is seen as the consequences of the trip of two British visitors to India: Mrs. Moore and Adela Quested. The adventures and misadventures that accrue to these two visitors set off the chain of events that makes up the novel. The former is an elderly British woman who was visiting her son, Mr. Rodney Heaslop, then serving as the City Magistrate in an out-of-the-way Indian city called Chandrapore. The ostensible reason for Mrs. Moore's travel to India was to accompany Adela Quested, who was engaged to her son Rodney. Moore's intent was to stay in India through the hot weather and to see her son marry Adela. Both Moore and Quested feel imprisoned in what they sense to be the British Indian ghetto. The self-imposed isolation of the British Indians is resented by these two recent arrivals.

They fret at what they perceive to be their lack of contact with India and the Indians while living in Chandrapore. What they are unaware of is that there are rules and rituals that serve to separate not only the colonial rulers from the ruled, but also that divide sharply the different groups that comprised the Indian populace—namely, Muslims and Hindus.

Unlike these two British visitors, the reader is made aware of the gulfs between the British rulers and their subjects at the outset. In the second chapter of the book, the members of the Muslim subculture are discussing whether it was possible to be friends with their rulers. The implication of the conversation is that British colonials changed their liberal nature once they came to India to govern—once in India, they turned racist with very low opinions of those they were seeking to govern. According to Hamidullah, a Muslim lawyer who had been educated at Cambridge University: "I give any Englishman two years, be he Turton or Burton…And I give any Englishwoman six months. All are exactly alike" (Forster, p. 4).[1] This early discussion among the Indian Muslims shifted eventually to nostalgia about the memory of the Muslim rule of India and elsewhere in the world: "India—a hundred Indias—whispered outside beneath the indifferent moon, but for the time India seemed one and their own, and they resumed their departed greatness by hearing its departure lamented; they felt young again because reminded that youth must fly" (pp. 8-9).

In the midst of this escapism of Indian Muslims, reality intrudes in the form of a servant of the British Civil Surgeon who, dressed in a scarlet coat, brings a message from Major Callendar, his employer, to Dr. Aziz, who is the leading Indian character in the novel. Aziz was being called to see Major Callendar at his bungalow. In response, Aziz rides his bicycle, which had neither light nor bell or even brakes. Along the way the bicycle has a flat tire, forcing him to find a tonga—a horse carriage. They were scarce that evening—it seemed most of the carriages had been drafted to transport the British Indians to their club, where a function was in progress. He does find a tonga, but instead of going to Callendar's house directly, Aziz goes first to dispose of his bicycle at a friend's house, and then "dallied furthermore to clean his teeth" (p. 10). But as his horse carriage approaches the part of town belonging to the British, Aziz worries about riding a tonga to visit the residence of a member of the ruling class.

There had been one case where an Indian riding a carriage was told to go back by the servants and approach on foot. Even though hundreds of Indians had visited the British Indians in their horse carriages, the book lets it be known, it was the exception to the rule, which become famous around town. By the time Aziz arrives at the home of his British superior, a very irritated Callendar had already left, having been angered by what he saw as stereotypical lack of responsibility on the part of the natives.

What compounds the problem for Aziz is the loss of his carriage to two rather pompous British ladies, who expropriated the tonga, while behaving all too rudely towards the native Aziz. The frustration of Aziz increases even more because Callendar's native servant is uncooperative despite being bribed. It appears that the British Civil Surgeon has not even left a message for his late-arriving subordinate. Snubbed and insulted by the two British ladies who stole his carriage, Aziz walks out of the part of town, usually called civil station, where British Indians lived.

Just outside the British Indian enclave of the town, Aziz finds and rests in a mosque. The mosque makes Aziz's thoughts to wander, and while imagining Islam's past grandeur, he notices Mrs. Moore enters the mosque. Having tired of the amateur theater at the British Indian club, Moore had decided to walk the neighborhood on her own. Initially, still smarting at the theft of his carriage, Aziz reprimands her for not taking her shoes off in the mosque. He assumed that any British woman walking into the mosque, being British, would fail to take her shoes off. After being told by Mrs. Moore that she has, in fact, observed this rule, Aziz's mood changes and he behaves more congenially. The two have a friendly talk and he escorts her back to the club—although a part of the conversation is used by him to vent his frustration for the slights he presumed to have suffered at the hand of the British Indians.

Back at the club, Mrs. Moore makes her companion Quested envious by telling her of her excursion to the nearby mosque. When Mrs. Moore tells her son, Ronny, about Aziz, Ronny reprimands her for associating with an Indian. Adela complains that they have seen nothing of India, but have been limited to seeing English customs replicated abroad. Although a few persons make racist statements about Indians and harp on their racial inferiority, Mr. Turton, the Collector, proposes to host a "Bridge Party" (to bridge the gulf between the ruling class and their subjects) at his residence.

The Bridge Party and Beyond

The Bridge Party hosted by the Collector, the closest thing to omnipotence in the town, is well attended; however, it was failure, for only a select few of the English guests behave well toward the Indians. Among these is Mr. Fielding, the schoolmaster at the Government College, who seeks to make up for the failure of the Bridge Party by hosting a small party at which he invites some Indians in addition to Moore and Quested. Heaslop saw the party suspiciously, and he was not happy that his mother and fiancé attended it. Even at this early stage, Mrs. Moore reprimands her son for being impolite to the Indians and for his overt lack of civility, which she labels kindness towards the natives. But her son replies that he is not in India to be kind; instead, his presence there is to maintain order, in other words to bring civilization to the natives. Her son's behavior offends her sense of values, political and spiritual.

Aziz accepts Fielding's invitation to attend the party given for Adela and Mrs. Moore. Professor Narayan Godbole, who talked about the nearby Marabar Caves, also attended it. It is noteworthy that he does not really reveal much about the caves and even manages to avoid being a part of the expedition to the Caves, which has rather disastrous consequences. In the meantime, Fielding takes Mrs. Moore to see the college while Ronny arrives to find Adela alone with Aziz and Godbole. Shocked, he chastises fellow British expatriate Fielding for leaving an Englishwoman alone with two Indians. Fielding reminds Ronny that Adela is capable of making her own decisions—a remark which would seem all too ironic later in the book.

To upstage Godbole, Aziz "volunteers" to arrange a picnic at the Marabar Caves for Miss Quested and Mrs. Moore, a promise he kept only after being forced into it later in the narrative. Aziz himself had no interest in them and knows nothing of the mythic legends associated with them, unlike Godbole, who does but fails to communicate it to others. The comically grandiose expedition to the desolate caves—complete with special train, elephants and potpourri of exotic native colors—turns into an unmitigated disaster.

Although Aziz, Adela and Mrs. Moore arrive at the train station on time, Fielding and Godbole miss the train because of Godbole's morning prayers, which seemingly lasted extra long. Adela and Aziz discuss her marriage, and she fears she will become a narrow-minded Anglo-Indian like the other wives of British officials. When they reach the caves, a distinct echo in one of them frightens Mrs. Moore, who decides she must leave immediately. The echo and the hot desolation of the caves terrify her, for it gives her the sense that the universe is chaotic and has no order. The location of the caves certainly may be seen as a representation of a spiritual wasteland. Aziz and Adela continue to explore the caves, and Adela realizes that she does not love Ronny.

As Adela and Aziz are going through the caves, which were dark, hot and uncomfortable, she asks Aziz, a widower, if he has more than one wife. The question upsets him and to calm down, he steps out of the cave; meanwhile, she feels she has been assaulted and fearfully runs out. The book does not explicitly indicate if there was really an assault on Quested. Nonetheless, thinking that she is being attacked, and feeling terrified, she seeks to escape. In the process, she is bruised while falling down the steep slope into the thorny shrubs. Miss Derek, riding a car that she had appropriated without the permission of her employer, an Indian Maharaja, rescues her. Both the car and the driver belonged to her employer, but given the skin-color of Miss Derek, there was little they could do. As a single woman, she was not well liked by the British Indians, married women particular, hence her employment in a part of India not directly administered by the British.

The Unintended Consequences of the Expedition

Derek brings Quested back to town. But the rest of those in the expedition to the caves have no knowledge of this emergency and they assume the missing Quested must have gone back to town with Derek while in a "healthy state." Whether on her own or under prompting by Derek, Adela, suffering from a bad case of nerves, accuses Aziz of being the man who attacked her in the cave. There is no investigation of the accusation. But, as a result of the charge made, no sooner does the party arrive at the Chandrapore train station than Aziz is arrested and simultaneously, his house was searched and his personal belongings were taken to the police station.

Even though the British Indians would have liked to lynch Aziz without any regard for due process, the political correctness demanded a trial. To show its sense of propriety, the ruling class even let an Indian judge preside over the trial since Heaslop, who would have normally handled the case, had a conflict of interest. In the course of the trial, it is revealed that her son has sent Mrs. Moore out of the country even though the hot weather would have made her journey dangerous in the age before air-conditioning was a household word in South Asia. Since she was being portrayed as a character witness sympathetic to Aziz, her reported departure leads to an outburst, with natives chanting Mrs. Moore's name. The seemingly religious chanting of Mrs. Moore's name according to the novel leads to a recovery of Quested's nervous condition; she was, ever since her visit to the cave, hearing a disturbing echo that was causing her to be on nervous edge. This echo is suddenly gone after the Indian crowd in the courtroom started chanting Mrs. Moore's name— Adela feels as though Mrs. Moore was communicating from beyond. Such implications of unexplained phenomena, like ghosts, are spread throughout the novel, hinting at another level of reality inaccessible to rational facts. Indeed in the third section, just such a paranormal reality becomes the subject of the novel.

Once the ringing in her ears stopped, Quested recalls that Aziz was not even in the cave when she thought she was attacked. She recants her charge against Aziz and, to the dismay of the British community in Chandrapore; the case against Aziz is dismissed. In the pandemonium, her British Indian companions who had until then made her into a symbol of British honor abandon her. She no longer remained a part of the British Indian community after the abrupt and surprising end of the trial.

After the Trial

Following the trial, Fielding gains new respect for Adela for having shown moral courage in the face of the hatred displayed towards her by the British Indians—they consider her an outcast. Ironically, the Indians also refuse to acknowledge the nature of the courage Adela displayed and want nothing to do with her either. After hearing Indians talk about retribution against Adela, Fielding attempts to persuade Aziz not to sue Adela for damages since that would be a great hardship for someone without a financial fortune. At Fielding's urging, Aziz relents and does not seek damages, much to the dismay of the other Indians who sought revenge. Adela leaves India with plans to visit Mrs. Moore's other children (and Ronny's step-siblings), Stella and Ralph, in England.

Meanwhile, Aziz hears rumors from his Indian friends, which insinuate that Fielding had an affair with Adela when she lived at the college. Aziz ends up believing these malicious, unfounded rumors even though he had doubts about the reliability of those conveying them. He goes on to imagine that in urging Aziz to drop his demand for damages, Fielding was seeking to enrich himself by marrying Quested. Because of this suspicion, the friendship between them begins to cool, even after Fielding denies the affair to Aziz. Fielding himself leaves Chandrapore to travel, while Aziz remains convinced that Fielding would end up marrying Adela Quested.

The Aftermath

Forster resumes the novel some time later in the Princely state of Mau, where Godbole now works for a Hindu rajah as a minister of education as well as a religious advisor. While the British directly ruled most of the subcontinent, there were about 400 Princely states that had internal autonomy and which were not directly administered by the British. Among them were Kashmir and Hyderabad. With the help of Hindu Godbole, Muslim Aziz has also moved to the same Princely state where he lives with his children. The move resulted in large part because the trial had pretty much destroyed his career as a doctor working for the British. This Princely state was autonomous but was kept under watch by the British Indian government. As part of this oversight, British officials visited states like this periodically, and one such visit brought Fielding to Mau for inspection of its educational institution, a college which existed only on paper, ironically named after Fielding by his former employee Godbole.

Fielding has married, and Aziz assumes that his bride is Miss Quested. Aziz stopped corresponding with Fielding when he received a letter, which stated that Fielding married someone Aziz knows. Fielding had written several letters to Aziz, but other Indians never delivered them to him. Fielding's wife was not Adela, as Aziz assumes, but rather Mrs. Moore's own daughter, Stella. She and her brother Ralph were visiting Mau with Fielding. Fielding actually meets with Aziz and clears up this misunderstanding, but Aziz remains angry, finding it difficult to shed the pent-up anger he felt toward Fielding for presumably having married the woman who destroyed his career.

Despite his misgivings, Aziz goes to the guesthouse where Fielding was staying and finds Ralph Moore there. The excuse for his visit was to take some medication for Ralph, who had been stung by a wasp. The wasps are a recurrent element in the novel. His anger at Fielding cools when Ralph invokes the memory of Mrs. Moore, and then, Aziz even takes Ralph boating on the river so that they can observe the local Hindu ceremonies—something the foreigners were not officially meant to do. Due to darkness of the night on account of heavy rain, their boat, however, crashes into one carrying Fielding and Stella. After this comical event, the ill will between Aziz and Fielding fully dissipates; however, they realize that because of their different cultures, they cannot remain friends and part from one another cordially.

Beyond Friendship

A very important part of this last section is the Hindu festival; its highlight was Godbole's involvement in religious ceremonies that took place. Through this ceremony the spiritual undercurrents present in other earlier sections of the novel are brought center stage.

For many of its readers, the main tension of the novel hinges not on the broader political and economic ramifications of colonialism, but on the dynamic question of whether or not the British Fielding and the Indian Aziz will be able to remain friends. While not discounting such a thematic reading, one can also argue that the focus of the novel is not limited to friendship in its conventional sense.

In the light of the last section of the book in particular, Forster provides clues to show that he saw friendship in a spiritual and symbolic light. Friendship and love between human beings is viewed as it is in Persian and Urdu ghazals—a poetic genre. The ghazals talk of love's physical consummation while endowing it with spiritual symbolism; the book itself makes it clear. The clues that promote such a reading would include a number of allusions in the book. In Chapter 31, reference is made to "The Friend—a Persian expression for God" thus investing a mystical aura on the nature of friend. Similarly, in the ending chapter of the novel, reference is made to the Hanuman temple and Saivite temple that "invited to lust." Clearly, this investing of friendship with the sacred and the profane is part of the theme—namely, the failure to consummate a friendship. But readers of the novel are being unmindful if they were not to notice how friendship has been invested with a mythic aura that combines in it opposites: the physical and the spiritual, the sacred and the profane, the mystical and the ordinary. In other words, the implication of the last section directs one to understand that the failure to consummate results from human scruples and hang-ups, not from external non-human factors. Further supporting this theme of aborted consummation are the references to the call to Krishna just before the end of Chapter 7: "Multiply yourself into hundreds of incarnations and be with all your admirers." Then there is the song in Chapter 36: "Radhakrishna Radhakrishna/KirhsnaRadha Radhakrishna." Clearly, what is being suggested is a consummation that does not follow the "accepted mode of discourse," the kind Browning immortalized in his "My Last Duchess" or the kind Quested and Ronny were to have entered into but failed to do. That there is a suggestion of androgyny is not surprising from a member of the Bloomsbury group of which Forster was a part; indeed, one of whose members, Virginia Woolf, wrote a novel *Orlando,* whose subject is androgynous.

The barriers sanctioned by the society must not bind consummation, the ending of the novel seems to argue. The failure of Fielding and Aziz to consummate their friendship is attributed by the narrative to the cosmic forces at the end; however, these forces, the horses, the earth and the sky, only echo the act performed by the two, Aziz and Fielding. It is they and their scruples, their hang-ups, their upbringing and their social circles that keep them from the "consummation." They only had to reach out and do it, but the two fail to do so. Then and only then do cosmic forces echo the denial initiated by the human protagonists. What the narrative of the novel attributes to impersonal, even cosmic forces driving Aziz and Fielding apart at the novel's conclusion, could more accurately be attributed to the complexity of interactions which take place across the largely unconscious and entirely prevalent barriers of discourse.

THE SPIRITUAL UNDERCURRENT OF THE NOVEL

The book has often been read as a reflection of the importance Forster attached to personal relations between individuals. It takes up yet another theme when it goes beyond good intentions, goodwill, culture and intelligence to show that tolerance, good temper and sympathy alone cannot lead to consummation. Instead it is conveyed to the reader that in a spiritual wasteland, consummation can be attained through the kind of attitude hinted at in the call to Krishna—of all the characters in the book, only Mrs. Moore and Godbole seem to reflect that. When she chided her son for not seeing God's love, she was echoing the need to accept people for who they are to minister to them, as Christ sought to teach. This is just what Godbole does in the "Temple" section, when he arrives at a balance between the state of being and becoming, and confers love without any qualifications or exclusion. He blesses even animals like wasps, which the Christian missionaries refuse to do in any earlier part of the novel.

Godbole's ecstasy in the last section of the book must be counter pointed with Mrs. Moore's loss of faith at the end of Chapter 14. Mrs. Moore learned that the "echoes" in the cave are only the product of human cognition and consciousness. They echo only what the human mind/conscious projects—just like at the end of the novel, when what the cosmic forces reflected was only the echo of what Aziz and Fielding projected. Godbole is an important counterpoint to the other characters; his behavior adds to the novel the motif of spiritual consummation, without which technological progress by itself would not change the human condition. The difference between him and other characters lies in his willingness to accept others just as they are, albeit, the book seems to suggests, incoherently and only while in the throes of ecstasy during his dancing during the festival celebrating the birth of Krishna.

The spiritual message of the book dramatized in the last section of the book, while important, especially for the postmodern readers, is a little difficult to incorporate within the MIS curriculum. But, a great work of art can be read at many levels. This is also true of *A Passage to India.* It can be read in ways that are more adaptable to the constraints of the MIS courses, in particular those dealing with system analysis. In the part of the chapter that follows, the focus is to show the relevance of the book to MIS and to suggest ideas about how to best use it as a useful resource in system analysis courses.

THE RELEVANCE OF THE NOVEL TO MIS PEDAGOGY

E.M. Forster's *A Passage to India* deals with relationships and interactions between British colonials and South Asian natives when the Indian subcontinent was a part of the British Empire—a jewel in the crown, it has been said. A major theme of the novel written in the 1920s is the ability of people to communicate with and befriend others with different backgrounds and cultures. The barriers to communication between different cultures, dramatized by the novel, persist even when human ingenuity is able to overcome technological impediments to human communication.

The book's title refers to a poem written by 19th century American Walt Whitman. It celebrates the completion of the transcontinental railroad across the United States, the laying of transatlantic telegraph cable joining the two sides of the Atlantic Ocean and the opening of the Suez Canal bringing Europe much closer to Asia. For Walt Whitman those three achievements, which occurred almost simultaneously, were testimonials to the triumphal human imagination. Those three accomplishments had the potential to promote human communication across physical barriers—oceans and continents. But Forster, the 20th century novelist, dramatizes the paradox rather than champion technology: the barriers to communications tied to human behavior and cultural constructs persist despite advances in technology. Having seen science and technology deployed to cause death and destruction on an unprecedented scale during the First World War, it would have been logical for someone like Forster to be skeptical about the ability of human beings to transcend the cultural, religious and personal gulfs that divide them.

Indeed, the ironic contrast between the skepticism of Forster's novel and the triumphant mood shown in the poem of Whitman is of special relevance to contemporary professionals involved with information technology and its effective use. They, too, find human behavior impacting information systems a more difficult impediment to overcome than it is to find the right technology itself. A disconnect between what is provided by information systems (ISs) and the needs of the users often exists and has existed for some time.

The disconnect causes companies to "squander billions on tech," as noted by the headline of a recent story in *USA Today* (Hopkins & Kessler, 2002, p.1). Dykman and Robbins (1991) point out the problem of "runaways" by noting how extensive and common the failures are: "75% of all large systems are either not used, not used as intended or generate meaningless reports. Many of these problems can be attributed to ineffective or incomplete systems analysis efforts." More recently, Marchand, Kettinger and Rollins (2000) have shown that similar problems still exist.

Knowing how human behavior impacts information systems is a very important factor to insure that MIS resources are to be used effectively. This requires a greater empathy for organizational cultures as well as skills in deciphering the organizational needs. The individuals making decisions in organizations may not be able to describe their needs—just as those seeing a doctor for health problems only know the symptoms but cannot make a diagnosis. Information professionals should be the ones who can understand, make a diagnosis and prescribe a remedy. This requires them to know more than the technical aspects of their profession. A better understanding of the limitations of technology and the relationship between human behavior and MIS must be taught in systems courses, if there is to be a more optimum use of the technology. To better understand interaction between technology and human behavior, one must start by having a greater empathy for the way people behave, individually and collectively. This is where the study of literature and humanities can help the systems professionals.

USING THE NOVEL AS AN INSTRUCTIONAL RESOURCE

The novel *A Passage to India* can serve as a surrogate for experiential learning in a systems analysis course by treating the subject of the novel, British India in the 1920s and the relationships between the ruling Anglo-Indian and the ruled South Asians, as a system and analyzing it by using the analytic tools of systems analysis. One could see British India described in the book itself as comprising of three sub-systems: the Anglo-Indians who ruled made up one sub-system, while South Asian Muslims and Hindus comprised the two other sub-systems. The characters belonging to each of the three sub-systems are unable to transcend their cultural prisons and relate to each other in a positive manner. The interface among these sub-systems and the individuals belonging to them, their failure to communicate with each other, as well as the factors that make such communication dysfunctional lend themselves to analysis and understanding through the lens of system analysis tools and concepts.

Students can use the techniques associated with system analysis to define each of the three sub-systems. They can also discuss how each sub-system perceives the other two as well as its own self-perception. They can then be asked to explain why the three sub-systems are unable to communicate well with each other. The focus on the dysfunctional communication among the three sub-systems can well serve the use of the novel in a systems analysis course. Another approach would be to have students study and analyze characters and decide which ones are stereotypical and which ones have depth.

Yet another way to make use of the novel would be by mapping the factors that led to the arrest of Aziz and the subsequent trial. It was an administrative decision, and usually such decisions are subject to checks and counter-checks. Administrators are also expected to attempt verification of the charges being made, not take them at face value. Clearly the decision to arrest Aziz was a wrong decision; the fact that it was made indicates a failure of such checks and built-in controls. The tasks assigned to the student could include the following:

- Map the series of events that led to the arrest of an innocent man.
- Isolate the factors in the system that failed.
- Suggest steps/systems control that could have prevented the making and implementation of potentially wrong decisions.

To help make optimum learning possible, the instructor ought to spend time discussing at least some of the chapters in class with students. These would show students how to analyze and draw conclusions by reading the evidence. Clearly, the analysis required must be based on a close reading of the text, understanding its nuances, both denotative and connotative. This is very different than experiments in a laboratory or field investigation. Since discussion of the entire book would be time consuming, it is better to focus on key chapters for class discussion, while having the students read the rest on their own and in groups. For example, students could be asked to analyze the second chapter, where Indian Muslims were discussing the possibilities of being friends with the British. The student analysis should be devoted to not only inferring what the Indian Muslims think of the British, but to draw out the cultural traits of Muslims themselves, besides what they say and how they say it. Other chapters that could be used for closer reading may be: Chapter 5 which shows British Indian characters; Chapter 6 where an Indian Aziz and a British soldier play the game of polo; Chapter 7 which describes the party at Fielding's college. In addition, sections devoted to the Cave expedition and the trial are likely to make for interesting discussion.

Clearly the students will need guidance from their instructors in dealing with analysis of evidence made available by reading a text. However, once they see how techniques used for flow charting and process mapping are applicable to literary texts, they will find learning experience rewarding.

CONCLUSION

The novel written by E.M. Forster can be used to supplement the teaching of systems analysis. Doing so seems highly relevant to multinational corporations of the 21st century, where managers and employees representing diverse cultures have to work together despite their cultural diversity. By using the novel as a supplemental resource, one can sensitize students to the cognitive, behavioral, linguistic and cultural factors that can impact on the communication of information, the raison d'etre for an information system. It is true that for many MIS academics, the idea of assigning a novel to their students would seem foreboding, yet the time it will take to read a classic novel is well worth the effort. Reading literature can be fun, it is food for critical thinking, it can improve communication skills, and it also happens to be a good teaching resource albeit underutilized in MIS classes.

REFERENCES

Adler, R.B. (1995). Teaching communication theories with jungle fever. *Communication Education,* 44, 157-164.

Berger, J. & Pratt, C. (1998). Teaching business-communication ethics with controversial films. *Journal of Business Ethics,* 17(16), 1817-1823.

Carson, R.A. (1994). Teaching ethics in the context of medical humanities. *Journal of Medical Ethics,* 20, 235-238.

Coe, T. & Merino, B. (1987). Future of accounting education. In Coe, T. & Merino, B. (Eds.), *Future of Accounting.* College of Business, North Texas State University, 1-6.

Coleman, J.S. (1976). Differences between experiential and classroom learning. In M.T. Keeton & Associates, *Experiential Learning.* San Francisco: Jossey-Bass, 49-61.

Coles, R. (1989). *The Call of Stories: Teaching and the Moral Imagination.* Boston: Houghton-Mifflin.

Cougar, J.D. (1995). *Creative Problem Solving and Opportunity Finding.* Danvers, MA: Boyd & Fraser.

Downie, R.S. (1991). Literature and medicine. *Journal of Medical Ethics,* 17, 93-96.

Dykman, C.A. & Robbins, R. (1991). Organizational success through effective systems analysis. *Journal of Systems Management,* (July), 6-8.

Forster, E.M. (1984). *A Passage to India.* New York: Harcourt, Brace, Jovanovich.

Green, B., Miller, P.D. & Routh, C.P. (1995). Teaching ethics in psychiatry: A one-day workshop for clinical students. *Journal of Medical Ethics,* 21, 234-238.

Griffin, C.L. (1995). Teaching rhetorical criticism with Thelma and Louise. *Communication Education,* 44, 165-176.

Hopkins, J. & Kessler, M. (2002). Companies squander billions on tech. *USA Today,* (May 20), 1.

Kennedy, E.J. & Lawton, L. (1992). Business ethics in fiction. *Journal of Business Ethics,* 11(3), 187-195.

Kolb, D.A. (1974). On management and the learning process. In Kolb, D.A., Rubin, I.M. & McIntyre, J.M. (Eds.), *Organizational Psychology: A Book of Readings.* City: Prentice-Hall, 27-42.

Marchand, D., Kettinger, W. & Rollins, J. (2000). Information orientation: People, technology, and the bottom line. *Sloan Management Review,* (Summer), 69-80.

McAdams, T. (1993). The Great Gatsby as a business ethics inquiry. *Journal of Business Ethics,* 12(8), 653-660.

McAdams, T. & Koppensteiner, R. (1992). The manager seeking virtue: Lessons from literature. *Journal of Business Ethics,* 11(8), 627-634.

Proctor, R.F. (1993). Using feature films to teach critical thinking: Multiple morals to the stories. *Speech Communication Teacher,* 7, 11-12.

Proctor, R.F. & Adler, R. (1991). Teaching interpersonal communication with feature films. *Communication Education,* 40, 393-400.

Serey, T. (1992). Carpe diem: Lessons about life and management from Dead Poets Society. *Journal of Management Education,* 16, 374-399.

Shepard, J.J., Goldsby, M.G. & Gerde, V.W. (1997). Teaching business ethics through literature. *The Online Journal of Ethics.*

Umapathy, S. (1985). Teaching behavioral aspects of performance evaluation: An experiential approach. *The Accounting Review,* (January), 97-108.

Walter, G.A. & Marks, S.E. (1981). *Experiential Learning and Change.* New York: John Wiley & Sons.

Webb, J. (1996). Inventing the good: A prospectus for clinical education and the teaching of legal ethics in England. *The Law Teacher,* 30(3), 270-294.

Zorn, T. (1991). Willy Loman's lesson: Teaching identity management with Death of a Salesman. *Communication Education,* 40, 219-224.

ENDNOTES

[1] All references to the text of the novel are to the paperback edition dated 1984.

Chapter XVIII

Great Plans – Little Planning:
A Corporate Case Study

R. Keith Martin
Fairfield University, USA

ABSTRACT

This case describes the near disintegration of a company due to uncontrolled growth, inadequate information systems and ineffective (or perhaps incompetent) decision making. Selesian Manufacturing Company, Inc., grew from a small, privately held operation doing business only in the United States, to a publicly held company with operations in several foreign countries. As the company's business expanded, the inadequacies of the founder/president's management competencies, and the lack of effective corporate information systems, resulted in serious organizational and operational problems. The case illustrates the problems that can develop quickly when an organization does not have defined goals, effective management and supporting information systems.

The case relates to an actual company, although its name and those of individuals have been changed in the case. It has been used effectively in an upper-division undergraduate course and, with some expansion, in a graduate course in information systems.

PROLOGUE

As a young man Charlie Henderson often could be found in his garage working on the old Ford he bought from an uncle, repairing a radio so that his mother could listen to her favorite soap operas or building some new contraption that some day might have some practical value. He loved to tinker with things mechanical. And, by his own admission he dreamed of the day when he would start his own company.

His dream came true. Charlie Henderson founded Selesian Manufacturing Company, Inc., to manufacture fish skinning machinery and paint can filling machinery, equipment that he designed; and component parts to specification, such as gears, shafts, conveyors and spar poles, used in logging equipment. Charlie was in charge of the production activities; his wife, Meredith, was the bookkeeper; and his brother, Richie, was the sales manager. Charlie oversaw all day-to-day activities. In total, the company employed 15 production, four clerical and four sales personnel.

PHASE ONE

Minimum sales and manufacturing information were obtained from the accounting system. It was a very basic system, although it did provide enough information about the company's operations so that Selesian was able to borrow money for expansion. If the company had an "information system," it was due to Charlie Henderson's intimate knowledge of the production and marketing activities. He believed that he acquired adequate detailed information through his direct involvement with all of the company's operations.

When Charlie Henderson founded the company, he had in mind several goals: to manufacture quality products, to be a "good neighbor" in the local business community, to inspire loyalty among his employees and to treat them fairly. He did not quantify these goals and, therefore, did not have clear objectives against which the company could be measured. As long as things were "going right" in Charlie's estimation, he was satisfied.

The company's products were well received in the marketplace, and over the years the demand for them increased significantly. In fact, the company became the leading supplier of fish skinning machinery in the fishing industry, and of component parts for logging equipment in the timber industry. It also held a reasonably competitive position for its paint can filling equipment. Charlie firmly believed that this all reflected the reputation for high quality that his company's products had achieved.

One of the basic problems with Charlie's management style was that he never really understood what "going right" meant. He knew that he could meet his payroll, that products were being manufactured and that orders were being received, but he didn't have any real comprehension as to the planning necessary to sustain the company's growth and profitability.

Charlie was active in community affairs, sponsored local and regional events, and encouraged his employees to become involved in their communities. And, he still considered Selesian as a small company, maintaining personal relationships with his employees, remembering such things as their birthdays, and the births and graduations of their children. Had he taken the time to think about it, Charlie undoubtedly would have believed that he had, indeed, achieved those goals he set years ago.

The increasing demand for its products required the company to increase its manufacturing and warehousing capacities, where it now employed about 80 production workers. In order to do so, the company required a major infusion of capital for expansion, and after consultation with friends, members of the financial community and business associates, Charlie Henderson decided to take the company public. At about that time both Charlie's wife and his brother retired from the day-to-day operations of the company. A new bookkeeper, Jennifer Simpson, was hired to take on the duties previously carried out by Meredith and her staff, which now numbered 10. Charlie took over Richie's sales activities, and the oversight of the now 14-member sales staff, while continuing his own responsibilities for production. Consequently, Charlie was spreading himself thin, and his ability to maintain that personal relationship with all of his employees, something that had been very important to him, began to slip away.

Since its founding, Selesian was the epitome of the paternalistic organization. Although the company did not provide a health plan, Charlie Henderson always looked after what he considered to be his employees' welfare. If a family was having financial difficulties, he often would add "something special" to the employee's weekly paycheck. Now, conditions were changing; the old ways were becoming archaic. The newer employees, particularly those in production, reflecting a more prevalent attitude regarding working conditions and employee benefits, and without having experienced the history of the company during its formative period, began discussions among themselves about health insurance coverage, and the potential advantages of unionization. In what proved to be a major tactical error, Charlie discounted the employees' concerns; he was unresponsive to what he regarded as being nothing more than "idle talk."

PHASE TWO

As a publicly held company, Selesian Manufacturing Company, Inc., had to provide information to its stockholders, regulatory agencies and its external auditors. Satisfying external demands for information about the company's operations presented a problem. The existing systems, for which low-level computing equipment was being used, had been developed to meet internal needs only. The new bookkeeper, coming under pressure to provide the required information for external use, soon realized that those demands could not be met with the current accounting system. As a first step in dealing with this problem, Charlie Henderson hired an experienced accountant, Mary Sartoros, from the firm serving as the company's external auditors to take care of the reporting requirements. The accountant quickly developed financial accounting procedures that would provide reports that met the company's legal requirements.

In an attempt to capitalize on his products' marketability, Charlie decided to expand into Central and South American markets, where his logging equipment was being used by subsidiaries of U.S. companies. His logic was that if those subsidiaries were using his equipment (having purchased them domestically and shipped them to the countries in which their subsidiaries operated), Selesian Manufacturing Company, Inc., could expand its own market (and significantly increase its profits) by selling to companies in those countries. His plan was to market through distributors franchised by his company.

As business continued to expand, and the number of production employees increased, Charlie Henderson admittedly began to feel the pressures and strain of overseeing all of the company's operations. Therefore, he delegated the responsibility for the company's two main functions, sales and production, to two long-time employees, naming them as vice presidents while he retained control over both product development and customer relations.

The sales vice president, Bob Stevens, had worked with Richie Henderson as a field representative and then as a district manager. In the latter position he had administrative, but limited planning responsibilities. Ralph Lederer, the production vice president, had been with the company since its founding, always working in production. Although Ralph was a foreman at the time of his appointment as vice president, Charlie Henderson dealt with almost all administrative responsibilities relating to the production activities. Consequently, both new vice presidents had limited experiences as managers.

Charlie Henderson considered his directives to the two vice presidents to be very specific: the sales vice president was charged with increasing sales volume, and improving the percentage return on sales; the production vice president was charged with increasing production efficiency, and improving the effective use of production facilities.

Bob Stevens and Ralph Lederer immediately set out to determine exactly what information they would need in order to meet the goals given to them. Since the goals were not quantified, each vice president set his own objectives, recognizing that valid standards should be established so that performance could be measured against them. Both vice presidents decided that they needed basic operating information that was not specialized, and was available from within the company. However, they decided independently that getting that information would require some modifications to the company's current procedures of data collection, processing and reports distribution. To meet the vice presidents' needs in the short term, considerable clerical effort within their individual departments would be required. The vice presidents had no experience within the international marketplace, and were not certain how they should be dealing with distributors in foreign countries. Their approach to determining their overall information requirements, therefore, was based on the assumption that what worked for the domestic operations would be appropriate for the foreign operations.

PHASE THREE

Based on her prior accounting experiences (which did not include clients with foreign operations), Mary Sartoros recommended that the company adopt a standard cost accounting system, revise the financial accounting system and upgrade the computer equipment to maintain these two systems. (The purchase several years ago of the relatively "low-level" computer equipment for processing accounting data had been done without conducting any feasibility study to identify the company's overall computing needs.) Others within the company who were reluctant to accept standards for valuing inventories expressed differing opinions as to what constituted meaningful marketing information that, in turn, would impact productions decisions. They also expressed concerns over the apparent complexities and costs of expanding the company's computer-based information systems. Because of these concerns, and a reluctance to change an accounting system that for years he had regarded as satisfactory, the president postponed the recommended action indefinitely.

As the need for non-accounting information became increasingly critical, a sense of desperation began to seize the company. Mary Sartoros was confronted daily with mounting requests for operational information, and in spite of almost heroic efforts, fell far short of meeting those requests. The capabilities of the current system simply didn't support her efforts. Many of these requests were coming from the two vice presidents who, feeling that they were not being served adequately by the company's information system, decided to develop their own systems.

Having been unsuccessful in obtaining information they deemed vital to their carrying out the charge given by Charlie Henderson, and sensing that their requests would always take second place behind the processing of accounting reports, the vice presidents became increasingly frustrated. Bob Stevens was aware that sales statistics produced through the accounting system contained significant inaccuracies caused by an array of deficiencies in the system, including the lateness of invoices, the omission of any sales territory designation on key documents and reports, and a lack of basic market information. He also realized that much of the information he did receive did not adequately reflect the results of the foreign operations. As a result, he created his own sales statistics and analysis group.

Ralph Lederer, the production vice president, could not understand why the existing system was not able to provide information for assessing operating efficiencies. Therefore, he took what he believed to be an expedient course similar to his counterpart in sales; he developed his own system, assigning attainable efficiency standards with which to monitor the performance of his operation. He decided that the valuation of inventories was an accounting issue and, therefore, he would not be concerned with it. However, he did take some steps to ensure that his system did encompass the distribution operations of the company's product lines, including shipments of equipment to foreign customers.

The creation of separate information systems, and the installation of computer work stations (which they purchased with their individual department's budgets) on which the systems were installed, was rationalized by the vice presidents as providing what they now determined to be essential *specialized* information to each of them. They did not see their developing separate systems as being either a serious policy issue or an operational problem. Their position was that the systems did not duplicate each other, and that each system was designed to meet the particular needs of different functional areas. But regardless of their arguments in favor of information specialization, all departments, including theirs, were obtaining their basic data, and some operating information, from the same source—the accounting system.

Charlie Henderson began to feel that the information he was getting from the two vice presidents, information that was derived from the separate systems, was either incomplete or unreliable. He was puzzled that although production costs had been lowered and sales had increased, profits also were lower. He became concerned that perhaps the company was selling in unprofitable markets. He wondered what impact the foreign markets had on the company's costs and income.

He was not able to find answers to these and other operating issues. No single information system in the company was designed to provide them. The several systems were both incomplete for their intended purposes and incompatible with other related systems throughout the company. The accounting system, although accurately reporting results for financial purposes, was not providing adequate information for operational decisions. While accounting techniques using a marginal or direct costing approach might have provided greater insight into the nature and behavior of the company's manufacturing costs, such improvements had not been made to the accounting system. And, the system was not designed to deal with issues, such as currency exchange rates, that occur in companies doing business in foreign countries.

PHASE FOUR

Selesian Manufacturing Company, Inc., was supporting an environment of multiple information systems—those designed for the specific information require- ments of a particular constituency to the exclusion of all other information needs (the two vice presidents), and those designed for the overall corporate (principally accounting) needs of a *national* company. Consequently, Selesian was impacted by rising costs due to the duplication of, or variations in, information as each system processed the same data to suit a particular manager's needs, and because of incomplete information about several areas of its business activities.

Fundamentally identical information was distorted by different interpretations, thereby causing breakdowns in communicating information throughout the company. The decision-making process was complicated by the continual demand on managers to evaluate conflicting information supplied by different sources. Staff members with specialized talents and skills, who were to develop, manufacture or market the company's products, were assigned to administer what amounted to routine accounting activities related to their areas of activity and responsibility. And, in reality nobody at Selesian really understood the complexities of being a "multinational" company.

Concluding that the information systems were inefficient and inadequate, the two vice presidents adjusted their organization's structure and expanded their own systems to provide for their evolving information needs. Neither one took into account that they were dealing in multinational markets where customs, laws, regulations and reporting requirements were different in each country and, therefore, would have a significant impact on the information they would need to operate their divisions effectively.

The production division, requiring more accurate estimates of sales demand, organized a planning department. The sales division, charged with the responsibility of moving the inventories generated by the production activities, established an inventory control department. And, since that division was also responsible for improving the return on sales, it set up a department to support selective selling decisions with detailed cost-of-sales studies based on product quality.

The existing multiple systems were not able individually to meet the information requirements necessary for effective decision making. Charlie Henderson began to sense this when he could no longer accept information without nagging doubts, and without sending a series of follow-up questions to his managers. Therefore, he took what he thought were decisive actions to resolve the reservations he had about the information being provided to him. He authorized the accountant to hire an analyst whose primary function was to work with the accounting department in identifying company-wide information needs, and in revising the current systems to meet those needs. He also hired a manager of international operations.

Unfortunately, because of the workload in the accounting department, Harry Becker, the analyst, became totally absorbed in the internal operations of that department. Although the financial accounting system was refined, it still operated within the same archaic framework. This was of little help to either the sales or the production vice president.

Jeremy Carlson, the manager of international operations, quickly determined that none of the computer-based systems throughout the organization were designed to provide the type of information that he needed to carry out his responsibilities—

being the "overseer" of Selesian's global activities. He assumed, however, that the systems being maintained by the two vice presidents could be modified to produce that information. He further assumed that since both vice presidents were responsible for activities that certainly were "international," they would be amenable to his requests for information and would adjust their systems appropriately.

Bob Stevens stated that he was not interested in the manager of international operations' problems. He concentrated on the information generated with his system in order to prove to the president that markets were providing an appropriate return, even though there were contrary indications from information generated by the company's accounting system. This took his attention away from generating new business for the company that, as the vice president responsible for the sales division, was his principal responsibility.

Ralph Lederer took a similar attitude. He maintained his own operating standards, even though there was no assurance of their accuracy. Nobody could tell if the "actual" costs of production, generated by the accounting system that contained prorated costs, allocations, deferments, accruals and certain "accounting adjustments for tax purposes," were any more accurate.

Neither vice president could determine by any quantified measure the impact that the company's international operations had on his division's activities.

Charlie Henderson had long held the opinion that if one understood the accounting reporting within the company, she/he would be able to discern what was happening in all phases of the company's operations. To strengthen the accounting department, he recruited a controller to improve external reporting, and appointed the accountant to be the company's treasurer, who would handle the task of providing shareholders and tax authorities with appropriate, and hopefully accurate, information.

The controller, Sarah Dunlop, assessed the company as being in what she believed to be a chaotic state, and hired a systems analyst and a computer specialist. Their hiring was justified to Charlie Henderson on the basis of accounting needs; the intention was that they would improve the accounting operations that, in turn, would provide better information to the operating units throughout the company. The systems analyst, Peggy Norris, directed her attention to streamlining accounting routines, and redesigning forms and reports. As this was being done, the computer processes were revised accordingly. An increased level of accuracy in accounting information was achieved, and the computer equipment was upgraded (and used also for some analyses of various operations within the company), but Charlie Henderson was not certain that the benefits were commensurate with the costs.

Some modest attempts were made to develop a corporate business plan against which actual performance could be measured. Comprehensive budgeting procedures were developed, but these potentially useful control tools were weakened significantly by their being "fitted into" the existing accounting information system.

PHASE FIVE

Charlie Henderson was aging rapidly. Analyzing past trends for purposes of short- and long-term planning had become an extremely time consuming and almost hopeless task for him. Therefore, he hired an administrative assistant, Bill Kendall, to help with those activities. Then, he hired a planning director, Paul Emerson, although the duties of that position were not defined.

By this time there was an abundance of operational reports available throughout the company. Five or six separate and independent information systems were in operation. Deciding on the relative accuracy of the information provided by each—separating the wheat from the chaff as it were—took an inordinate amount of time and energy of the president, the vice presidents and managers throughout the company. Obtaining information that was useful in supporting the decision-making process received very little attention. And, too often in staff meetings, the company's experiences to this point were minimized as being nothing more than the growing pains expected of a company evolving from a small to large, and domestic to international, enterprise.

Then, to add to Charlie's woes, employee discussions regarding unionization, and extended employee benefits—including, but now not limited to health benefits—increased in their intensity. Charlie Henderson wondered if he was losing hold of his company.

EPILOGUE

Selesian Manufacturing Company, Inc., is clearly a company in serious trouble. Management took many actions that, by themselves, may have been worthwhile and undoubtedly were well intended. The divisions and departments that were set up might have improved the operations of the company; they are not atypical of those often found in manufacturing concerns. The personnel that were hired might have been qualified to provide valuable service to the organization; there is no indication that they acted irrationally or without regard for the company's well-being. But, setting up organizational units for parochial reasons, and hiring staff without a rational/coherent/planned approach to the company's needs is costly and unproductive. To assume that a company can expand its operations into the international arena without major corporate changes is short-sighted at best, and foolhardy in the main.

Can the company survive its own foibles?

SUMMARY

Selesian Manufacturing Company, Inc., certainly is experiencing both short- and long-term difficulties. What Charlie Henderson was facing, although he didn't recognize, or was unwilling to recognize, was the fact that the "entrepreneurial spirit" does not often translate into sound business management. The company, therefore, provides a portrait of an organization whose founder had *great plans*, but did *little planning*.

This case study was developed for use in courses in information analysis and systems design, and in strategic planning. It also could be used in courses in strategic management. Selesian Manufacturing Company, Inc.'s experiences illustrate the problems that can, *and probably will*, occur because of incompetent, or perhaps misguided, management, poor decision making and inadequate information; the ways in which related problems develop; and the possible solutions to those problems. Each of the phases described in the case might be treated as individual units, with students analyzing what occurred in the company during the phase.

The *teaching objectives* of the case are to provide students with an opportunity to examine the profile of an organization for the purpose of understanding: the types of problems that confront entrepreneurial companies as they expand their operations, particularly if done so without a cohesive plan of action; the importance of mechanisms for maintaining and disseminating relevant and effective information throughout an organization; and the importance of well-conceived plans for expanding the personnel base of a growing organization.

By role playing as consultants to the company, students have the opportunity to identify actions that might provide stability within the company, improve its operations, and ensure its long-term growth and success.

Students are asked to review the case, and then prepare a detailed analysis of the company's actions as described in it. In developing the analysis they are to consider the following (some ideas for discussion are in italics):

- The president's control, or lack thereof, over the company's growth, and the related informational needs of management.

   As an entrepreneur who built the company from scratch, and knew everything that was taking place, the president never applied reasoned management techniques to the running of the company. His deficiencies in such techniques did not become apparent until the company began to expand rapidly, and his effectiveness in controlling the company's activities became elusive.

- The president's questions to the vice presidents: Are they ones he should be asking, or be expected to be asking?

The president should be able to ask any question about the operation of the company. The issue here is that he had *to ask about these items. Information should have been provided to him on a routine basis that would have made asking these questions unnecessary.*

- Actions of the vice presidents in developing their own systems.

They may be understandable under the circumstances, but clearly were not in the best interest of the company. The two vice presidents should first have identified their common needs and the ways in which they could have been met with common systems, and second discussed their individual or departmentally unique needs and the ways in which common systems, or sub-sets of such systems, might meet those needs.

- The need for the personnel added to the staff, and the manner in which they were hired (e.g., were the positions necessary, and would different types of staff been more beneficial to the company).

Each new employee was added in a haphazard manner as a response to real and/or perceived problems. No thought was given to the role these employees would have in the company's operations once the problem(s) that led to their being hired were resolved. Certainly, the planning director, assuming the usual functions of a position with that designation, was hired far too late. Also, hiring a systems analyst and a computer specialist at the same time suggests that some high-level technology was needed to solve all of the company's problems. Hiring the computer specialist probably should have been deferred. There may be other approaches, at least in the short term, that would help stabilize the company.

- Actions that might have been taken in any of the phases that would have helped the company avoid the problems it incurred.

And that's what the case is all about. What could have been done?! Students are asked to present their analysis.

ASSIGNMENT—PART II

Charlie Henderson wants to bring stability to Selesian Manufacturing Company, Inc. He is convinced (at last) that the company cannot survive if the current practices regarding planning and decision making, information systems development, the scope of its operations (domestic and international) and perhaps its present organization structure continue as they are now.

Students are asked, as a friend of the president or as a consultant to the company, to describe the course of action they would recommend to ensure as much as is possible the long-term success of the company.

Again, the students are asked to analyze the current situation and recommend a course of action for the company.

AUTHOR'S COMMENT

The use of cases provides students, particularly at the undergraduate level when their direct business experiences may be limited, an opportunity to analyze actual corporate situations, management decisions and operational strategies. A key to the effectiveness of the case method is that there is no single "right solution" to the issues raised in the case. Students are required to consider a set of facts as presented in the case, to analyze and evaluate the impact that events described by those facts have had on the organization, and to apply reasoned judgment in forming both their critique of what has taken place and their recommendations to the organization's management for future action. The case method, as a "pedagogical laboratory," enriches the students' academic experiences by incorporating a robust component of reality into their course work.

About the Authors

Fawzi Albalooshi is an Assistant Professor in the Department of Computer Science at the University of Bahrain, Bahrain, since 1996. He completed his graduate studies at the University of Wales in the UK, were he was awarded his master's degree in Computer Science and doctorate degree in the field of Software Engineering. He developed research interest in the area of educational technology since he joined the Department of Computer Science as one of its faculty members and was involved in a number of projects related to educational software development and implementation. Other areas of research of his interest are object-orientation and computer-aided software engineering.

*   *   *   *   *

Muhammad Ali teaches in the Computer Science Department at Tuskegee University, USA. He has also taught at the National University of Science and Technology in Pakistan. He obtained his PhD from George Washington University and has taught courses in Parallel Programming with MPI; C++ Programming for Engineers; FORTRAN Programming for Engineers; and JAVA Programming for Engineers. His research interest deals with computer communications including telecommunications, ISO standards on computer network protocols, ISDN protocols, network management standards, computer network security architecture, security services and mechanisms, and cryptology.

Eshaa M. Alkhalifa is a member of the ruling family of Bahrain who is more of a researcher than a regular academic. She introduced the concept of adaptable Multi-Media Intelligent Tutoring Systems as a direct result of her findings in Cognitive Science that question current beliefs in mental representation.

Derek Asoh obtained his MSc in Electrical Engineering from the Marine Transport Institute, St. Petersburg, specializing in automation. He subsequently taught electronics and control systems at the Yaounde National Polytechnic. He is currently a Fulbright Scholar in the multi-disciplinary Information Science Doctoral Program at SUNY/Albany. His research interests include systems and application development and evaluation, knowledge management and business performance. His recent research has been presented in several conferences, including the Hawaii International Conference in Systems Sciences, Information Resource Management Association and Systemic, Cybernetics and Informatics. He is an IT Consultant and a Reviewer of the *Rockefeller College Review Journal,* SUNY/Albany.

Joseph Barjis presently works as a Research Associate in the Department of Computer Science of the University of Reading and a Lecturer at Thames Valley University, both in the United Kingdom. From 1998 to 2002 Dr. Barjis worked at Delft University of Technology, and from December 2001 to June 2002, he worked as an Assistant Professor of Computer Science at Rijswijk Institute of Technology, both in The Netherlands. He worked in the spring semester of 2001 as a Visiting Assistant Professor in the Department of Computer Science, Tennessee Technological University, USA. He earned an MSc degree with Highest Honors with an overall GPA of 4.97/5.0, and a PhD with an overall GPA of 5.0/5.0, both in Computer Science. Dr. Barjis has published three book chapters and more than 70 scientific-research papers. He was awarded the medal, "Excellence in Study," "for excellent academic results"; The World Order of Science-Education-Culture, "in recognition of scientific achievements"; and "The Best Paper Award" of the 1999 Summer Computer Simulation Conference, Chicago, USA, for his paper presented at the conference. In January 2002, Dr. Barjis was invited by the Marquis Who's Who in the World (V.I.P. Code: WO203003E) to submit his biography for the 20th edition of *Who's Who in the World*, and after the review and selection process, his biography was recommended for publication in the 20th edition. Apart from his professional field, Dr. Barjis is interested in sports (taekwon-do, yoga, swimming), literature and poetry, languages and traveling around the world.

Sheila B. Bato received her Bachelor's of Science in Management Information Technology at the Ateneo De Manila University, where she is currently taking up her master's degree in Computer Science. Ms. Bato is a full-time faculty member at the Ateneo De Manila, teaching courses, such as Web Page Design and Introduction to Information Technology. She is also doing consultancy work for a systems development project at the same university.

Salvatore Belardo is an Associate Professor of Management Science and Information Systems at the University at Albany, USA. He holds a PhD in Management Information Systems. Dr. Belardo has published widely in a number of top journals and has been recognized as one of the most prolific authors of decision support systems-related research, as well as one of the top 10 authors in terms of citations in the journal *Interfaces*. He has published several books, including *Trust: The Key to Change in the Information Age* and *Innovation Through Learning: What Leaders Need to Know in the 21st Century*.

Apiwan D. Born is an Assistant Professor in the Management Information Systems (MIS) Department at the University of Illinois at Springfield, USA. She earned a PhD in MIS from Southern Illinois University at Carbondale (SIUC). Her dissertation title, "Exploratory Study of Information Systems Infrastructure and its Link to Performance," received a doctoral dissertation award from SIUC. She holds a BS in Statistics (honor) from Chulalongkorn University, Bangkok, Thailand. She has master's degrees in MIS (MSMIS) and in business administration from Mississippi State University. Dr. Born recently received the Master Online Teacher Certificate from the Illinois Online Network and the University of Illinois. Since 1999, she has taught online graduate courses including Introduction to MIS, Technology Management and a graduate project seminar. Her research interests are effective strategies for Web-based teaching and learning, student assessment in an online learning environment and impacts of information systems infrastructure on organizations.

Lisa J. Burnell is an Assistant Professor in the Computer Science Department at Texas Christian University, USA. Her previous experience is in the Aerospace and Transportation industries. Dr. Burnell has a PhD and Master's in Computer Science and a BA in Mathematics, all from the University of Texas, Arlington. Her research interests are probabilistic reasoning, decision-theoretic inference and software engineering methodologies. She may be reached at L.Burnell@tcu.edu.

Jakov (Yasha) Crnkovic is an Associate Professor of Management Science and Information Systems, School of Business, University at Albany, New York, USA. After earning a BS in Mathematics and Computer Science, he combined it with Economics (MS) and Computer Information Systems in Business (PhD) through education at the Faculty of Economics, University at Belgrade, Yugoslavia. Before joining the University at Albany, he taught graduate and undergraduate courses at the University at Binghamton, College of Saint Rose; University at Belgrade, Yugoslavia; and University of Miami, Florida. His research is in the areas of decision support systems, management of information technology, system simulation, e-business and networking. He is author or co-author of more than 10 textbooks (in Serbian and English) and over 60 publications.

John R. Durrett is an Assistant Professor of Information Systems at Texas Tech University, USA. He received his PhD from the University of Texas at Austin in Information Systems, and his MBA and BA from West Texas A&M. His research and teaching interests are distributed systems design, e-learning and network security. He can be reached at john@durrett.org.

Bea V. Espejo is a Faculty Member of the Department of Information Systems and Computer Science of the Ateneo De Manila University, where, for the past two years, she has been teaching undergraduate courses in multimedia, Web design and information technology. She is also currently finishing her MS in Computer Science, concentrating on Computer Aided Instruction, at the same university. She is highly involved in the e-learning efforts of the university and aids other faculty members in developing and implementing their courses online.

Emmanuel Fernandes is currently a PhD student at the Faculty of HEC (business school) and CENTEF, University of Lausanne, Switzerland. His research interests include new technologies and e-learning. He received his diploma in Computer Science from University of Savoie, France, in 1995. He worked two years as a Development Engineer in the financial field for the Credit Agricole. He is currently responsible for the ARIADNE CDS of Lausanne University and Project Coordinator of one of the Swiss Virtual Campus projects on e-learning: General Chemistry for students enrolled in a life science curriculum.

Maia Wentland Forte is currently Vice-Rector in charge of Finance, Informatics and Statistics and Director of the HEC-Lausanne MBA program, Switzerland. She is Professor at the Business School, dispensing a Business and Information Technologies course in the frame of the MBA program. Her research interests include continuous education, open and distance learning, and knowledge management systems. She is member of the Swiss National Science Foundation, a member of the Swiss Virtual Campus Steering Committee and a member of the executive committee of the ARIADNE Foundation. She is also a member of several scientific committees (Fuzzy Economic Review, Society for Fuzzy, Multi-Valued Logic in Economy and Management) and lecture committees (Sciences et Techniques Educatives (ed. Hermes), International Journal of Chaos Theory Applications).

Tomaso Forzi (Dott-Ing) graduated in 2000 with a degree in Management and Production Engineering from Milan University of Technology (Politecnico di Milano, Milan, Italy). Between 1995 and 1998 he was exchange scholar at Aachen University of Technology (RWTH Aachen, Aachen, Germany) within the EU Program TIME (Top Industrial Managers for Europe), as well as Student Assistant at the Laboratory for Machine Tools and Production Engineering (WZL) at the same university. Between 1998 and 1999 he was a Guest Scholar in the Department of Industrial Engineering at North Carolina State University (Raleigh, NC, USA). Between 1998 and 1999 he conducted research work for the Ford European Research Center (FFA, Aachen, Germany) as well as for the Institute of Industrial Technologies and Automation, National Research Council (ITIA-CNR, Milan, Italy). Since 2000 he has been working as a Researcher in the E-Business Engineering Department at the Research Institute for Operations Management (FIR) at Aachen University of Technology. His current research focuses on e-business engineering, virtual organizations, entrepreneurial strategy and business modeling within a networked economy.

Stuart C. Freedman is Professor of Management and Chair of the Management Department at the University of Massachusetts Lowell, USA. His field of specialization is Organizational Behavior. In addition to his work in the area of online communication, Dr. Freedman's research interests are in organizational reward and control systems, the dynamics of groups and teams, and planned organizational change. His articles and reviews have been published in such journals as *Administrative Science Quarterly, Training and Development Journal, Personnel Journal, Journal of Applied Social Psychology* and *Global Competitiveness.* Other publications have appeared in the *Proceedings of the Information Resources Management Association, Eastern Academy of Management, Decision Sciences Institute* and others. He holds a PhD from Cornell University.

Jan Frick is employed as Associate Professor and Department Manager at the Department for Business Administration, Stavanger College, Norway. He holds a Master in Science in Operation Management and ICT from the Norwegian Institute of Technology in Trondheim, Norway (1980), and a PhD in Development of Industrial Collaboration Network from Aalborg University, Aalborg, Denmark (1992). Dr. Frick has previously worked at the research institutes SINTEF and Rogaland Research Institute and at the industrial collaboration institutions Jærtek and TESA. Dr. Frick has managed the Nordic PhD course, "Managing International Research and Development Projects" (1998-2002) and the Norwegian research project on e-learning, "NettLaeR" (1999-2002). Since 1992, Jan Frick has been the manager for the Norwegian part of the internation research network, Internation Manufacturing Strategy Surveil. He is a member of the IFIP workgroup 5.7 "Integration in Production Management" and has been published at several international conferences and journals.

Joaquim Borges Gouveia has a history of more than 20 years concerning teaching and the management of research projects. He has a diploma and a PhD in Electrical Engineering (FEUP, Portugal). He is currently a Full Professor at Aveiro University, Portugal, where he is the Head of the Management and Industrial Engineering Department. He was the Project Leader concerning the research and development of the EFTWeb project. His main interests are e-learning and distance education, research and technology management, and innovation. He is involved in a number of projects concerning the use of technology for e-government and acts as adviser for a number of organizations, including the Portuguese government.

Luís Borges Gouveia spent five years in industry working at an IBM VAR, where he participated as a Project Manager in several projects implementing Videotex systems in the early '90s. He has a master's degree in Electrical Engineering (FEUP,

Portugal) and a PhD in Computing Science from Lancaster University, UK. He is an Assistant Professor at Fernando Pessoa University, Portugal, where he participated in a number of projects related to technology innovation applied to education. His main interests are ICT use for education settings, e-learning and distance education, and virtual environments for collaboration. More recently he is involved in a digital cities project.

Fabrice Holzer graduated from the University of Lausanne (Switzerland) with a degree in Social and Communication Science. He experienced a wide range of demanding project work within R&D product development while working for almost five years with Petrel Comm.™as R&D Manager, before its sale to Cable and Wireless PLC. After a short mandate as developer with the IMD International "virtual campus" team, he joined the CENTEF Department at the University of Lausanne in February 2000. He is currently in charge of eBioMED.ch project management, a Swiss Virtual Campus national call program. He is involved in research concerning concept navigation and individualized contents delivery system.

Kris Howell is Assistant Professor of Computer Information Systems at Colorado State University–Pueblo, USA. She has been teaching computer courses at the college level since 1986. Her current teaching interests include: Visual Basic; Introduction to Web Development with HTML, JavaScript and XML; and Systems Analysis and Design with UML. She earned a PhD from Colorado State University–Fort Collins with a cognate area in Computer Information Systems. Dr. Howell has also been Co-Owner, Analyst and Programmer for JaK Rabbit Software, Pueblo, Colorado, for over 13 years. She also serves as Faculty Advisor for the local student chapter of the Association for Information Technology Professionals.

Carol M. Jessup is an Assistant Professor of Accountancy at the University of Illinois at Springfield, USA. She holds BA and MA degrees in Accountancy from Sangamon State University. Her PhD is from Saint Louis University in Business Administration with a concentration in Management and a minor in Public Policy Analysis and Administration. Courses taught include: Accounting Information Systems, Federal Taxation, Financial Management of Nonprofit Organizations and online courses in Administrative Uses of Accounting. Her research interests include accounting information systems, issues related to online teaching and learning, interpersonal trust and Jungian psychological type. She was recently awarded the Master Online Teacher Certificate from the Illinois Online Network and the University of Illinois.

Esther E. Klein is an Assistant Professor of BCIS at the Zarb School of Business, Hofstra University, USA. She received a BBA/MBA in Statistics/Operations Research from Baruch College/CUNY and a PhD in CS/MIS from the Graduate Center/CUNY. Prior to her academic career, Dr. Klein was a Senior Statistical

Analyst at Pfizer and a Project Leader at PASNY. She also served as a Consultant in Microcomputer DBMS and authored two primers on DBMS. Dr. Klein's research interests include collaborative technologies and organizations, GSS, creativity and gender in computer-mediated decision-making groups, ethical issues in CMC and leadership in computer-mediated contexts. She has had articles published in various journals, including *Computers in Human Behavior* and *The Journal of Leadership Studies*, and in various proceedings such as those of AIS, DSI, IRMA and NEDSI. Dr. Klein is the recipient of the "Best Published Paper of the Year" award by *The Journal of Leadership Studies* for "The Impact of Information Technology on Leadership Opportunities for Women: The Leveling of the Playing Field" (Summer 2000). She has been a guest speaker at academic forums, and is a member of ACM, AIS, DSI, IEEE Computer Society and IRMA.

Peter Laing (Dipl-Ing, Dipl-Wirt-Ing) studied Electrical Engineering at Aachen University of Technology (RWTH Aachen, Aachen, Germany) and graduated in 1999. Between 1997 and 1999 he gained comprehensive experience in the field of new mobile communication technologies at ComNets (Chair for Communication Networks, Aachen University of Technology) where he developed a computer-based simulator for new wireless communication protocols. In 2001 he received his second degree in Business Administration at Aachen University of Technology, after he enrolled there for Business Science in 1999. In addition, since 1999 he has been working as Researcher at FIR (Research Institute for Operations Management at Aachen University of Technology), and at the moment he is Manager of the project Z-Online (see case study). His main research areas are e-business engineering, controlling of strategic targets, risk management in entrepreneurial networks and advanced e-commerce solutions.

Kathy S. Lassila is Associate Professor of Computer Information Systems at Colorado State University–Pueblo, USA. She has over 13 years of experience in the information systems field in positions ranging from Computer Operator to Field Services Division Manager. Her current research interests include community informatics, the social and organizational impacts of IS, Internet law and system development methodologies. Dr. Lassila's research has been published in the *Journal of Management Information Systems, Topics in Health Information Management, Journal of Information Systems Education* and numerous conference proceedings. Her current teaching interests include: senior IS field project, programming languages, object-oriented analysis and design, and IT strategy.

Tommaso Leo is Coordinator of the MODASPECTRA project, as well as Full Professor in Automatic Controls at the University of Ancona, Italy. He has served as Dean of the Faculty of Engineering from 1990 to 1996. He has been Chairman of Robotics, Automation and Human Movement Analysis programs at DEA and responsible for the e-learning initiatives of Ancona University. He worked in analysis and modeling of human motor behavior, in measurement systems and techniques, in signal processing and optimal filtering methods, in adaptive control and system identification, in friendly interfaces for medical use of the movement analysis, and in the development of Web-based applications for learning and accreditation. He is author and co-author of about 200 scientific contributions, and editor of some scientific books and special issues of scientific journals. He is member of IEEE, of the International Society of Biomechanics, and of the International Society for Postural and Gait Research. Presently, he is the Coordinator of the PhD program in "E-Learning: Methods and Techniques for Computer Assisted Education" offered by the University of Ancona.

David Lewis is Professor of Management at the University of Massachusetts Lowell, USA. His areas of interest and specialization are operations management, management information systems, the management of quality and international management. Dr. Lewis has presented over 85 papers at professional conferences, and has published numerous articles in a broad range of professional journals. His current research interests include issues in online education and quality assurance. Dr. Lewis holds a PhD from the University of Massachusetts Amherst.

Marlene P. Mana is a candidate for the Master's of Science in Computer Science program of the Ateneo De Manila University, The Philippines. Over the past three years, she has been a Systems Analyst of the Ateneo de Manila University, implementing its various information system requirements. She is also an Instructor at the same university, teaching MIS majors their Introduction to Management Information Systems and Systems Analysis and Design courses.

R. Keith Martin is Professor of Information Systems and Operations Management, and holds the Stephen and Camille Schramm Chair in Business, in the Charles F. Dolan School of Business at Fairfield University, Connecticut, USA. Dr. Martin was Dean of the School for 11 years, and during two of those years, also was Acting Dean of the University's Graduate School of Communication. Previous appointments include on the faculties of Baruch College of the City University of New York and the University of Washington; the Management Advisory Services Department of Price Waterhouse; IBM and its subsidiary, The Service Bureau Corporation; and Campus Merchandising Bureau, Inc.

Athar Murtuza teaches Accounting at Seton Hall University, USA. His interests include cost/managerial accounting, information systems and communication of information. Even though he has taught accounting for 20 years, his doctoral degree was in literature. He subsequently obtained an MBA with accounting emphasis and is a Certified Management Accounting (CMA). His book, published by John Wiley, argues that the documentation process need not be just archival; instead, it ought to be an occasion to learn and to re-design. During 1999-2000, Dr. Murtuza spent his sabbatical in the Religious Studies Department at Yale University, studying Islamic financial ethics and antecedents for accountability.

Svend Øvrebekk has attended the Norwegian Institute of Technology. From 1977 to 1980 Svend worked for the Nordic Power Exchange. From 1908 to 1997 he work at the Stavanger Technical College. Svend's current responsibilities while working for RKK includes developing Internet-based and videoconference-based methods that are easy to use and non-expensive so that they may be used by teachers and schools.

Maurizio Panti is Associate Professor of Computer Science at the University of Ancona, Italy. Previously he was a Researcher at the University of Urbino and the University of Salerno (1971/74) and Assistant Professor at the University of Ancona (1974/1984). He teaches Data Bases and Fundamentals of Computer at the University of Ancona. He has managed the Computer Centre of the same university, and now is member of its Academic Senate. His research interests concern, databases, information systems and agent technologies for IS integration. He serves as a member of the program committees of international conferences such as CAISE, WMC02, SEBD and CoopIS, and has served as referee for many international journals.

John W. Priest is a Professor of Industrial and Manufacturing Engineering at the University of Texas at Arlington, USA. Dr. Priest is author or coauthor of more than 130 technical articles, predominately on the product development process, design for manufacturing and technical risk management. Between 1978 and 1999 he worked on government task forces to improve the product development process, including decision support systems and knowledge management. Prior to joining academia, Dr. Priest worked full time for Rockwell International Communications (now Alcatel), Texas Instruments and General Motors.

Michael Sautter holds a MPhil in Educational Research from the University of Tromsoe, Norway. He has also trained as a teacher at the University of Bergen and has formerly worked as a Teacher at primary, secondary, and high school levels. He also worked as a Teacher's Trainer at the University of Bergen. He now works as a Research Scientist at Telenor Research and Development with a special focus on ICT and Education, ITC-supported learning and collaboration processes at work, and man-machine interfaces.

Andrew Stein is a Lecturer in the School of Information Systems of the Faculty of Business and Law at Victoria University, Australia. He has contributed to the *International Journal of Management, Journal of Information Management* and *Journal of ERP Implementation and Management.* His research interests include enterprise systems, student transition to university, e-procurement applications and the e-marketplace business models. His teaching includes ERP Implementation, Enterprise Systems and Strategic Information Systems.

Steven F. Tello has extensive experience in the development and delivery of technology-enhanced training and education for college and K-12 faculty. As Associate Director of Distance Learning at the University of Massachusetts Lowell, USA, he is responsible for the operation and development of the university's online program. He has taught in the university's Multimedia Certificate Program, and conducted numerous workshops on the educational use of multimedia and the World Wide Web. Most recently, he initiated the development of the university's Online Teaching Institute, which provides higher education faculty with an orientation to online pedagogy. Dr. Tello holds an EdD from the University of Massachusetts Lowell.

Salvatore (Sal) Valenti is a Senior Researcher at the University of Ancona, Italy. He has been a member of several research projects funded by the Ministry of Instruction, University and Research (MIUR), by the National Research Council (CNR) and by the European Community. His research activities are in the fields of Computer Based Assessment and Distance Learning. He is member of the WAOE© World Association for Online Education, and is a board member of the *Journal of Information Technology Education.* He is serving as reviewer for *Educational Technology & Society* and for *Current Issues in Education.* He has been Chair of the track on "Virtual Universities" at the 2002 International Conference of the International Resources Management Association. He is author of more than 60 papers published in books, journals and proceedings of international conferences. Currently, he is a Faculty Member of the PhD program in "E-Learning: Methods and Techniques for Computer Assisted Education" offered by the University of Ancona.

Ray Webster is a Lecturer in Information Systems in the School of Management Information Systems, Edith Cowan University, Australia. Prior to that, he worked in the University Centre for Complementary Learning, Thames Valley University, UK. He has also worked and taught in countries such as Turkey, Israel and Malaysia and has consequently developed an interest in cross-cultural aspects of his research. His research interests include the fields of user-centred design for educational technology systems, human-computer interaction and information systems in education. His doctoral research is based in the Centre for Advanced Learning Technologies (CSALT) in the Dept. of Educational Research at the University of Lancaster, UK.

Bahram Zaerpour is Director of the CENTEF (Centre of Technologies for Education and Learning) at the University of Lausanne, Switzerland. His research interests include open and distance learning and information and communication technologies for education.

Index

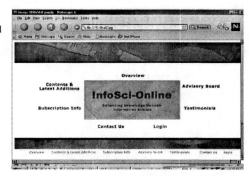

International Journal of Distance Education Technologies (JDET)

The International Source for Technological Advances in Distance Education

ISSN: 1539-3100
eISSN: 1539-3119

Subscription: Annual fee per volume (4 issues):
Individual US $85
Institutional US $185

Editors: Shi Kuo Chang
University of Pittsburgh, USA

Timothy K. Shih
Tamkang University, Taiwan

Mission

The *International Journal of Distance Education Technologies* (**JDET**) publishes original research articles of distance education four issues per year. **JDET** is a primary forum for researchers and practitioners to disseminate practical solutions to the automation of open and distance learning. The journal is targeted to academic researchers and engineers who work with distance learning programs and software systems, as well as general participants of distance education.

Coverage

Discussions of computational methods, algorithms, implemented prototype systems, and applications of open and distance learning are the focuses of this publication. Practical experiences and surveys of using distance learning systems are also welcome. Distance education technologies published in **JDET** will be divided into three categories, **Communication Technologies, Intelligent Technologies, and Educational Technologies**: new network infrastructures, real-time protocols, broadband and wireless communication tools, quality-of services issues, multimedia streaming technology, distributed systems, mobile systems, multimedia synchronization controls, intelligent tutoring, individualized distance learning, neural network or statistical approaches to behavior analysis, automatic FAQ reply methods, copyright protection and authentification mechanisms, practical and new learning models, automatic assessment methods, effective and efficient authoring systems, and other issues of distance education.

For subscription information, contact:

Idea Group Publishing
701 E Chocolate Ave., Suite 200
Hershey PA 17033-1240, USA
cust@idea-group.com
URL: www.idea-group.com

For paper submission information:

Dr. Timothy Shih
Tamkang University, Taiwan
tshih@cs.tku.edu.tw